LEARN

Information and Reference Sources and Services

Dr. Anil Kumar Dhiman

and

Smt. Yashoda Rani

Ess Ess Publications

4837/24, Ansari Road, Darya Ganj,
New Delhi-110002
✆ : 23260807, 51563444
Fax : 011-51563334
E-mail: info@essessreference.com
url:http://www.essessreference.com

First Published 2005

ISBN : 81-7000-455-1

Price : 750/-

Published by :

Ess Ess Publications

4837/24, Ansari Road, Darya Ganj,
New Delhi - 110 002
Phone : 23260807
Fax : 23274173
E-mail: info@essessreference.com
url:http://www.essessreference.com

Printed at :

Printline, New Delhi

Contents

Learning Library Science Series

Each book in this series has been written to provide in-depth knowledge of the basics of Library and Information Science and is in accordance with the B.Lib.Sc. syllabus of major Indian universities imparting the said course. To make this work series more comprehensible for the students, the books under this series have been written in Question-Answer format and the language used is very simple, easy and understandable. This series has been divided into six parts, each of which is dedicated to one basic aspect of library and information science.

The present series consists of six books in all, its first part deals with Learn Library and Society, second is Learn Library Management, third is Learn Library Classification (Theory), fourth being Learn Library Classification (Theory), fifth, Learn Reference Services, Information Services and Their Sources and the last and sixth book is Learn Computer Basics and its Application in Libraries. This gives a comprehensive and complete coverage to almost all the syllabi of most of the Indian universities imparting Bachelors' Degree in Library and Information Science (B.Lib.Sc.).

Although this book has primarily been written, keeping in mind the students making an attempt at the above mentioned Degree course, but it is hoped that this book shall find its place with anyone who is interested to know and learn more about the basics of library and information science. Not only the students, but the teachers of library and information science can derive equal benefit from this series. The books are equally suited to librarianship, library science students and library staff seeking to upgrade their skills.

Authors

Acknowledgements

It is indeed difficult to write one book and writing such a series of books is naturally much more difficult but this series could finally see the light of the day, but this could never have been possible without those innumerous books which have been consulted at every step and we are grateful to the authors of all those books, naming all of whom would not be humanly possible. We are thankful to Mrs. Sheel Sethi and Mr. Sumit Sethi, the owners of Ess Ess Publications for giving us an opportunity to present this voluminous work to the readers. We would also like to record our thanks to our friend, Mr. Sushil Kumar of IIT, Roorkee for his kind help. We feel indebted to Sh. Ram Lal Dhiman, Smt. Kamla Devi and Ms. Alka Rani who helped us at various steps. Last but not the least, we are thankful to our son Aman who could not get much of our attention while we were working on this work.

Anil. K. Dhiman
Yashoda Rani

Acknowledgements

1
Information Services: Concept, Need and Purposes

Q. : Discuss the meaning and scope of Information Service. How far does in differ from traditional librarianship ?

or

Describe the Information with suitable examples and explain the specific purposes for which Information services are needed ?

or

What do you mean by Information ? Explain the need for providing information services at the national and information levels in modern times.

or

Discuss the usefulness of Information Services in the library.

Or

What do you mean by Information? Discuss its role in modern society.

Ans. The word 'Information' is used to define various meanings such as knowledge, information, telling, understandings, message and data etc. The data are collected as result of a study involving observation, experimentation or survey. These are the facts and figures that are not currently being used in a decision process and usually take the form of historical records, that are recorded and filed, without immediate intent to retrieve for decision making. Data are normally mutually exclusive and have definite limits. The data need to be stored and made available to the users.

In simpler terms, the processed data are the information.

Data ⟶ | Process | ⟶ Information

Information consists of data that have been retrieved, processed or otherwise used for informative or inference purpose, argument or as a basis for forecasting or decision making. The way in which the data of a message are structured is crucial to their effect as information.

Definition of Information/Information Service

Information can be defined in the following four ways:-

(i) as a process,

(ii) as an intangible entity,

(iii) as a thing, and

(iv) as a commodity.

(i) Information as a process

Information indeed is a process of becoming informed. On being informed man, it is knowledge-base and behaviour change. If these changes do not take place, then it can be easily said that one is not informed. In fact information is all pervasive, one cannot imagine his life without it. Even the cave man was informative and quality conscious. Rather he was more careful about both the concepts as he was the producer as well as the users of his tools and weapons. Today, at every moment we need information decision-making. In the words of Michael Buckland, To have been informed is to be in a state of knowing something. Becoming informed denotes a change in what we know. It may commonly but not necessarily include knowing something. Becoming informed denotes a change in what we know. It may commonly but not necessarily include knowing more. News may arrive that contradicts rather than confirm what we knew and leaves us in greater doubt. We may feel that the new information leaves us knowing less that before. More to the point, it is not so much that we know less but that we know differently. The ideas that we had held have not disappeared, but our belief in them has changed. Physically receiving a text or other information does not guarantee that the recipient becomes informed. There are major barriers to access information –

(a) Cognitive access: The recipient must have sufficient expertise to understand or at least misunderstand the information. Either leads to a change in knowledge.

(b) **Acceptability** : The recipient must be willing to accept information, believing it to be true and not rejecting it as awkward-one would know of the rejected assertion but that is not the same.

Thus it is true that information is a process of being informed. For example, after looking at one's watch, one becomes informed about the exact time. Thus information reduces uncertainty and helps in decision making.

(ii) Information as an intangible entity

Unlike tangible objects information is an intangible entity, which can be used and shared but can not be consumed like tangible goods. The person who gives information does not lose information, but the recipient gets the information. In case of tangible goods, the goods are exchanged and sold, and the seller loses the goods. But information can not be imagined without its container or carrier. In this context, the human, documentary, and institutional sources of information come to out mind with the change of format, the content will not change. Therefore, being an intangible entity, information can be shared and used but not lost and consumed.

(iii) Information as a thing

Libraries and information centres deal with information as a thing. Information, when communicated via a recorded medium becomes a thing. Libraries and information centres acquire books and other documents to cater to the information needs of the end users. Physical objects such as data and documents are referred to attributively as information because they are regarded as information, having the quality of imparting knowledge or communicating information. In fact, every object is information. The value of the object as a source of information is user and time specific. A person who already knows about that object is not informed time and again, because that information has already gone into that person's knowledge-base after having the temporal effect.

(iv) Information as a commodity

Information is sold and purchased everyday, but it is very difficult to measure information and its value like tangible goods. It is very easy to measure a piece of cloth or any other tangible good, but it is very difficult to measure information and ascertain its value. The price of information is fixed on the basis of its cost of production and the profit margin of its producer, rather than on the basis of its value to the user or the society at large. Information has paradoxical properties, if it is useful, it is worth paying for and worth supplying to others. But unlike other commodities, one can share information with others and yet still have as much as one did before. Scarcity is a determinant of price, but as information can be disseminated indefinitely, it is not obvious how ordinary notions of scarcity and price apply to information, it is not obvious how ordinary notions of scarcity and price apply to information. Since knowledge can be beneficial in a variety of ways, so useful knowledge and, therefore, information-as-knowledge and information-as-thing can be well worth paying and worth sharing with others.

Thus, definition of information is perhaps less conventional, but it arises from experience, has proved useful in practice, has a sound theoretical foundation and today is widely accepted. It has some characteristics as :

— What we take in from outside to feed our knowledge so that we can function successfully and achieve our aims.

— What is necessary and what is available in given situations for this purpose. This definition of information takes account of some of the particularities and unique features, which distinguish it from other material resources.

— In order to have value, information has to be transformed by human cognitive processes into human knowledge without which no products of tangible value can be produced or exchanged.

— Where inflows of the information necessary to maintain knowledge and support appropriate action are blocked, disaster can follow either quickly, as in aircraft disasters or catastrophic failures in chemical processes, or in the form of gradual run-down into incompetence and chaos, as in organizations which are grossly mismanaged, under financed and understaffed.

— If it is hoarded for the exclusive use of a limited number of people, it can actually fail to achieve its full potential value for those who hoard it, but if it is exchanged and traded, the value resulting from its use, increases for all parties to the transactions.

— Information value lies in its use. Value is derived from and is added to by those involved with the process of its transfer. Its ultimate value derives entirely from the perception of its recipient and user as to what benefits they see accruing from its provision.

— Information is a diffused resource, that enters into all the activities of businesses and forms a components of all products and services that are sold. It also has the paradoxical quality of being usable for measuring the value of other things, but not of itself. As far as the libraries or information centres are concerned, they contained information in the form of books or microfilms and magnetic devices, or CD-ROMs and Internet etc.

Thus, in the context of library the function of 'Information Service' is an activity to find out what is already known on a particular subject or topic and make it available to the reader. Therefore to make libraries effective and useful, the librarians need to be well informed of the latest-developments in the universe of knowledge to satisfy the need of users.

Role/Need of Information and Information Services

Every society has its own critical resource. In agricultural society, labour was essential input, in industrial society, capital played a pivotal role, and in information society, information has become a strategic resource besides men, money and materials. In fact, it has become the sixth need of the members of the emerging information society after air, water, food, clothings and shelter. Therefore, preservation and access of information is an essential factor in human progress. It is also an essential input for decision-making. We can not imagine the information society without understanding the nature of information. In all field the need of information is unevitable. Even the economy of the country is dependable on the information provided. The following factors are responsible for justification of the importance of information.

1. To Maintain and Organize Research Power and Work Projects

In the age of explosion of the universe of knowledge, the scientists and researchers cannot do the investigation and specialization both in a given time. They are always curious and anxious to know the latest developments and changes in the related subject. Therefore, they need an Information Scientists who can help them in retrieving of information after selecting out of collection.

2. To Make Use of the Huge Publications Which Grows Rapidly

The main objective of information science is to control the flow in publications and to start the supplement electronic organizations as well as to mechanise and automation of the technical libraries.

3. Organisation and Collection of Specific Literature

Industries, trade and commerce, research and scientific organizations gives much importance to the literature related with research projects instead of conventional literature. To collect, organize, and the new techniques or information retrieval is quite necessary. To do this job, information service is required.

4. Management and Decision Making

Information provides a means of improving the management of enterprises and services of all kinds. It has become a vital component in the dynamics of social evolution. As knowledge advances and its applications become more diverse and call for further research, precise information concerning the state of problem is necessary before action can be taken. Importance of decisive information occur at all levels of management.

5. Intellectual Awareness and Updating

It includes the services related to make plan, consultation, surveys, field jobs, reporting etc.

6. Industrial and Commercial Need

Every day, there is a continuous increase in industry of every field. In order to minimise the expenditure, cheap cost, more useful, increase in production, the research and development (R and D) are in progress. It has become essential to establish information centre in the library to do these jobs. The industrial libraries provide the information services very satisfactory.

Thus in order to ensure a balanced growth, the governments, particularly in the developing countries, must develop adequate information policies and information infrastructures. To create information awareness and promote its use, efforts must be made to spread information literacy. It means, people in all walks of life must be aware to find, retrieve, and use information strategically. Information can affect the stake of people positively or negatively. If knowledge is power, information is instant power because it can be used instantly.

Keeping in view the power of information, it must be managed and used strategically.

Information Service and Traditional Librarianship

Since long, reference services have been providing in the traditional libraries while in the modern libraries it is known as 'Information Service'. Before 'Information Service' the similar to this service was reference service. There are some differences in these two; which are as below:-

1. The main objective of reference service is to make the readers self dependent in information retrieval. Therefore, the new readers are given an orientation in the beginning as an introduction.

   In the modern sense- information service is the main job of special libraries. Here the readers are acquainted with the future demand of the related subjects. Thus, the readers are not required to give an introductory orientation.

2. Much emphasis is given to provide the desired literature to the readers in reference service while, in 'Information Service', the desired specific information is collected and is provided to a particular class of the readers.

3. In providing reference service, short range information is provided speedily on demand of the readers while in information service, the providing of new information related with their subjects to the specific readers is a continuous process.

4. Reference librarian waits to the readers when information scientist acquaint himself initiating and solve the problem with a view to updating.

5. Reference service and decentralization of the knowledge in revised form is the information service.

6. Reference service is provided through reference assistants while in information service, the mechanical devices are also used.

7. Reference service is multi-subject oriented while information service is specific subject-oriented.

8. Reference service is an intellectual activity of all libraries while information service is the heart of special library.

Q. : Defining Information, discuss its nature and generation.

or

What do you mean by 'Data', 'Information' and 'Knowledge' in the context of library and information activities. Discuss the various activities which helps in generation of information.

Ans: The information is usually defined as organized or processed data which certainly add something to the knowledge in human beings.

A data is generally - what, which can be numerically expressed; that is, quantified, quantifiable or objective. Data are highly repetitive but Information is not highly repetitive or quantified or quantifiable. It is characterised as narrative and subjective. Data are number or unit facts, frequently repeated. Whereas, information is an idea. Information is a symbol or a set of symbols, which has the potential for meaning.

A knowledge is the information conserved by an individual at one extreme, and the humanity as a whole at the other extreme.

The information communicated to an individual may bring a change or transformation in him or may not. Data undergo the process of cognition, which results in a specific data structure called the information function of data. The information function then operates on the recipient's knowledge-structure resulting in a new knowledge structure. If the users already know the information communicated, it will have no effect. The concept of information has three immediate consequences:

(a) Information and data are not identical;

(b) Information is independent of the state of knowledge of the individual; and

(c) Effective information changes the state of knowledge of the recipient. Every information possesses certain characteristics, which are :

(i) Origin/Source

The validity of information will depend upon the origin or source. Before information is communicated to a user, one should check the origin or source of information (or message), but always it is not possible for us to check the origin of the information. In such a case, we must check the source from whom or from where the information is received.

When the information is received from a valid, reliable and genuine source then only, it should be considered for communication to a recipient or end user.

(ii) Message

The information to be communicated should be checked as to whether it possesses the following characteristics or not.

Accuracy : The information to be communicated must be accurate, i.e., it must meet the exact requirements of the recipient. It should be precise and free from error.

Appropriateness : The information must serve the purpose of the user. All the information relevant to the purpose of the user should be collected and presented to him so that his just needs are satisfied.

Timeliness : The information should be timely. The value of information depends on timeliness as timely information saves losses and wastage, avoids duplication and saves from going on unintended lines.

Comprehensiveness : The message must be understandable. It should include all the relevant information. It should be in a simple and understandable language.

Explicitness : It should be clearly and fully expressed. The message should not leave any doubt in the mind of the user as to its validity and comprehensiveness, etc. The recipient must be able to receive the message in straight and clear terms.

Availability and Accessibility : The information must be available and accessible to the user. Otherwise, there will be no use in merely communicating about the existence of a particular piece of information.

Verifiability : The verifiability has two implications. Firstly, the message should be verified for its validity, accuracy, appropriateness, comprehensiveness, etc., before it is communicated to the recipient. Secondaly, when the communication is not direct or from a known source, the recipient must be able to verify on his own about the validity, etc., of the message.

Bias free : The information should be bias free. It should not try to impose opinion on the user or influence him. It should not have any slant to one among alternatives without any positive reason or based on a principle.

(iii) Medium

An individual scientist receives information through numerous media; may be oral, by speaking and listening; documentary, by reading and writing; and visual by displaying and observing.

The message should be communicated through an appropriate medium. In order to increase the effectiveness of the message a combination of two or more media may be used. For example, script and photographs; tables and graphs; etc.

(iv) Recipient

From the point of view of the recipient, information should possess the following characteristics:

Adaptability : The information should be adaptable for a new use, need and situation, etc. It should be enabled to be used for a purpose or in a way different from that for which it was meant for.

Cost-Effectiveness : The information should, improve the performance of a system at an acceptable cost or at no cost, or should reduce the cost without unduly effecting performance. It is desirable to define a unit of cost of the relevant reference found for the user, since this takes the system's performance into account.

Generally speaking costs tend to rise with the number of documents processed and particularly with the exhaustivity of the search process. On the other hand, costs can be reduced by a more rigorous acquisition policy based on an examination of the distribution of sources among the retrieved references.

Currency : The information should be timely available. It should be not obsolete as well. Timely information will be of high value and cost-effective also. Currency should be regarded as one of the basic characteristics of information.

Nature of Information

Information in the symbolic means by which one mind influences another mind. Information is data that has been processed into a form that is meaningful to the recipient and is of real or perceived value in current or prospective actions or decisions. The giving, orchestrating, and taking of information is a basic source of power. Power is the ability to get things done that one wants to be done. Like weapons and money, information can be used by agents to exercise their will over stakeholders and to achieve their own goals.

It can also be used in a way that deprives a few stakeholders of their ability to achieve their own goals. People who acquire, process, store, disseminate, or use information to achieve their own goals can either harm or significantly benefit other people in the process.

Features of Information

Information is unique among resources and it is essentially human in its origin. As Information originates in the mind and is intangible, it has some different characteristics that clearly distinguish it from other kinds of resources and the sources of wealth. In fact, information is human, expandable, compressible, substitutable, transportable, diffusive, and shareable. Collectively, these features make information a unique resource, the use of which creates some rather unique ethical issue. Some of features are :

(i) Humanity : Information itself exists only in the human mind. What is observed, remembered and can be retrieved and what it then analyses and integrates; it is the input and output of human perception and imagination and is given and taken by human minds. Tangible goods can be touched, but information being intangible entity can not. Information, therefore, is what the giving and taking minds observe, imagine, remember, analyse, compare, relate, rank, organize, intuit, or integrate. Since information is a mind-based human entity, it is manipulated in a different way than are tangible items. Data-strings of symbols may be manipulated physically, electronically, or optically, but information-the sense we make of the symbols and the meaning we attribute to them-results from an inherent psychological process and is moved, shaped, built, and destroyed by human mind.

(ii) Expandability : Information tends to expand with its use as new relationships and possibilities are realized. Abundance and overload are greater problems than scarcity. The primary limits to the expendability of information is the amount of time, the giving and taking minds have available and their capacity to observe, reflect, analyse and integrate, because attention is our most valuable psychological resource.

(iii) Compressibility : Complex messages can be compressed, concentrated, consolidated, integrated, and summarized. Entire video movies can be transmitted using only a fraction of the binary bits originally required to capture them. During this process some significant information may be lost. Therefore, the uses of information should be mindful of this possibility.

(iv) Substitutability : Information can replace men, money, and materials in most economic processes. Substitutability is one of the major sources of information's power. It can be used to improve the human condition, as well as to cause the harm.

(v) Transportability : Information can be moved globally at the speed of light. Using the modern communication technologies, the messages can be sent farther, faster, and considerably cheaper. Moreover, with the Internet and the web, the traditional constraints of space and time stand collapsed and real-time access to information is possible. The cost of information communication has also come down. We have moved from telegraph to fibre-optic-networks through telephone lines. Fibre-optic technologies currently being installed promise even another quantum leap in performance. Thus information is explosively transportable. In less than a century, we have witnessed a major dimensional change in both the speed and volume of the movement of information, a change in transportability of resources greater than the multi-millennial shift from foot travel to supersonic jets. This means that today, the bad and well as the good that information does can be realized quickly, virtually anytime, anywhere across the globe.

(vi) Diffusibility : Information is hard to contain. Being intangible, it leaks out and disperses. Information once leaked out can not be taken back. Motivated minds are even more eager to acquire information. This is one of the reasons that many traditional methods of containing the flow of information, such as provisions for confidentiality, secrecy, and intellectual property rights, are in practice, so difficult to apply effectively today.

(vii) Shareability : The most significant economic feature of information is that it is not depleted with use, rather it can be enhanced with use, as with training, propaganda and advertising. In fact, information by nature can not give rise to exchange transactions, can give rise to sharing transactions. Things can be exchanged, but ideas can't. Ideas can be shared only. Information can be sold many times and yet retained by the vendor. It can be decomposed and reconstituted in a way unimaginable with physical materials. It can have significant value one day and worthless the next day. Information was always important, but what is new is the sheer volume of information available today. The basic challenge today is in providing realtime access to quality information. Quality information should be timely, precise, accurate, quantifiable, verifiable, accessible, free from bias, comprehensive, appropriate, clear, engaging and affordable, because information is always user-specific and time specific. The two unique features of information are that the vendors dose not lose it even after selling it, and information does not suffer from scarcity syndrome.

Information - generation Process

Information is the product of different types of human activities and events, or incidents. The activities are undertaken by individuals or by organizations to achieve specific objectives. Events are things that happen, occur or take place. If there has been no activity or an event taking place, there would be no information. Some of the important activities, through which information is generated, are :

(i) Research and Development : Some activities are deliberately undertaken with the specific objective of creating or generating information. Research activity falls in this category. Research organizations in science, technology, social sciences and humanities have been established specifically for this purpose. Research is a creative work undertaken on a systematic basis in order to increase the stock of knowledge and use it for the benefit of man and society. It is a highly organized activity throughout the world which continuously creates a large mass of new information.

There has been a dramatic increase of both research institutions and researchers in all branches of knowledge. More and more funds are allocated for conducting research. The progress of a nation is also often judged by the percentage of national income that is spent on research. The outputs of research constitute a major part of information handled by the library and information services. Over a period, there had been a large-scale accumulation of this organized body of information and to this stock is continuously added, the products of the current research activities. This phenomenon is characterised by the term "information explosion."

Research activity is not confined to the research institutions alone. The academic institutions-colleges, universities etc., also undertake and consider research as one of their major tasks, besides imparting formal education to the students.

(ii) Surveys and Censuses : Besides research and academic institutions, there are also organizations which are set up specifically to gather statistical information through censuses and surveys. This may be considered as adjunctive research activity. One of the most important examples is, the Office of the Registrar General which is established to conduct decennial censuses to collect population data which is the basic information about the demographic characteristics of the country.

(iii) Government Activities : There are also activities undertaken by many organizations for generating information as a by-product. The most important organizations in this category are the governments and their agencies. They perform, their tasks as a matter of routine. For example, the police department has been set up for the maintenance of law and order. It is their routine administrative task. The activities of these departments, in turn, generate information about such burning topics as dowry deaths, terrorism, atrocities perpetrated on the backward community and like. The massive development planning exercises undertaken in successive Five Year Plans by the Planning Commission and State Planning Departments generate an enormous amount of information on all dimensions of socio-economic issues. A major part of the information both statistical and descriptive variety needed by the social science researchers and decision-makers in governments, business and industry emanates from the governmental sources. The reasons are obvious. There is no area of activity in the life of a nation in which the government is not involved.

Besides these administrative organs of the government, the legislative and judicial bodies also contribute to the growth of by-product information, e.g., the basic sources of legal information are the legislatures which enact various laws and the judiciary which interprets the laws when disputes arise in their implementation.

(iv) Other Activities : Another source of by-product information is the business and industrial organizations whose activities throw up business and industrial information.

Besides, the contributions of individuals is also involved in information generation. The literatures fiction, novels, stories and poems written by them ultimately become a major source of socio-cultural information and they mirror the social conditions of specific periods.

Q. : What do you understand by 'Reference Service' and 'Information Service'? Discuss by giving examples the types of Reference and Information service.

or

Explain the types and purposes of Reference Service and Information Service.

or

What do you understand by reference service? Explain the impact of reference service on its parent organization and the users.

Ans. The library functions that are common to all kinds of libraries are acquisition, organization and dissemination of information. It is the last function i.e. dissemination of information with which reference and information services are associated. Reference service in the library is concerned with direct, personal assistance to library users seeking information. Whereas information service is provided in anticipation of the needs of the users of information. Both, the reference service and the information service promote the use of library material, connect the users with the library documents and meet the information requirements of the users. The depth and range of these services vary with the type of library and the kind of users a library is designed to serve.

Concept of Reference Service

The basic concept of reference service is derived from Sanskrit word, sandarbh meaning to "weave or to collect together", coordination, weaver. The basic principle is to coordinate two and more things to be gather. Thus, reference service to coordinate between two things as a bridging channel.

In the context of library there are two things-Reader and the book. The efforts to coordinate between the reader and the book is 'Reference Service'. As a result the distance between reader and book is reduced. Thus, with a view to aware the readers with their wanted subject matter or query, to understand the actual need of the reader and are made related efforts is 'Reference Service'. It also include personal contact, searching the literature, collecting the information, to attract the reader satisfying at the maximum level efforts. The main factor of reference service is the reader, therefore the need, nature, literary taste and status of the reader should be considered while providing 'Reference Service'. It is variously defined as under :

Dr. S.R.Ranganathan : "Reference Service is the process of establishing contact between a reader and his documents in a personal way". Document means all the documents likely to be of use to him at the moment. The reader and the book are two separate having its personal entity. It is not possible to do all this for a reader without an intimate understanding of his precise interest at the moment. To get this understanding, there must be a intimate communication between the librarian and reader. From first step to last, the librarian will have to be personally administering to the needs of the reader.

American Library Association defines reference service as "The provision and organization by a library service which is directly concerned with assistance to readers in their search for information on various subjects, and in using the resources of the library on various subjects, and in using the resources of the library in study and research."

Besides, there are many other definitions which help us to comprehend what reference service in a library actually means:

James Wyer defines reference service as "that part of library administration which deals with the assistance given to the readers in their use of the resources of the library" and "Direct or sympathetic and informal personal aid in interpreting the library collections for study and research."

William Warner Bishop defines it as "Reference Service is organized effort on the part of libraries in aid of the most expeditious and fruitful use of their libraries".

Samuel Rothstein means reference work to be the personal assistance given by the librarian to individual readers in pursuit of information. By reference service he implies further, the definite recognition on the part of the library of its responsibility for such a work and a specific organization for that purpose.

A.H. Wheeler states that "Reference Service is so greatly a matter of variables and intangibles that attempts to evaluate the department and its operations are rather baffling."

Thus, there has to be an intimate communication between the Reference Librarian and the Reader in order to establish without loss of time contact between the reader and his books and this communication or personal service may be termed as reference service. It is the personal service to each reader in helping him to find the sources of books answering his interest pin-pointedly, exhaustively and expeditiously.

Information Service

Information service is the developed part of reference service. Reference service is the traditional or classical while the information service includes latest technology techniques like mechanised and computerised help as a source of find and retrieval the information to provide reference service.

By reference service a reader is provided the literature desired by them while the information service provides them information retrieval. Both reference service and information service are mainly for establishment of contact between the right reader and the right book at the right time and in the right personal way and the effective method of fulfilling this need is through reference service.

Reference service includes the direct, personal aid within the library to persons in search of information for whatever purpose and also various library activities especially aimed at making information as easily available as possible. Dr. Ranganathan says that all the techniques developed towards library services lead to mechanisation and the mechanical aids have their limits. As the library service is to the intellect, it has to be rendered in a personalised manner and not in a mechanical way. There seems to be a necessity for an intermediary between the reader and his documents and this is what is looked after by a reference service which in turn has become a specialised function developing upon specially assigned personnel. Reference service enables libraries to deal with knowledge and not just volumes. Reference services are provided by human efforts and reference whereas information services are mainly based on technical devices, computer and other latest technical methods. Generally a difference is made between reference service and information service, but these are not two but one.

Reference Service Vs. Information Service

In literature, the terms reference service and information service are used synonymously. Some experts refer them as two different kinds of services. The differences enumerated are as follows:-

Reference Service	*Information Service*
It is a Traditional Service	It is a Non-traditional service
Emphasis is to provide documents	Emphasis is to provide Information
User is given the material or directed to locate the material	Attempt is made to provide exact information
Aim is to instruct the user	Less concerned towards instructing the user
Service is provided on demand	Service is provided in anticipation
It is a passive service as Library staff waits for the user to approach and make demand	It is an active service as Library staff does not wait for the user to come but provide service to keep user well informed

Now-a-days, reference and information services, are considered together the same. The reference services as responsive service provided to users in response to their request and information service as anticipatory service provided in anticipation of the needs of the users.

Functions

The functions of Reference and Information Service from the above definitions can be enumerated as follows :—

1. Supervisory function
2. Information function
3. Guidance function
4. Instructional function
5. Bibliographic function, and
6. Appraisal function

1. Supervisory Function : This consists of maintaining efficient reference service through proper organization of facilities, selection of materials, direction of personnel and study of the readers. The readers are provided speedy reference service saving their time according to the volume of their need and availability of the sources in the library. The trained professional staff are appointed to provide the efficient services to the readers. The readers are provided help by the collection, its arrangement and accessibility having after studying the nature and psychology of the readers. These all activities are needed for a good management and are done in reference service.

2. Informative Function : The information functioning part of a reference librarian consists of answering an apparently simple question to supplying information based on search in the collections of the library combining in bibliographical techniques with competence in the subject of enquires. The mechanism and techniques adopted at the library are not generally appealing and lack the personal touch. There is need for human agency for putting the books and other reading material into active use by those who would be benefited by them. There is a certain amount of artificiality of books. Personal methods might perhaps induce the readers to appreciate the value of books better. Thus to collect various information for its retrieval for further use and also to select proper reference tools are the functions of reference service as a part of informatory.

3. Guiding Function : The guiding function includes readers advisory service, which is vocational involving recommendations of good books, guidance for self education and possibility prescription of certain books for certain mental, physical or emotional ailments. The reference librarian has to be considered while performing these duties to the readers accessing to their nature, tendency and likings. Efforts are to make them library oriented. Guidance is also given for its structure, various author, title variations and to consult them. Some readers are coming to the library to know the business information, scholarships etc.; they are given these answers as a guidance.

4. Instructional Function : Instructional function includes the informal and formal library teaching to use the library better. The bibliographical function consists of furnishing bibliographies to meet the requirements of the clientele. The objective of the library is to provide the best and efficient services to the readers for their research and development. To achieve this objective it is the duty of the reference libraries to impart training of familiarizing with the available reading material and the new techniques adopted in the library.

5. Bibliographic Function : Bibliographic function includes the preparation of various types of subject bibliographies on demand of the readers according to their needs and tastes.

6. Appraisal Function : As the reference librarian provides assistance with the help of reference tools, it is very essential to have a through knowledge of these tools. Evaluation of the reference tools is very essential as it would involve selection and acquisition of right type of reference material and knowledge of how to get the most out of these material.

The main functions may be:

— Assisting users at all levels in the use of library tools and library collection.

— Attending to enquiries received from the library users in person, over the telephone, via online, e-mail, fax or through correspondence.

— Preparing 'reading lists' and conducting literature search and compiling bibliographies on request.

— Helping in research by compiling special indexing and abstracting services in anticipation of demand.

— Making arrangements for inter-library loans.

— Providing facilities for photocopying of reading lists, periodical articles etc. and building up good reference collection based on user's needs.

— Building up reference tools like Union Catalogues etc. for providing effective Services.

Types of Reference and Information Services

There are wide range of reference and information services offered by present day libraries. The nature and scope of these services vary with the category of user and the type of library. The category of users the libraries normally serve are students, teachers, researchers, professionals, planners and policy makers, common public and children etc. The type of libraries can be Public, Academic or Special. The reference and information services that are offered can be broadly grouped into two categories viz., Responsive service and Anticipatory service. Responsive services are offered in response to the users requests while anticipatory services are offered in anticipation of demands from the users.

1. Responsive Services

Responsive services are provided in response to the requests from the library users. Request may be for finding general information about the library, its layout, how to become a member, how to use catalogue or for finding answer to particular question or getting particular document from the library. These services can be broadly enumerated as follows:

(i) Provision of general information

(ii) Ready reference service

(iii) Assistance in searching and locating documents

(iv) Long - range reference service

(v) Compiling a subject bibliography

(vi) Assistance in the use of collection and library tools such as catalogue including online library catalogue, reference books, and online database etc.

(vii) Inter-library loan

(i) Provision of General Information : General information is sought by user who visit the library for the first time. Such readers need directional guidance in the use of library such as general layout of the library, where bound volumes of periodicals are kept, where current issues of periodicals are displayed? Or reference and text-book section of the library etc. Such type of directional guidance is frequently provided by the libraries.

In school, college and university libraries, now regular 'user orientation' or 'user initiation, programmes are organized for the new entrants in these educational institutions. The programmes are organized for new students every year in the beginning of the academic session. The contents of these programmes normally cover the following areas:

Objectives of the library and its Organization, collection of the library and its location, catalogue of the library and how to use it, general rules and procedures of the library, lending and borrowing facilities, reference and information services etc. The user initiation programme may be in the form of a lecture by the librarian followed by a tour of the library. Some libraries prepare audio/visual kits for this purpose and some distribute library brochures containing all the information. Whatever may be the format of these programmes, basic objective is the same i.e., to introduce the library and its services to the new users.

(ii) Ready Reference Service :This service is concerned with providing answers to fact finding questions such as what, where, who, when and how types. These kinds of needs are clearly understood without much discussion and the sources required are usually fairly easy to identify. Such services do not take much time and hence are known as *short range reference service.* This service is distinguished from the purely directional guidance in that the reference staff need to consult some sort of reference source rather than simply answer from personal knowledge. The professional requirement for the reference staff here is the knowledge of reference source, their contents, organization and presentation, besides the skill to match the query with the appropriate reference source which contains the answer. The following table presents a few illustrative examples of typical questions and the possible sources to find the answers:

Questions Relating to	Possible Reference Sources
Words/phrases, their meanings and usages; synonyms, antonyms etc.	Language dictionaries, Thesauri
Technical terms in different subjects	Technical dictionaries, Special glossaries.
Literature references	Bibliographies, Indexes, Abstracts and the like.
Persons	Who's Who, Biographical dictionaries.
Places	Geographical dictionaries, Gazetteers; Atlases and Maps.
Facts about a country, background information on a subject.	Statesman's Yearbook, Encyclopaedias.

(iii) Assistance in Searching : This service is concerned with the searching and locating of the documents in response to specific request from the user. The queries such as I have to write a paper on different breeds of horses, where can I find the information? I have to make a comparative study of communism and capitalism, where can I find the information? Such queries, depending on the user's needs, lead to carrying out specific searches, finding the required document(s) and giving to the user. While in ready reference service answer is in the form of a data i.e., short answer from the reference book, but in this type of service answer is in the form of one or more documents containing the information. Such query is also called as 'bibliographic inquiry'. Specific search questions constitute the greatest proportion of reference questions in school and academic libraries as well as in many special libraries. The time taken to answer such questions may take 10 minutes to an hour or more. The time factor also depends on what is available in the library, librarian's knowledge of the sources in the library. And if the document is to be procured through inter-library loan it may take the days.

(iv) Long Range Reference Service : Long Range Reference Service is generally provided to a specialist who is seeking information for research work or to solve a particular problem. Information sought may be too specialised in nature, it may be too recent, it may be related to earlier period it may be in another language. This type of service is more common in special libraries. The request may come from a professor, a business executive, a professional or a scientist. In long range reference service, information is searched in several sources like books, periodicals, non-books material etc. In case information is not available in local library, the sources of other libraries are explored and material is borrowed on inter-library loan. Sometimes to provide this service informal sources are also consulted. Since to provide this service wide range of sources are consulted the time taken is much longer therefore, such service is also known as *long range reference service.*

The marshalling of facts and figures from a wide range of secondary and primary sources, together with the need to write background notes and explanations, would call for the highest expertise in reference service. In such instances, the user may be an active researcher, a celebrated author, a report writer, or an industrialist urgently requiring data on complex legal and regulatory matters. It is also possible that the person may be well-versed in his subject of enquiry and the reference sources pertaining to the field. The help, the person might seek from the library, would be like research assistance which would provide all the reference notes and materials that may be needed for his project. No doubt such reference and information support has to be of a high quality.

In handling such long range and often intricate reference questions, it would be useful to learn the procedures and practices that are usually employed for the purpose. These may be conceived as a series of steps, as given below:

— Reference interview;

— Determination of the subject of enquiry with a precise enunciation of the topic;

— Identification of the primary sources that may provide the answer, through searches from secondary and tertiary sources;

— Spotting the places of possible answers to the topic;

— Listing all the references with notes and explanations;

— Organizing and presenting the collected information in the form of a report acceptable to the user; and

— After getting the feedback, fill up the gaps to complete the process of reference and information support.

The most important step here is the 'Reference Interview', which would determine the entire course of action for operating successfully. The process of dialogue between the user and a member of the reference staff is termed as 'Reference Interview'. This technique would demand high communication and articulation skills to elicit the exact nature of the inquirer's need for assistance and research support. The useful details that would eventually emerge from this dialogue would be highly useful in conducting the search for finding the necessary answers. These details are:

— Objective of the question and its modification in the course of the interview;

— Personal characteristics, particularly with reference to the persons' co-operative tendencies;

— Depth of search required on the subject of enquiry and his knowledge of the sources; and

— Expertise available in the library.

Once this preliminary step is handled well and the relevant details of the question collected, the rest of the steps may not be very difficult, provided the reference staff know the procedure of search and the relevant bibliographical and reference tools.

(v) Compiling Subject Bibliographies : Another very important reference service offered by the library is to compile subject Bibliographies or request. Sometimes such bibliographies are compiled on regular basis or in anticipation of user's needs. At times, bibliographies are compiled on special occasions such as during the seminars and workshops to provide participants with the latest literature on the subject. University and special libraries offer this service more frequently than the public library. Some of the important aspects that call for attention in such compilations are :

— Objectives and purpose;
— Selection of topics;
— Scope of the topic in terms of its full ramifications;
— Coverage with reference to types of documents;
— Coverage with reference to the age of reference;
— Mode of presentation of entries;
— Supporting indexes;
— Updating procedures, if necessary; and
— Mode of production.

Short bibliographies on topical subject areas may also be compiled on certain occasions to highlight some recent literature.

(vi) Assistance in use of Library and Library Tools : Assistance in use of library and library tools is provided to the user so that he may be able to use the library most profitably. To provide this service effectively, it is important that reference librarian should have positive attitude towards the profession. He should be friendly in nature and willing to help the user and should be professionally competent to establish rapport with the user. All these attributes not only enhance the image of the library but also encourage the library user to approach the library staff without hesitation and with confidence.

(vii) Inter-library loan : Inter-library loan refers to borrowing a publication from other libraries when the same is not available in the local library. The local library should have arrangement to borrow publications from other libraries on Inter-library Loan to satisfy the information needs of their users.

2. Anticipatory Services

Anticipatory information services are provided to library users in anticipation of demand for such services to groups of users but not individually. To provide these services user's information needs are assessed and services are designed accordingly. Initially the service is provided on trial basis and when response is satisfactory then the service is regularized. Such types of service are more common in special libraries. Generally following type of services are offered :-

— Current Awareness Type

— Abstracting Service

— User Advisory Service

— User Education Programme

(i) Current Awareness Type : To keep the users abreast of the current development in their respective field of interest, current awareness type of services are offered. This involves scanning the newly available documents, selecting items relevant to the needs of group or individual, recording them and disseminating to the users on regular basis. Some of the common services are :

— Title Announcement Service

— Selective Dissemination of Information

— Newspaper Clipping Service

Title Announcement Service : This service keeps the users well informed of up to date information in their area of study and research. To provide the service, current issues of the periodicals are scanned and articles relevant to the needs of the user are selected, bibliographical details of the selected references are noted down and these records are accumulated to be issued as bulletin on periodical basis. To speed up the service sometimes content pages of current periodicals are xeroxed, cumulated and disseminated to the users. Sometimes in addition to current periodicals, newly acquired books, patents, conference proceedings are also covered in current awareness bulletin.

Selective Dissemination of Information : This is a highly personalized current awareness service provided to individuals or to a group working on common project or on limited subject filed. The basic concept of "SDI service is mattering the incoming new information with the interest of the user. SDI service is that service within an organization which concerns itself with channelling of new items of interest from various sources to those points within the organization where they can usefully serve someone's interest. It endeavours to present indiscriminate distribution of new information and avert the resulting danger of not communicating at all". With the help of computers this service can be performed most effectively. Basic aim behind this services is that neither user is provided with too much of information nor he is made to miss information essential for his study and research.

Newspaper Clipping Service : This service is concerned with scanning the daily newspapers, selecting news items of interest of the user community, cutting these items, arranging them under broad subject headings and circulating to the users on daily or weekly basis. Back files of newspaper clippings are also maintained for retrospective use. This service brings to the notice of users information about current events, activities and personalities. The service is generally provided to R and D managers, govt. officials, researchers and media persons.

(ii) Abstracting Service : This service is for providing current and retrospective literature on chosen fields with abstracts as well as citations of articles and papers appearing in current journals, and also reports, conference papers and proceedings. The aspects which needs attention in the production of abstract bulletins are:

— Subject identification
— Selection of items to be included
— Sources
— Citation practice
— Preparation of abstracts or using author abstracts
— Presentation of entries
— Supporting indexes
— Frequency
— Physical production

(iii) User advisory service : This service deals with providing reading guidance to the individual. The aim of this service is to motivate the readers to use the library and inculcate good reading habits in them. Such service is more often offered in school and public library. This service helps the readers to select right book for educational and recreation purposes.

(iv) User Education Programme : The terms 'User Education', 'User Orientation' and 'User Assistance' overlap and sometimes are used interchangeably. User Orientation is concerned with acquainting new users to the library, such as objectives of the library and its organization, collection of the library and its location, general rules and procedures of the library, reference and information services etc. of the library. User Assistance deals with providing personal assistance to the users in the use of library tools and its resources. User assistance refers to helping an individual rather than a group.

User Education connotes a more educational activity which is concerned with motivating the user and developing a skill in the user to find and search information independently for study, research and recreational purposes. User Education and User Orientation programmes are offered to group of homogeneous users. User category may be school children, college students, research scholars, academic staff, etc. Contents of these programmes vary with each category of user. However, basic objectives of these programme are same i.e., to create awareness of the availability of different sources of information in relation to user needs and developing necessary skill in searching and finding information independently using these sources.

Reference and Information Service from Electronic Sources

In traditional literature search, the librarian searches in number of issues of printed indexes and bibliographies to find answers to a query. The issues are manually picked up from different shelves for searching. Once the relevant references are found, bibliographical details of each item is recorded manually. The entire process is quite time consuming. Now a days most of the printed international indexing and abstracting services in different disciplines are available in computerized database form. Many major reference tools like encyclopaedias and dictionaries are also available in electronic form. These databases are stored on remote computers for online searching or stored on CD-ROM disks or made available for searching on the internet. For online searching, the computer terminal in the library is linked remotely via telephone lines or other means. The librarian by sitting on the local computer terminal logs on to the computer thousands of miles away and can access these databases by simple search commands. The search results can be viewed on the screen and relevant references can be downloaded and printed on the local computer. The librarian does not have to buy these databases but can access them online as and when required by making payment for each search. Online international databases can also be accessed through online service provider. There are three types of online service providers, commercial online vendors, commercial publishers and Government Institutions. Commercial online vendors do not produce any database but make them available by hosting them on their computer with requisite search software. Commercial online vendors provide access to large number of databases eg. DIALOG provides access to over 6000 databases. Second type of online service providers are commercial publishers who provide online access to databases produced by them eg. H.W. Wilson and company. Third category of online service providers are Government Institutions such as National Library of Medicine (NML). NML provides direct online access to over 40 databases in the field of medicine and related areas. Most of the database producers are bringing their databases on CD-ROM disks also. Many reference works such as Oxford English Dictionary, World Bank Encyclopaedia, Academic American Encyclopaedia etc. are available on CD-ROM. When databases are stored on CD-ROM disk then library can purchase these disks and search them directly. Large number of bibliographic and full text databases are also available for searching on the internet. Searching computerized databases is convenient, and it saves time and allows in-depth searching. Computerized databases are also more current than their printed version as these are updated continuously on daily or weekly basis.

Impact of Reference Service on Parent Organization

The impact of reference service on the parent organization, the users and various aspects of librarianship may be seen as under :

(i) Library support : Reference service helps the users to get right kind of documents and information at the right time, thus saving their time. It assists the researchers to avoid duplication of work and helps them in the introduction of new ideas. It makes information available to decision-makers to take right decisions. Thus, reference service also attempts to fulfil the objectives of the parent body. A satisfied user serves as a friend of the library and can be helpful in getting greater support for the library. If the reference service is poor, then it will create a poor image of the library. Thus, the library may loose support from its users and the parent body.

(ii) Library service : The experience shows that the impact of reference service leads to increased demand for library services including reference service. In order to improve the situation, the reference librarian makes an effort to educate himself finding out more about the users and their requirements, the sources of information, produces better tools, uses better techniques and methods, etc., which leads to better reference service. As a result, there is more effective use of the library. The produces a cycle of reference service and better use of the library.

(iii) Organization of the library : Reference service is considered as an important service. Organization of a library takes it into consideration. Therefore, library catalogue is placed near the stacks and reference collection is put near the catalogue. Reference section is located near the stacks and the library catalogue. This is done to suit the provision of reference service and for the sake of users.

(iv) Circulation of documents : Reference staff would know about the quantity of demand regarding various documents on the basis of their reservation by users, In case, a book is in more demand, then reference section would tell the circulation section to put it in the reserve section. Similarly, it can indicate whether or not a given reference book should be allowed to be borrowed. Reference staff can help circulation section to decide the period of loan for different categories of documents.

(v) Book selection : Inter-library loan records kept by this section would point out the weak areas in the collection. It would indicate as to which books need to be selected. Similarly, on the basis of the queries received by it, it would be able to make suggestions for selection of various kinds of documents.

(vi) Acquisition : A user might make a request for a book already on order. Then the reference section would approach the acquisition section to acquire the book as early as possible. This might necessitate the sending of a reminder to the vendor. If a book is urgently needed, the reference section might request the acquisition section to acquire the book immediately. The above kinds of possibilities would also arise for the acquisition of reference books. If these are acquired late then this would badly affect the provision of reference service. This leads to the fact that the implication of reference service for acquisition section would be to acquire-books in time.

(vii) Classification : A reference librarian can make suggestion about arrangement of documents on shelf. He can tell whether or not broad classification is desirable in a given library. He would be able to point out to a classifier unhelpful placing of books or mistakes in classification.

(viii) Cataloguing : A reference librarian can provide help to a cataloguer and vice versa. In order to serve as a finding list, a catalogue needs to provide minimum bare information but in order to satisfy the requirements of reference service, more information would be required than otherwise is given, such as information about imprint, collation and notes, etc. A reference librarian would also insist on uniformity, consistency and accuracy of details.

Besides, in order to have full impact, the reference staff should improve their efficiency and become more alert. The degree of impact would be the measures of their capability and effectiveness.

Q. : Mention different theories of Reference Service. Explain the usefulness of Dr. Ranganathan' five laws of library science in providing reference service.

or

'Reference service is a necessary implication of laws of library science'. Discuss the statement.

or

Explain briefly as to how the five laws of library science provide directional guidance in the provision of reference service in libraries.

Ans. : A Modern Library, with a few exceptions, is regarded as a service institution, and its aim is to enable the users to make the most effective use of the resources and services of the library. This type of library acquires material, possesses it and makes available for use rather than preserve. It allows open access to its collection and provides service to its users. It is expected to convert potential users into habitual users. A habitual users is the one, who goes to a library regularly and uses the library as a matter of habit.

In order to make potential users into habitual user, it is essential to establish a desired kind of contact between user and the document. So, reference service is the process of establishing the contact between a reader and his documents in a personal way. It is quite clear from the definition given by Dr. S. R. Ranganathan that "Reference service is a personal service to each reader in helping him to find the documents answering his interest at the moment, pin-pointedly exhaustively and expeditiously."

Theory of Reference Service

In USA after 1826, it was realized that the traditional role of librarian was no longer adequate to meet the needs of the readers. Samuel

Swett Green who first stressed the need for reference service insisted that furnishing the reader with catalogue and reference book was insufficient. Instead, he advocated the need for personal guidance and interpretation of library to the users. However, when the need for reference service realized, the concept of reference service became a debatable point for a long time. The attempts have been made to discuss the degree of assistance to be given to the readers there is still a difference of opinion and due to lack of adequate theory, the reference librarian do not know the precise nature of service to be rendered by theory.

Reference service from its very beginning has been the subject of a variety of concepts and definitions. Up to first two decades of twentieth century, a few librarians were for personal service to scholars, but by 1920, the concept of reference service began to change. The idea of subject specialization was given by Melvil Dewey as early as 1907, but it was towards 1930 that the desirability of subject specialization was at long last, realized. It was the world war II which drove home the necessity for speedy dissemination of information. As the conveying of information came increasingly to be regarded as a major formation of the library, the provision of assistance to the user become accepted as a central responsibility of the librarian rather then a marginal activity. With the passage of time, the concept of the libraries as information or documentation centers rather than a book distribution centers, became a reality. The 1946's and 1950's were an era of library technology, the librarian was more concerned with acquiring and organizing, classifying and cataloguing the material. In the 1970's, the need for planning library services as part of the educational cultural and scientific planning has been realized. To the librarian therefore, it is an era of intensive reference service and reference services no longer means issuing a book or even finding a list of information for the reader. It mean entering into partnership with those engaged in all types of intellectual endeavour, putting to full use his bookmanship, his professional knowledge of recorded information in all its variety, for the benefit of the uses.

In, 1930, James I. Wyer identified three distinct concepts of reference service as below :

1. Conservate or illiberal theory,
2. Liberal or generous theory, and the

3. Theory of middle state.

1. Conservative or Illiberal Theory : This theory decides the limitations of the librarian to provide assistance to the readers at personal level only. This assistance should be limited at personal level and directive only. No need of initiation of the reader is needed. He shall trace the required information himself and shall be provided service on demand only.

2. Liberal or Generous Theory : This theory favours to the readers for their help at without any limitations. They should be provided the information service at its maximum.

3. Theory of Middle State : According of this theory, a librarian should adopt a medium way for reference assistance. The readers should be provided assistance at the level of considering the limitations of the resource available in that library. If the man material is adequate the services can be rendered in the maximum way accordingly. If the situation is little adverse or resources are less, then readers should be satisfied by only the directions.

Various thinkers have given various principles or theories. The main teaching of all these principles is that while rendering services to the readers the consideration of sources must be taken into consideration.

Dr. S.R. Ranganathan and Five Laws of Library Science

In 1940 the first edition of Dr. S.R. Ranganathan's "Reference service and bibliography" came out dealing with a theory of reference service. He is of the view that reference service is based on five laws of library science. These are discussed below :

(i) First Law and Reference Service : The first law of library science is "Books are for use". According to this principle the efforts are to be made for making the reading material usable. This law implies that personal service should be rendered to help the reader to help himself so that the books in the library are used with maximum advantages and satisfaction. Books selected to suit the individual needs and accompanied by factful guidance, should be the response to individual requests for personal service. The individual needs are varied and the personal service on the part of reference librarian should effect contact between the right reader and the right book at the right time and in the right manner. In this personal service, the reference librarian should be prepared to consult specialists and experts whenever necessary. The librarian should be a friend, philosopher and guide to everyone who comes to use the library and his duty should be to serve the readers.

(ii) Second Law and Reference Service : Second Law is "Every reader his/her book". Here emphasis is given to the reader. A reference librarian should know the reader and his requirements, so that he can provide right books/ information to every reader. The first thing is to know the need psychology of the readers coming in the library. Some special skills are to be developed in reference librarian and other staff, to make enable them to acquire skill to know about the readers, their characteristics, their want etc. The reference staff have to find out how much help could be given to every reader to find sentiments of the readers. It is also necessary for the reference librarian to have a vast and thorough knowledge of books and book collections. As it is known that knowledge we know ourselves have limitations while the knowledge where it can be traced in reference sources, so it is not feasible to depend upon memory alone, the librarian has to depend upon the aid books to discharge his obligations in helping every person to find his books. Bibliographical aids, reference books, catalogues etc. are the aids that must be mastered by the reference staff or the librarian.

(iii) Third Law and Reference Service : The Third Law of Library Science is "Every book its reader". If we say that every document its reader or in the context of the information society every information its user it would be better. In the present era of information explosion, each and every information or a bit of formation is useful for the researcher or reader. So micro-documents as well as macro-documents are meant in this connection. This Law gives emphasis on documents/ information. The demand of the third law will meet with the help of directories, bibliographic, catalogues encyclopaedias and other reference books. The effectiveness of the law depends on the capacity of the reference books present in the library and information centers. Reference books are mute by nature; they can not make the journey to the world to find out their respective readers. This entire journey will have to be carried with the help of reference librarians, so as to establish a personal contact between the reader and the document.

(iv) Fourth Law and Library Service : The Fourth Law of Library Science is "Save the time of the reader". Here the factor "time" has been used because researchers are our national economy and we should not waste their time by looking here and there for each and every document.

The flow in publications has made reader to confuse and he is not in a position to locate and trace his query from the collection. It may waste his valuable time and delayed in research which is useless after such a time. Therefore, some personal initiation is necessary to get the reader acquaint himself with the collection and its correct use. Therefore, the adequate trained professional staff should be provided in a library which will save the time of the reader.

(v) Fifth Law and Reference Service : The Fifth Law of Library Science is "Library is a growing organism". In particular the documents in the library continuously grow in quality and quantity. As a continuous process and natural phenomena, the books, readers, their need and the library grow. There is a vast increase in publishing world not only in books but also in the periodicals, magazines, reports proceedings. The readers are engaged in research which requires more and more queries. This all can be done with the help of reference service only. Reference librarians should keep themselves well acquainted with of the new documents/ information and with secondary periodicals so as to keep track of all the documents coming out in the subject.

Thus in the above manner, the laws of library science have their own message as far as reference service is concerned.

Q. : Explain the nature and range of Reference Service in a special library.

or

Reference Service is a hub of all library activities, justify this statement in the context of a University or a College Library in detail.

or

Discuss by giving examples, the need for providing reference service in a public library.

or

Explain the nature and range of Reference Service in a Public Library.

Ans. Reference service is the service, which is provided to a user on demand on personal basis. According to Dr. Ranganathan contact between the right reader and right book at the right time by a right person, is the reference service. He has emphasized on personal service by human assistance.

The objectives of the library be achieved by reference service itself only. The all activities of the library are revolving around the reference like, book selection, acquisition of books, periodicals work, classification, cataloguing, orientation, display of books, circulation all are useless if these sources are not utilized properly and it is possible only through reference service. The collection of the library can be used only when a reference librarian provides human assistance making its use effectively.

Reference and Information Service in Different types of Libraries

The nature and scope of reference and information services depend on the category of user and on the type of the library, though basic objectives of the service remain the same i.e., to meet the information need of the user, promote the use of library collection and help the user in finding and seeking information for problem solving, study research or recreation.

Dr. Ranganathan has given stress on human assistance while providing information service. He has given the following reasons for human assistance.

(i) Psychological Needs : A reader goes to the library needs a psychological initiation to satisfy his tempo. Dr. Ranganathan says that reader should be given personal human assistance. He believes if he is not provided the ready reference answers to his queries, the tempo for curiosity of knowledge shall be down. Therefore, there should be provided to right reader, the right book at right time.

(ii) Artificiality of Books : Due to speedily advancement in printing technology and computer offset printing and other new techniques of publications, at one side, when the complications in use of this flow of publications, the other. As a result it has become very difficult for reader to use the stored books in the library without personal assistance or reference service.

(iii) Artificiality of Cataloguing : In order to make usable the collection of reading material in the library, certain devices are used like book selection, book order, periodical work, classification cataloguing, accessioning organization and display of books, and charging and discharging them. But a catalogue is the mirror of a library collection by given author, title and subject approach and is prepared with a view to help the readers,. It's use is so difficult that a reader or new reader in particular is unable to consult it without human assistance or freshers initiation or to explain the reader - what, why and how to use this catalogue. Therefore Dr. S.R.Ranganathan said "....... Book selection, book order, periodical work, classification, cataloguing, accessioning, organization and display of books, and charging and discharging them, will become fruitless unless proper reference service is done, indeed reference service alone can lead to the ultimate fulfillment of a service library and of the laws of library service".

Though reference service is provided in all types of libraries whether it's a public or academic or specialized. The size of staff space and number and types of reading collection depends and decided at the needs of its objectives and clienteles.

(i) Academic libraries

Academic libraries comprise school, college and university libraries. Objectives of these libraries are to support the basic functions of the academic institutions.

(a) School Library : It is the school library where children are first exposed to a library. Good reference service in the school library plays a vital role in developing positive attitude towards the library. Efforts should be made to inculcate good reading habit in children through Reader's Advisory Service, by setting up book exhibitions and celebrating book week involving children's participation. School children should be instructed to use the library and its resources. Teachers should be encouraged to integrate course curriculum with the library and provided with necessary documents for this purpose. It is also equally important to build good reference collection comprising audio/visual material, illustrated dictionaries and encyclopaedias for different level of children viz., primary school, high school and higher secondary school children.

(b) College Library : User community serve in college library comprises teachers, undergraduate and postgraduate students. Reference services provided to students normally consist of instructions to students in the use of library, assistance in locating specific information or documents, answers to fact finding questions, inter-library loans and sometimes compilation of bibliographies.

Training college students in the use of library and its resources offers challenging opportunities to college library to make significant contributions towards educational objectives. However, the task is not easy, since college life offers a lot more attractions than the library as a resource center. Therefore to impart successful training, teachers cooperation is must. This can be done by integrating library resources with course curriculum and involving teachers in the user education programs.

(c) University Library : The three principal clienteles of the academic library are undergraduate, graduate students and faculty members staff. The reference service has also three aspects viz. (1) Instruction in the use of books and the library (2) Guidance in the choice of books and (3) information service.

Undergraduate Students : Normally service to undergraduates is directly related to course assignments. The students generally want a easy way of getting at the book and if we place several choices before them they will select their choice. Students are more interested in the successful completion of assignments than in its educational value. At the undergraduate level the students curiosity is limited upto the text books and little reference queries.

Graduate Students : They are probably the heaviest users of library and reference service. A graduate student might have already had a certain proficiency in the use of library. He will require initiation only upto the literature and secondary reference tools in his own field. Now a days there has been the practice in western countries and to a limited extent in our country too, to offer some literature course or training in the use of information. In the university libraries, the functioning of providing information service, the graduate students are themselves expected to learn as to how to find information for themselves. The reference department need not have to provide any kind of active or on demand information service.

Faculty Staff : The faculty staff consider themselves as experts and will not like any instruction. They may seek assistance only when a member works outside his speciality for research. Faculty members do not also require guidance in the choice of books and they will seek assistance only in locating and obtaining material not available locally. As regards information services only in cases where limited or predictable research interest in specified fields are to be catered for sort of specialized information service can be offered.

Reference service may be provided to the readers by a central reference department in the main library building or decentralized in the departmental libraries. The current awareness service, selective dissemination of information, comprehensive literature, search or preparation of state-of-art services, compilation of bibliographies are the usual specialized information services.

As far as Information services are concerned, these are provided to the teacher and researcher only. The time factor is the most important for this group of readers, since they have lack of time. Therefore the students and teachers should try to find out information.

The teachers and the researchers guide to the students and they should provide the education as follows : -

1. The answer of factual questions.
2. List of documents should be prepared and be given to the teachers
3. To search the literature for teachers.
4. To bring the translated literature from other library and make available them.
5. CAS: Current awareness service.

Thus in an university library, the students should be given the text books and curriculum, necessary information and secondary sources to the researchers.

(ii) Public libraries

Public libraries serve general public comprising children, housewives, businessmen, professionals, students, teachers etc. with different educational background. The public library is mainly used for recreation, information and education. Reference service in public library comprises providing general information, assistance in searching and locating documents, ready reference service and sometimes long-range reference service. Most of the questions handled by the library are of fact finding type or for background information. To serve the user community better, the library should survey to find out the needs and interests of the user community, about local institutions and local personalities. The following are the reasons which create the demand of reference service in a public library.

1. To acquaint the accessibility of the library to a new person. If the coming member is fresh and coming first time in the library,

no matter he might be a student, social servant, leader, politician, he is not aware with the collection of books and periodicals and the method of its use. Reference service is provided so that he can acquaint with the tools like catalogue, classification and the available literature.

2. Certain devices like classification, cataloguing and bibliographies are needed to give some teaching at first so as to make its use accessible.

3. The new comer reader in the library wants to know the answer of his queries which can be answered by tracing from various reference books which are called reference tools. It is not easy for a new comer to consult these reference books and to get the answer of their need. Therefore an orientation to use these tools is necessary so that the reader can be trained and acquaint with these tools.

4. Every library has its own rules and systems of collecting the reading material. To make its use convenient, reference service is provided.

5. Public libraries are regarded as the "Public Universities", which are spreading the knowledge amongst the society without any discrimination. Today the libraries are not merely a collection of storing books only but responsible for quenching the thirst of knowledge of the society and its need. The ambition to get the knowledge and to make it a public habit continuously, personal assistance is needed, and the reference service makes it feasible.

6. The personal guidance of the librarian and assistance to consult the collecting books and other reading material to satisfy the need of the reader approached there in.

7. To make available the assistance for research and development, inventions business research, with the needy material as books and periodicals.

8. In a democratic pattern of society and its success, it has become very essential to acquaint every citizen of the nation with the biographies of popular leader, their life, work and contribution, by teachings, which is only possible in a public library by reference service.

9. To cater the needs of the society and its people for an healthy

entertainment for the use of their leisure time, the reference service is needed in the public library.

10. Various persons of the society coming to public library are in need of manuscripts, bibliographies, indexing and abstracting services as well as the translation, all these editing services are to be provided essentially through reference service.

(iii) Special libraries

Special libraries comprise those libraries which specialise in particular subject or group of subjects (e.g. S and T libraries, Social sciences libraries, Medical libraries etc.) or particular collection (e.g. Picture libraries, Electronic libraries, Sports libraries etc.) or serve particular user community (e.g. libraries for blinds, prisoners, patients etc.). Most of these libraries are attached to parent organization and serve the needs of parent body. Reference and information service in these libraries include responsive as well as anticipatory services. Provision of information services in anticipation of demands is regular feature of special libraries attached to R and D institutions. Information services are very well organized in these libraries.

Mainly the following are the reasons of providing reference service in a specialized library.

1. To provide current awareness services.
2. To provide and make available the periodicals published articles and publications.
3. Retrieval of the information with the help of subject bibliography.
4. Selective dissemination of information services, to provide to the readers.
5. Service of national documentation centres and specialized information centres to find answers to specific reference questions.
6. To distribute the accession list etc. to the libraries.
7. Special libraries provide expert use of union catalogues and other bibliographical apparatus to exploit the resources at other places, this is possible through reference service.
8. To provide the assistance for research work.
9. To make available the publications of the information related to the institution.

10. No library itself is complete, therefore inter library loan and its services are adopted as co-operations, reference librarian in special library perform this duty well.

11. To save the time of the reader in special library so that their important urgent academic assignments can be fulfilled.

Generally a special library has to answer of fact findings, periodically important, the detailed information. To answer these questions a reference department of a special library should give the following services :-

1. Information Service : The reference librarian provides the information for research in these libraries. These information can be ascertained and search from the help of documents. Sometimes reference staff has to prepare charts, cartoons, reports and diagrams and to give it to the scholars for their research projects.

2. Literature Search : The employees in special libraries have the full knowledge of documentation, depth knowledge of the subject related with the problem. In order to make available the research material to the scholars they search and collect it from the published material. To do this job they consult handbook, encyclopedia, indexes, abstracting periodicals, bibliographies etc.

3. Current Awareness Service : Current awareness service is the latest service to be provided by the help of new reading material and other to be published from time to make available. It is given with a view to updating of the knowledge. CAS, includes collections of periodicals, listing of periodicals, the indexing of selective articles, or preparing of abstracting of the articles published from time to time.

4. Inter-Library Loan : No library can claim for having a rich collection. It is not possible to keep all the published book available in the library as every library has a limited financial budget. Therefore the book are demanded and taken on inter-library loan from different libraries and returned after the work is finished with thanks.

5. Translation Service : Today the books and periodicals in science and technology are published in different languages and script while the researcher has the knowledge of limited one or two languages, as a result he is unable to use this all published material of different language. To solve this problem the translation services are provided, which is a technical job. Either it should be done by the library self or from the centres of documentation or translation.

Thus, in a special library the reference service is provided.

Q. : What is meant by "reference service'? Discuss various types of reference services.

or

What do you understand by 'Ready Reference Service' and 'Long Range Reference Service'? What is their importance?

or

Discuss in detail the difference between Long and Short Range reference services and describe them briefly.

or

Discuss the main features of Long rang reference service. Explain by giving the example, the categories of library material which are generally found useful for this service.

or

"Preparation, Service and Assimilation are the process involved in reference service". Explain.

Ans. Reference services help the user to define and identify his query correctly, bearing in mind how he intends to use the information, since this can affect the choice of source. The reference personnel then inform him what catalogues, directories, files, secondary publications or databases to consult to seek out the relevant information for himself, explaining, if necessary, how the user should go about his search. Alternatively, they themselves do the search for the user, if desired so by him i.e., the user.

Generally, following types of questions are asked by the users.

(i) **Directional type :** Where to find what? This type of guidance is generally needed to users who come to the library for the first time. He only needs to be directed. User may seek assistance in locating desired library materials or services rendered by the library. He may ask - *Where is the reference section? Where to get photocopies? Where computer related books are kept*? These are the straight forward directional type questions and can be answered by library guides, graphics or through multimedia. After providing directional type information, reference librarian might say, *If you do not find what you want, please come back.* Further, accompanying the user to the appropriate source or site may also provide or opportunity to explore the information in more depth.

(ii) Instructional type : In today's rapidly changing technological scenario, user may not be aware of the new information technology, retrieval mechanisms, operation of computer, CD-ROMs, Internet, etc. He may like to seek instructions about their use. Instructional (how to use?) guidance may be provided to the user for their proper use. He may ask -*How to search CD-ROM database? How to search Internet or send E-mail? How to operate microfilm reader? How to operate OPAC?*, etc.

(iii) Factual type : User may ask for factual or fact finding information which can be provided by the reference librarian without much delay. These type of questions are generally ready reference types. The answer can be found out from the reference sources placed near the reference desk. He may ask- *What is the length of coastal boundary of India? What are the addresses of Indian, American, and British institutions conducting course in library and information science? Who was awarded the Novel Peace Prize this Year?*

(iv) Exhaustive type : Exhaustive search deals with research level questions and are time consuming. These are also known as long range reference questions. These type of questions require strategic searching from a number of specialized sources which may or may not be available in the library. User may ask about *nuclear stockpiles world over*, he may like to *compare the ranges and warhead carrying capacities of missiles developed by various countries, strength of armed forces of India, China and Pakistan*, and so on.

Depending upon the questions asked by the users, and time taken in answering them, the reference service may be :

1. Ready reference service
2. Long range reference service

1. Ready Reference Service

This service, which serves in a very short period or in such a short period of moment, is called 'Ready Reference Service'.

American Library Association defines this as, "Direct reference service consists of personal assistance provided to library patrons in pursuit of information."

According to **Dr. S.R.Ranganathan,** "Ready reference service is reference service finished in a very short time in a moment if possible."

The above definitions gives the concept of ready reference service on time bound or means that service in which answer is given to the reader in a moment or say in the least time. It is the fact finding service. The main factor of the service is service. Being service motto, the answers are provided to the reader immediately without wasting of time. This type of service provides the answer of the students by consulting various reference tools like Encyclopedia, Dictionary, Yearbook, Biographical Dictionary, Index etc.

It is not essential that the answer should be given from the reference books or anything other text material. If the librarian knows he can use by memory too, but it will not be an authentic. Therefore the reference tools must be used to provide authentic information.

This type of reference service is needed for:

(a) Nature and history of reference books.

(b) Nature of the readers.

(c) National economy.

Methods of Rendering Ready Reference Service

The Reference librarian has to ready forever to collect, and find out the information for various books to satisfy the needs of the readers. Therefore he should be well acquainted with the latest devices used and techniques adopted in the library. There are three following steps for providing ready reference.

(i) Preparation

(ii) Service

(iii) Assimilation

The ready reference is the result of joint effort of the above three steps. The preparation and assimilation is the indirect action while the service is the direct aspect.

(i) Preparation : Preparation means to be prepared himself a reference librarian acquainted with the library collection and new additions so that he may provide ready reference service form the available resources. He will unable to provide the guidance until and unless he makes thorough study and knowledge of these services. The process of preparation relates with the following three types of reading material, to have full acquaintance and familiarity with these in preparation.

(a) New reference source : A Librarian is supposed to have the full knowledge of new additions as well as the collected books and other forms of literature. He will be fully confident while answering of the queries, if he had studied these all.

(b) New editions of reference service : The information in the available books is not up to date until unless new editions of these are not consulted. Therefore a reference librarian should be aware with facts of changed editions. Due to rapid growth in research, new changes are unevitable. The various books including latest edition should provide the informations but sometimes the difference is shown or some variations in the provided information which is due to the following reasons :

(i) Involvement of various different persons in the preparation of reference book.

(ii) To collect the information date of different places and different persons.

(iii) Works, figures and informations are examined carelessly.

(iv) Latest information of figures and tables do not submitted even at the time of publication.

(v) Incomplete and defective information.

(vi) To get the required information just before the publication.

The above mentioned adjustments are to be considered by the reference librarian while giving ready reference to a clientele.

(c) Fugitive material : The fugitive material is in the form of newspapers and periodical cutting, pamphlets, prospectus, advertisement. The fugitive material is supposed to be very helpful in providing the service in the special libraries.

(ii) Service : After having prepared as above mentioned process, reference librarian is ready to provides direct service to the reader. The different readers of varying interest come to the library for getting information as well as for dense study or specific purpose. Some of them are regular comers and some of them are not. Few readers wants to get the required information without coming to the library. Some readers are quite busy. Therefore the services to be provided to these all categories have differences in providing of service. Thus, while serving to them the attitude of the librarian is different according to their categories. For example - to some he is a teacher while to the other a friend. Thus, the three categories of services which are provided are, as follows :

(a) To train a new reader for fact analysis.
(b) To guide the regular reader.
(c) To provide the factual data to the readers.

If we understand the reader and his need, the half the battle is won. It means the a & b, first two steps point helps to train the reader so that he may be aware with reference books and get his desired information self. The last point is for the reader himself. Dr. S. R. Ranganathan stressed that the last work to be done by the reader alone.

In the special libraries, there is a lack of time with the reader. The reader in these library is a scholar of research and so busy that he should be provided information in a very short period.

(iii) Assimilation : After completion of the job provided to the reader, the librarian should analyse it again and satisfy himself whether the information provided to them is correct or wrong. An account of the jobs performed, information collected should be maintained.

2. Long Range Reference Service

This service is that which takes too much time to provide the information to the researchers, to collect the required information after a great search and investigation. The time consuming factor is being taken into consideration for its specialities. The following are three points and elements :-

(i) Time : Long range reference service takes much time. Therefore Dr. S.R.Ranganthan has stated that in long range service few questions can be answered in half an hour while few questions may take full day or few weeks or so.

(ii) Sources of Information : In ready reference service the query is answered from the available reference books like dictionary, encyclopedias, directories and finishes within library premises only. While in long range reference service the search beings from the library resources - like books, periodicals, bibliographies, abstracts, microfilms, and if needed the information is collected from the other libraries to which scope may go upto the national or international level. If the information is not available then tries to contact the original source of the information.

(iii) Nature and scope of the Information : In short range reference service, the queries are of general interest and are based on the facts. The librarian has no difficulty in answering because the most answers can be given from the resources available in the library but in the process long range reference service the questions of the queries are complicated due to the following reasons:-

— Wide scope of the subjects.
— The subject is either quite new or ancient.
— The subject may be a regional and geographical.
— The subject is related with any of a particular caste, creed, religion or thought.
— The subject is interlinked with many aspects.
— Complication of the language.
— The translated form of the old subjects.
— The lack of adequate reference collection to answer.

Need and Utility of Long Range Reference Services

This is needed due to following three reasons :-

(i) Flow in literature
(ii) The interdisciplinary nature of subjects and
(iii) Language problem.

(i) Flow in literature : In modern times the 'Education for all' concept has given a tremendous rise in the publication as a flow. Today there are number of books and other form of literature, which are the source of media of expression. Researchers' view that today's time is of periodicals and newspapers. The updating information of the subject is available in the periodicals and magazines only, without these publications a researcher can not do his research.

(ii) Inter-disciplinary nature of the subjects : Every day research and inventions has increased the subjects in multi-directional and multi-dimensional field. To make more useful and creative of the every branch of knowledge is interfering to the other and taking a new shape as a result it becomes for a reference librarian to locate the answer in a short period. Due to lack of time, long range reference service is not only a need but also very essential.

(iii) Language problem : The speedy transportation, the source of communication have made the globe very small. Today every nation is providing literature in his regional language and supplying it to the other part of the world. A researcher doing research on his topic shall be required information available in any part of the world. No matter in which language it is available. But it is difficult to understand in other foreign language. The researcher and the learned persons involved in research projects needs translation of these literature available in different script. The translation work is the work of reference service of long range nature.

Rendering of Long Range Reference Service

The following three steps are to be needed in long range reference service.

1. Preparation : The first step of providing long range reference service is preparation. For this it is very necessary that a reference librarian should :

(i) Be aware of the knowledge of all the subjects in general and depth knowledge of the specialized in particular.

(ii) Know the interrelations of the subjects.

(iii) Know the reference books and other sources, its structured arrangements and techniques of use.

(iv) Know other than conventional methods and books, the bibliography, abstracts, periodical publications, dictionaries reviews etc.

(v) Know subject wise arrangements of newspapers cutting to know the contemporary knowledge of economic and political events.

(vi) Collect unpublished material of research dissertation submitted already as well as research in progress.

(vii) Know the general collection of reading material of the library.

(viii) Prepare himself mentally and physically both before providing service to the readers.

2. Service : Most important aspect is to provide service. To satisfy the curiosity of a reader is standardised and authentic is the certificate in the real sense. The service is in the three stages :

(i) Librarian should know the correct problem and its answer pointedly, only then he shall be in a position to answer it.

(ii) Search of literature - Having after decided the correct problem of the reader the search of required literature starts.

(iii) If the literature is searched then answer or report shall be given to the reader. If the material is not available in the library the inter-library loan facility will be used and the material shall be taken as loan from other.

The readers coming to the library are of two types - a general to specific. General readers want general information and create personal relations too in the library as they have much time while the specific readers don't have much time as they are busy in doing research or in doing deep study of the subject. Both the readers are to be satisfied by the service.

3. Assimilation : Under this process the professional staff of the library including head are always in a mood to adjust the readers demand by way of analysing their questions and mutual exchange of ideas, and thus solve the problem. Moreover, through reference books, newly published reference sources with new editions, bibliographic abstracts, indexes, makes their knowledge update so that the service can be given in update manner.

Reference librarian makes contacts to national documentation, international abstracting, indexing and abstracting documentation centres.

Thus all the activities performed to answer of subjects and general is called as assimilation. This makes librarian as popular by these services. Dr. Ranganathan has given stress of human assimilation in reference service.

Difference between Ready Reference & Long Range Reference Service

Factors	*Ready reference service*	*Long range reference service*
Time	Between few minutes and half an hour.	Few questions may take less than half an hour but some may take a whole day or even weeks.
Sources of Information	Ready reference sources of information, namely, dictionaries, encyclopaedias, yearbooks, directories, biographical dictionaries, maps, atlases, handbooks, manuals, etc.	Search starts with ready reference sources but is continued to other soures of information like pamphlets, ordinary books, periodicals, un-published documents etc. In case the resources of the library do not

		provide the required information then search may be directed to resources of other local libraries. If local libraries are not able to provide the answer, then search may be attempted to libraries in other parts of the country. The libraries in other countries can also be explored. If required, the institutions and individuals (may be scholars) can be contacted. A library in this context would also include information centres documentation centres etc. Here, the aim is to exploit all possible resources of information. The above is a description about the ideal situation.
Nature of Information sought	Here we are mainly concerned with facts.	Here we are concerned not only with facts but also other types of information. Information sought may involve exposition of a problem from a particular point of view. Information sought may require systematic search in periodicals. Information may be too specialized. It may involve expression of an opinion or a point of view on a particular idea. It may be too recent so that it may not have been included in reference books. It may be related to an earlier period, likely to be found in early works. Information could be such, which may have to be collected from large number of sources of information. The required information may be available only in foreign language sources. It may have appeared in a source of information not possessed by the library but may have to be borrowed from another library.

The concepts of ready reference and long range reference services are relative ones. In a library with poor sources of information, even search for mere facts sometimes becomes long range reference service. Similarly due to lack of ready reference books on India, certain questions which should have ordinarily belonged to the category of ready reference would get converted into long range reference service. The same can be said about the capability of a reference librarian. An experienced and a capable reference librarian would be more successful.

If proper record of answers to queries belonging to long range reference is maintained, then next time, if the same or similar question gets repeated, help should be taken from the records. In this way long range reference service would get converted into ready reference service. A good reference librarian should take maximum advantage of his experience and maintain such recorded information systematically. Similarly preparation on the part of a reference librarian is extremely important. For example, if a library is receiving many queries with regard to recent events, in that case maintenance of a press clipping tile can serve an extremely useful purpose. This will help him to convert otherwise long range reference service into ready reference service.

2

Organization of Reference & Information Services & Department

Q. : Discuss the various factors you would keep in view while organizing a reference or information department in a public library.

or

How will you organize reference or information department in a University library?

or

Write a short note on organization of reference information department.

Ans. : As reference and information services are a measure of the strength of a library in meeting the information needs of users, which to a large extent determines the success or failure of the library, no effort should be spared in organizing and managing these services with efficiency and speed. Almost all-large and middle size libraries entrust these services to a separate division.

Usually there is an organized separate reference department in the university and large public library. In the small library the services are performed by the librarian along with other jobs. In the medium class library the work is delivered to one employee of the library or professional person. But being there is an independent department in the university and large library, therefore an independent post of Reference Librarian is provided.

Reference department of the library is that department which directs readers directly or indirectly to motivate them for use of library in an effective way, not only to the readers but to those who are indifferent about the library and non-readers category.

The success of the department depends upon an efficient organization and administration. By making a study by survey about the need, psychology and capacity of sources, the reference department is established.

Generally the following three points are to be considered while establishing reference department which are common for all categories:

(i) To be provided best service.

(ii) Maximum facility is to be provided to the readers.

(iii) Every reader his book' is to be followed means, every reader shall be entertained.

Thus to make and run a reference department the following aspects should be considered before it is started : -

1. Location

Being heart of the library, the reference department must be placed at first story of the main buildings so that the readers of all categories can utilize the reference department. There should be library catalogue, periodicals department and other specific literature of reference room available so that these can be used as and when needed. This department should have an adequate space having a rich collection of reference books.

2. Organizing

Organizing refers to the creation of an operational structure of the reference division. The structure is determined on the basis of analysis of work and jobs of all the different activities of the division. An illustrative organizational structure is given below:

Reference Division

Reference Services	Anticipatory Services
Directional Guidance	Bibliographic Compilations
Current Awareness Services	SDI
Reference Desk	Newspaper Clipping Service
Ready Reference Service	Indexing Service
Long Range Reference Service	Abstracting Service
	User Education Programme

3. Furniture

The Almirahs provided should be easily accessible. In the height, these should be in lower height than the room and the depth of the shelves must be adequate to make provision of keeping books properly. Besides, the comfortable chairs, tables, reference desk, vertical file, should be available in reference department. There should be provided good lighting and adequate air. The dais of the reference table should be in half moon round shape. The desk should be equipped with an arrangement of keeping cards, files etc.

4. Equipment and Stationery

There are needed conventional and modern instruments and devices in the reference department. Generally, the following instruments are kept in the reference department: -

(i) **Telephone:** In a public and university library it is must. Now-a-days, Internet, fax are also essential part of the kit of instrument. But in small library it is not an essential need, as the readers come personally here.

(ii) **Reference file:** While in service period, various files are maintained. These references are to be preserved for future use.

(iii) **Vertical file:** These files are used to keep the record of temporary reading material like, tables, charts, diagrammatic representation, handbooks, commercial catalogues, price lists etc. These are arranged in alphabetical order as well as alphabetical subject arrangement.

(iv) **Daily Diary:** The questions/queries, which can not be answered from ready reference, are being noted in this diary. Besides query, the details about the reader like, address, telephone no., when he will come again, are noted therein. This diary can be used in public library but not very much useful in academic library, as the questions asked in academic libraries are immediately disposed off.

Other than the above material, the clippings of newspapers, files, reading and writing material, cards, papers, library manual and the directory are maintained in the library.

5. Staff

As far as the reference department and its organization are concerned, two things are very important:

(i) collection of adequate reference books and

(ii) Selection and training of suitable professional employee for reference service.

Staff is the backbone of library. If a number of persons are engaged in information services, then their work must be coordinated by the head of the section. He should by training, experience, and personal qualities be capable of directing people. Thus, he should possess qualities of leadership, which will enable him to get the maximum out of his staff. At least one professional should be made available for providing information services during all the hours, the library is kept open. During peak hours, more professionals should be employed keeping in view the demand.

It is essential that a distinction be made between professional and non-professional jobs. The professionals should attend to professional work leaving non-professional work to be done by others. In case, a document is to be located a non-professional worker can do the job, whereas if it is the compilation of a bibliography or a documentation list, the job should be assigned to a professional.

6. Reference Collection

Information services are usually provided through well-organized organizations like library, documentation center, clearing house, referral center, information center, databank etc. Their organizations perform their function either independently or as units of the larger organizations or systems or networks. Today, library is rightly known as information center, which aims at identifying, collecting, storing, processing, including cataloguing, classification of documents, printed books, periodicals, manuscripts, reports, theses and other reading material such as audio-visual photographs, maps, microfilm microfiche etc; and displaying them for circulation reference and study.

Reference books are the essential base tools of reference services. Therefore good qualitative and quantitative collection should be made in the library. There cannot be collection of the same type in all the libraries. The readers of a library come as per the geographical location. Means every library has the various readers and various place. Therefore the questions and queries asked in the library is also different according to need of the readers, which is also effected by the geographical factor. Hence the collection of the book in reference library should be acquired keeping in a view of the demand of readers.

While in a public library the all-main reference collection should be provided where in a university library the following is needed: -

(i) The main collection of the tools submitted or represented.

(ii) Specific reference books.

(iii) Very specific collection.

The reference material should be arranged in a scientific way so that it can be made accessible for use. Generally it's a separate hall or a room consisting of sub divisions. The books are classified according to the best used or according to their popularity and are arranged in a classified order keeping in a view the need of readers.

In case the library has been computerized, then there should be a computer terminal at the reference desk. This shall go a long way in improving the service. Provision of various technologies can enable the services to become more efficient and effective.

7. Library Manual

A mannual provides the entire information about the library. It should be provided in the reference section of the library. Every year the new edition with all changes must be published. The following information's are provided in this manual: -

(i) The importance of the library and its use.

(ii) The period of working of library.

(iii) The short and concise history of the library.

(iv) The library departments and services provided by them.

(v) Library rules.

(vi) The plan of library project and map.

(vii) The staff list with designations.

(viii) Library committee and its officials list.

(ix) Visiting book and its what others say about the library as suggestion book.

To run reference department in an effective way the following points are to be considered:

1. As the reference tools are very costly, as such an adequate budget should be provided.
2. Reference collection should be acquired according to the need and taste of the readers.
3. The library should make a policy to purchase the reference book consisting of various members.
4. Skilled and professionally trained staff personnel should be appointed.
5. Adequate place- space must be provided for Shelving, Counter and readers sitting and Internet searching etc.

Q. : What is a reference book and its various categories? How are they helpful in primary reference service?

or

What is a reference book? How does it differ from an ordinary book? Describe the categories of reference books.

or

Define a reference book. Discuss its kinds and features with examples.

Ans. : The queries asked by the readers are answered with the help of reference book. Therefore the base of reference services is the reference book, provided. Appropriate and adequate reference book means which provides the right answer to the right reader within a reasonable time and the reader satisfied fully.

The reference books are those which are published with an objective to get a specific information. The arrangement in these books are quite different than other books of common collection. These are arranged in such a way that user can get his desired information very easily, where in general books the given subject matter is arranged in order of respectively chapter. In the reference books, the matter is arranged, not only subjectively but also arranged in alphabetical or classed so that reader can see books easily in a short span of time. Due to this discontinuity of subject these books are not studied from first to end in one sitting but are referred for a specific purpose only.

Characteristics of a Reference Book

(i) They are not meant for comprehensive reading.

(ii) They usually concentrate on facts.

(iii) They are normally not issued in loan but are kept for use in the library only.

(iv) The arrangement of information is such that it can be conveniently and quickly recalled.

(v) It is a miscellany of information or facts.

(vi) The information included in them is collected from a vast number of sources.

(vii) They are consulted for definite items of information.

(viii) They are intended primarily for occasional consultation and are not the meant for continuous reading.

Importance of Reference Books

In the modern age of literature explosion, it has become very difficult for searching the required material. The need may be for general reading or for research, the readers should be given the answer without a loss of time. It shows the importance of library. In order to run library in an efficient way, few sources or tools or say devices are to be used. While providing reference service, these sources are reference books.

In this age of explosion of knowledge the information factor is most important. The information should be made available within limit of time. Business persons, administrators, researchers and students etc., all are be provided the proper answer of queries or need information speedily. To do this reference books are needed and these have an important role.

Kinds of Reference Books

Broadly speaking, the reference books may be divided into two types as under:

(i) **General Reference Books :** These are the books which does not deals with a particular subject but as a whole one subject or information on few subjects is explained. The scope of these books is popular for historical information of the subject not current.

Examples : Encyclopedia Britannica, English Hindi Dictionary etc.

(ii) **Specific Reference Books :** These books are written for a specific subject to provides specific information. These are edited after collecting the information from various sources so that these can be used speedily filed only.

Examples : Mc Graw Hill Encyclopedia of Science and Technology, Dictionary of Economics etc.

On the basis of varying need of the readers the reference book can be divided into following categories: -

1. Dictionary

Any book, which explains the meaning of a word/words of a particular language or languages, arranged alphabetically is Dictionary.

In a more broader sense it includes the meaning of a word, meaning of a line, definition, pronunciation, original word or its origin, different verbs, Orientation of the letters, Synonymous and antonymous, spelling, new terminology, abbreviations used, foreign words, lovoktis, idioms and phrases, etc.

Examples:

— Oxford English Dictionary, Oxford Clerendon Press 1933, 12v.
— Manak Hindi Kosh, Prayag, Allahabad, Hindi Sahitya Sammelan.
— ALA Glossary of Library Terms, Chicago A.L.A. 1943.
— English-Hindi, Hindi-English, English-Sanskrit, Sanskrit-English Dictionary by Kamil Bulke.

Usefulness of Dictionaries

1. Quick Reference tool for meaning and other aspects of words.
2. Serve as tool for language standardization.
3. Serve as a language recorder of historical development.
4. Facilitates communication among different languages.

2. Encyclopedia

These are known as an ocean of the knowledge. It deals with the all branches of knowledge in depth or one subject, an informative essays in details and depth, which are arranged to use in alphabetical order and subjectwise classified index is provided at the end of volume. Multi volume encyclopedia provides a guide volume as well as the index volume containing one separate volume in one entity.

Mainly these deal with the historical information of a subject and non-living person's biography of great leader, subject's facts and findings analysis and provides basic facts and figures.

An encyclopaedia may be general encyclopaedia or subject encyclopaedia basing on the coverage of subjects.

1. General Encyclopaedia

Examples:

— Collier's Encyclopaedia - 24th vol. Annual revision. 1949-51 (First Published)

— Encyclopaedia Americana - 30Vols. Annual revision. 1929-23 (First Published)

— The New Encyclopaedia Britannia. 15th ed. 32 Volumes. Annual revision. 1974. published earlier as Encyclopaedia Britannica since 1768-71, 1st Ed.

2. Subject Encyclopaedia

Examples :

— McGraw-Hill Encyclopaedia of Science and Technology. 6th Ed. New York: McGraw Hill Book company, 1987, 19 Volumes and Index.

— Encyclopaedia of Library and information science. 1968-35 Vols. Supplements, 1-Dekker.

Usefulness of Encyclopaedia

1. Most used sources for introductory or background information.
2. Most comprehensive coverage.
3. Bibliographical references led to further study.
4. Facts and illustrations helps a lot.
5. Gives idea of a particular period.

6. Gives different point of views on a give topic.

3. Biographical Sources

It contains the short biosketch of very specific persons of reputed fields. Their short life details, with the pronouncing name is given. It lists of the great persons like-Date of birth, genealogy, education, works, practical life, writings, main incidents, experience, achievements, marital status, post held, address, expiry date and the contribution to the society etc.

Examples :

— Who's Who- India-Ed 4. Delhi, INFA Publication, 1972.

— International Who's Who, 1973-74. London, Europa Publications.

4. Geographical Sources

Geographical Sources consist primarily of geographic representation. These are made use of to find out answers to geographical questions, which are concerned with information about places such as- cities, towns, mountains, lakes, rivers, forests etc.

Uses : The distinct advantage of geographical works over more generalized reference books is that:

(i) They give information for smaller units not found in general works.

(ii) The Information given often will be more precise.

(iii) Since they are limited to one area, they are usually easier to use.

The following types or sources of information are recognized, which can be used for getting geographical information: -

1. Bibliographies and indexes.
2. Encyclopaedia
3. Dictionaries
4. Sources of statistics
5. Biographical sources

But geographical sources used in reference work may be sub-divided into following sub-categories:

(a) Gazetteer : The types of sources of reference service provides the information about the queries of geographical questions, like, cities, places, mountains, lakes, rivers, forests, its location, other particulars, places of interest, institutions public life, available facilities, climatic conditions, transportation, population etc. For example - location of Agra-longitude and longitude, Distance between Kolkata and Mumbai. The population of Canada, Density of population, largest city of India in area etc.

— Gazetteer of India, Delhi Publication Division, 4 vols.

— Webster's Geographical Dictionary, Springfield Mass, Merrium.

(b) Atlas : This may be an independent publication or it may be along with the other books as a part of it. It provides the information of the questions related with the area of a nation or any particular place, city of country, rivers, mountains, lakes, sea, oceans, islands, bay of roads, railroads and climatic conditions etc. It is a collection of the facts as mentioned above.

Examples:

— National Atlas of India - S.P. Chatterjee Ed. Kolkata, National Atlas organization.

— Hammond's Complete World Atlas, New York, Hammond.

(c) Maps : This is useful reference source for consulting the square, angles of lands etc.

Examples:

— India in Maps. India Publication Division.

— International Map of the World or Millionth map. London, British Ordinance, Survey.

— Tribal Map of India, Kolkata. Anthropological Survey of India.

(d) Guide Books : The books published with the information of any city, country or a particular region, provides to the travelers, as to how to go, when to go, where to visit, hotels, sight seeing etc., are the guide books.

Examples :

— Fodor's Guide to India. New York, Fodor Modern Guides.

— Bharat Darsan Mala. Manager of Publications, Delhi.

5. Ready Reference Sources

The ready reference sources are those which help in locating the right and factual answers to questions. They contain brief, pinpointed answers. They are further sub-divided as follows: -

(a) Yearbook

(b) Almanacs

(c) Directory

(d) Hand books and Manuals

(e) Statistical sources

(a) Yearbook: It is a compendium of the statistics or fact of the preceding year or the previous year. It is published annually.

Examples:

— India : A Reference Annual, India, Ministry of Information and Broadcasting, Publication Division.

— Bowker Annual of Library and Book Trade Information, New York, RR Bowker.

(b) Almanac: It's an annual publication, provides information of the astrology, and as a calendar of the year.

Examples :

— Rectories Panchang, Kolkata; Regional Meteorological Center; Nautical Almanac Unit.

— Information Please Almanac, London, Whitaker.

(c) Directory : This is a list of classified and alphabetical arranged, which contains the list of the residents of a nation, businessmen, institutions etc. It lists the business and trade of a national personalities for business purposes.

Examples :

— All India Telephone Directory; Baroda; Indian Export Trade Journal (4 parts).

— International Library Directory. London, A.P. Wales Organization.

(d) Handbook and Manuals : It is a treatise on a special subject, containing concise information in simple language, small enough to be held in hand.

A 'manual' is a corresponding word derived from Latin term 'manuals'. It means a guidebook, compensations book, an abridged handbook or a treatise which can be referred for guidance in any occupation art or study. They are related to "How to do something" by means of specific and clear directions.

Examples :

— Book of Facts, a collection of Genuinely Interesting Facts about Things around Us. Bombay, Jaico.

— Sukti Sager, Ramshamear Gupta, Lucknow, Publication Division.

— Handbook of Special Librarianship and Information Work. Ashworth, Wilfred Ed. London, ASLIB.

(e) Statistical Sources : Statistics is concerned with collection, classification, analysis, interpretation of data or facts.

Statistical sources are those which provide the information about the facts or data in the numeric form. Statistical information is provided in any type of source.

Examples:

— Demographic Yearbook, UNO.

— Yearbook of Labour Statistics of ILO.

— Oxford Economic Atlas of World.

— UNESCO Statistical Yearbook.

6. Bibliography

A Bibliography is the list of books and other material written by one author, or on one subject, or about some place, during one period.

It is a list of document together for some purpose, usually to bring to the notice of the reader, an exhaustive or select list of documents relevant to the pursuit of his enquiry or study.

Examples :

— Cumulative Book Index: a world list of books in the English language, New York, Wilson.

— British National Bibliography London, Council of British National Bibliography - Weekly, Monthly and Annual.

— Indian National Bibliography, Kolkata, Central Reference Library.

7. Index

It is very useful source to get an information of a periodical publication which systematically indexes the contents of periodicals usually within specific subject field. It is a systematic list which specifics or indicates the contents topics, names or other information in a book or any other document.

Examples :

— Readers Guide to Periodical Literature, New York, H.W.Wilson.

— Indian Press Indexes. Delhi Library Association.

8. Abstracts

This is periodical publication by the process of dividing and grouping in classification. This is a printed or mimeographed publication which consists of abstracts of currently published, periodicals, articles, pamphlets etc, issued by a special library and distributed periodically to its clientele.

Examples :

— Indian Library Science Abstracts (Q). Kolkata, IASLIC.

— Library and Information Science Abstracts (Q). London, ASLIB.

9. Serials

The serials are periodical publication, issued at regular intervals in successive parts, bearing numerical or chronological designations and intended to be continued indefinitely, e.g. periodicals, newspapers etc.

Examples :

— Statesman's Yearbook.

— Ulrich's Periodical Directory, N.T.R.R., Bowker.

— Ayer's Directory of Newspapers and Periodicals, Philadelphia-Pa-Ayer.

— Asian Records, New Delhi.

— Reader's Digest, New York (Monthly).

— Hindustan Times, New Delhi.

10. Patent

It is a certificate document between an inventor and the state administration, consisting the agreement between these. This literature is used as a reference tool or source, which specifics the design or manufacture, usually of an invention and the document granting exclusive right to the inventor or patentee to produce, use, sell or get profit from the invention for a fixed number of years.

Examples :

— Official Gazettes of United States Patent Office.

— Official Journal of the Patent Office, U.K.

11. Micro Documents

In order to preserve the knowledge of scientific and industrial research and of other subjects, for the use, the libraries has started to collect the information in the micro-literature. This is a short document on a specialized topic which embodies micro thought. An article in a periodical is a micro-document, while the periodical itself is a macro-document.

Examples :

— Guide to Newer Educational Media; Films, Phonorecords, Radio slides, Television, Chicago, ALA.

— Unesco Catalogue of Colour Reproductions of Painting prior to 1800 and from 1800 to 1961, Paris.

12. Audio -Visual Sources

These are the sources which provide knowledge by hearing and seeing the aids, are the audio-visual aids. The aids includes the material, such as gramophone, records, tape recordings and various visual aids like filmstrips, films, lantern slides used as an adjunct to teaching or lecturing. The reference library is equipped with apparatus for screening and listening and for storing audio-visual material.

Examples :

— Educational Film Guide (Q) -N.Y., Wilson.

— India Education (Ministry of). Annotated Catalogue of 16-mm Educational Films in the Central Film Library, New Delhi.

— Hall, David Records, N.Y. Knopf.

13. Government Publications

The documents which are published by or by order under its right, are the government publications. These are published by government or departments or commissions in the form of books, periodicals, and reports. These are the official records by the authority of the government and are authentic, standardized, cheap and subsidized.

Examples :

— Kothari Commission, Report on Education and National Development 1964-66 Delhi, Manager of Publications, 1966.

— Radhakrishnan Report of the University Education Commission, Delhi, Manager of Publications 1949 - 2v.

14. Fugitive Materials

These are perishable nature materials needed for a particular time. This is also named as Ephemera, which includes pamphlets, cuttings and other materials of ephemeral interest and value.

15. Current Information Sources

These are very essential part of our daily lives, which provide us latest, day-to-day information and inform about the recent happenings. Newspaper, magazine, television etc provide such information.

The various source of current information are:

(a) Indexes to newspapers.

(b) Indexes to general periodicals.

(c) Radio and television broadcast.

(d) News summaries.

Examples :

— Data India, New Delhi : Press Institute of India 1976.

— The New York Times Index, New York: The New York Times, 1851.

— Kessings Record to World Events. London, Kessings Publications, 1931.

— Asian Recorder, New Delhi, Asian Records and Publications, 1955. Weekly.

Besides, now-a-days new Audio-visual sources in the form of CD-ROM, Databases and Internet resources are also included under reference documentary resources.

Q. : State the criteria for evaluation of a reference book.

or

What is a reference book? How does it differs from an ordinary book? Give the various criteria for evaluating a reference book.

Ans. : Based on the use, we may divide books into two categories as below:

(i) Books which can be read consecutively for inspiration, enjoyment or information; (ii) Books which are designed to be consulted or referred to from time to time for a specific piece of information. Ordinarily, these do not lend themselves to continuous reading. Broadly speaking, any book can be called a reference book, provided the information contained in it, is so organized that it becomes readily accessible.

The first category consists of ordinary books and the books of second category are called reference books.

An ordinary book possesses the following characteristics:

It is made of continuous exposition. It is developed sentence by sentence, paragraph by paragraph, chapter by chapter. There is a link at each stage. There is an element of continuity. In case of a biography of a person, it would normally be developed from childhood to death and later influence. In a novel, the novel develops through stages; there is an element of continuity. Ordinary books can be read continuously from cover to cover. Ordinarily, these are allowed to be lent out by libraries.

Whereas, a reference book is designed by its arrangement and treatment to serve certain purposes. A reference book usually possesses the following characteristics:

(i) It is meant for consultation for a specific piece of information. Of course, works like dictionaries, encyclopaedias, yearbooks, etc., provide information directly but works like bibliographies, indexing and abstracting services do not provide information itself but point out the sources which may contain information.

(ii) It is not meant for continuous reading. No one is expected to read a dictionary or an encyclopaedia or a directory from cover to cover.

(iii) Very often, a reference book may consist of disjointed entries of varying length. For example, one entry in an encyclopaedia may have no relationship with the next entry. These entries may have been brought together merely due to the incident of alphabetization. In other words, we can say that a reference book usually lacks continuous exposition.

(iv) It is usually not lent out because reference books are required from time to time for consultation. One never knows, somebody may require it at any time. Thus, its use is restricted to the library building itself.

(v) Information in a reference book is so organized that the required information can be located promptly and exhaustively.

Reference books form the very basis of reference service. Of course, the reference staff has also to consult other materials at times to give service. Due to the nature of their use, these are usually kept in a separate sequence in a library.

Evaluation of Reference Sources/books

In order to achieve a thorough understanding of reference books, it is essential to know how to evaluate a reference book. A reference librarian should know the criteria of evaluation of a reference book. "The librarian must ask at least four basic questions about a reference work: What is its purpose? Its authority? Its scope? Its proposed audience?. Reference books are different in their purpose from ordinary books; therefore, a different approach is required for their study and evaluation. It is convenient to lay down checkpoints for their appraisal. Mr. Louis Shores has guided the methods of evaluation of reference book, which are as below:

1. Authority

To be authoritative a publication of reference use, we should see the background of the author, editors, joint author including publisher too. If the one publication is written by more than a person who are responsible for its thought contents is, we should search and evaluate the background of the all writers. Besides it should be verified whether book is new or old. If the new edition, then is it update or not?

2. Scope

To know the scope of a specific reference book in size, volume, circulation the following four points are to be considered: -

(i) Purpose: To know the purpose of the book, we should know the contents, and preface of the book. Having after knowing the purpose, we should evaluate whether the book achieved its objectives or not? If yes, how far the targets are achieved ?

(ii) Coverage: The related book must be evaluated by its conciseness or detailed particulars.

(iii) Up-to-dateness: The reference book is useful till it is updated. Its old editions can not fulfil the need of required information. Therefore newness is main important point. This should be compared with other updated material.

(iv) Bibliography: It should be carefully observed that a bibliography at the end is provided or not. It will be very useful for the readers to consult the related bibliography used in references.

3. Treatment

While evaluating a reference book, it should be measured from all the angles of the status of the book, viz., its language, style and presentation, authoritativeness and standardization. There is a fear of biases towards a subject or a country or an author; therefore it should be evaluated from the point of view of biases.

4. Arrangement

The collection of a library is useful if it is easily accessible. If it is complicated in its arrangement then reader will not be in a position to use them immediately. The reference books generally arranged either in classified or alphabetical or in chronological or geographical orders as per the needs of the clientele. Therefore the arrangement of the information must be easily understandable and accessible. The alphabetical index provided in the end of book alongwith a bibliography of related reference material to be consulted, will be an added virtue and it should be evaluated in plus side.

5. Format

The physical appearance of the reference book should be attractive by colourful, printing and diagrammatic with good binding. The inner side of the book should be indicated with the super quality diagrammatic representation, photographs etc. While purchasing a reference book, these virtue points must be considered.

6. Special Feature

Every book has its specific characteristics and virtues. While acquiring a book it should be considered with its special feature. In the same way if one book attracts a specific reader it means it is forever good.

Conclusion: After having gone through all the check points conclusion may be drawn about usefulness of a reference book for the type of library or for the type of user. Sources for information for the evaluation of a reference book are:

Title page, Preface, Table of contents, Introduction, Text and Index etc. By evaluation the kind of reference books/sources of information the good library service will be rendered to the users according to their need.

Q. : Discuss the role, qualities and qualification of a Reference Librarian of an University library.

or

Explain the role and functions of a Reference Librarian in a special library. Discuss the qualities and qualifications to be possessed by him.

or

"The efficiency of reference service is largely dependent on the quality of the reference librarian", discuss by giving examples.

or

What should be the qualities of a Reference Librarian? How will it differ in different types of libraries?

or

Stating the objectives of the information services, justify the appointment of a good Information/Library officer in a library.

or

Discuss the qualities of a Reference Librarian.

Ans. : The aim of information service is to keep its users well informed with wither information which may of uses to them and in the form which is most usable to them. All information activities and services are aimed to the user. Thus, user is the focal point of any kind of information service. There are various kinds of users and their needs are very complex. Hence, on the basis of type of information wanted, information service may be various types i.e., current awareness type, selective dissemination of information, abstracting, indexing and bibliographical services, data services, translation services etc.

An information officer is the one, who provides information service in special library or documentation center or information center or information departments. He is sometimes called by the name

Information Scientist, or Documentation Officer, or Intelligence Officer, etc.

Information officer plays a significant role in information handling and information transfer. The main objective of an information officer is to provide potential user with timely and relevant information with least possible cost. An information center is known by his behavior and capabilities of providing right information to right seeker at right time. Libraries have different jobs because of variations in the jobs performed is due to specialties of every library. But broadly speaking few common functions are the same in every library, which are as follow:

1. Supervisory Work

The head of the reference department is the reference librarian. He is the monarchy of that department. Reference department to run library smoothly performs the following jobs: -

(a) Directing and inspection of duties and jobs performed by subordinate staff in the library.

(b) Selection of reference material in a library.

(c) To call the meeting of subordinate professional staff of library to solve the departmental problem.

(d) To make coordination with the other departments of library.

(e) To keep the documentary records safe and maintain statistics.

(f) Annual reports, its preparation and to present to the librarian.

(g) To make future plans for improvement.

2. Directive Work

In order to make the optimum use of the reading material in the library, the reference library has to do the following work: -

(a) To assist the reader in use of reading material and also to make a coordination between reader and reading literature by personal assistance.

(b) To make acquaint devices used in the library like, cataloguing, classification etc.

(c) The use of reference books and how to get the required detail from these sources.

(d) To listing the researchers, consultation of periodicals and to get desired information out of these sources.

(e) To assist and guide to the new readers to reach upto the reading material.

3. Informative Work

(a) To answer the factual questions which relates in the incidents, facts, statistics and data's etc.

(b) To answer the questions to be asked on telephone.

(c) Literary search or to provide long-range reference service.

(d) If the sufficient reading material is not available particularly in regard of the questions asked, then to make available the literature on inter library loan for providing information.

(e) To train the readers for self-searching the information.

(f) To render the services of CAS - Current awareness service, Translation service, Photostat and Information service etc.

4. Guidance Work

In a public library, readers come for consultation of the book in the library. Some of them might be of a new ones, they are in need of proper guidance. The reference librarian may provide his services in the following manner :

(a) He provides information to the reader to select his proper business. He also gives the books of related topics.

(b) He provides the books to the reader in such a way that he get the knowledge gradually.

5. Documentation Work

The documentation work may provide :

(a) A bibliography of the book needed.

(b) On demand the translation of the particular required literature.

6. Evaluation Work

The success of a department depends upon what we did and what we achieved. A continuous self-evaluation must be taken into consideration to know as to how much level objectives are achieved? Without evaluation, no future plan can be implemented or even planned. Therefore, a reference librarian always see the last record for self-evaluation. A reference librarian has to do the following jobs:

(a) To keep the record of questions asked by the readers, which may helpful to know how many questions are asked.

(b) Also a record of those questions which could not be answered.

(c) Survey work and its report.

7. Other Work

Other than the jobs mentioned above, a reference librarian also has to do the following work: -

(a) To create the curiosity of the reader and to motivate for use, to organize book exhibition, lectures, seminar on the subject etc.

(b) By the continuous use of cataloguing few mistakes are brought into notice of librarian and thus to remove these anomalies.

(c) To make acquaint with the new reference books received in the library to the readers as well as to staff.

(d) To make coordination with the order Libraries and Documentation centers.

The above mentioned efforts are to be filled in by every type of library and reference librarian of the institution.

Qualities and Qualification of Reference Librarian/Information Officer

The Chief of the reference department is the Reference Librarian. Now-a-days, he is also called by the name Information Officer as he also assist in providing information to users. His qualities must be of worth while. His virtues like quality, qualification, meritorious academic record, sweet and amicable nature, and dedication makes popular not only to reference section but also the library and its parent organization.

1. Personal Qualities

The following qualities are must in the personality of a Reference Librarian or Information Officer.

(a) Patience : Patience is must for reference librarian/ Information officer and it is an important virtue. The different readers come to the library, few of them are educated, uneducated, rich, poor, short or high tempered persons, confused mind, etc., it is his duty to hear them patiently and solve their problems. Therefore the reference librarian should not be a short/hot tempered but be a cool and calm behavior person.

(b) Sound Mind having Independent Views : He should be with sound mind and sound health. A person of short tempered/hot tempered or touchy cannot be a successful librarian. This type of person will spoil the image of the library and will be harmful for a reader instead of beneficial to him.

Reference librarian should be a man, free from all restrictions and stress. He should be courageous to say clear position. If the things will be putting in a clear position it will be more beneficial to the readers.

(c) Studiousness : Knowledge is changing fast. To be remain updated in the subject field, a person is to be very alert and habitual of regular reading. In the same way when a librarian is teacher of teachers, he will have to be very updated in the subject field in which he deals.

(d) Soft-spoken, Pleasant Personality and Healthy: Reference librarian should be a sober having sweet disposition. He should behave properly in a friendly manner with the readers. The pleasant personality person shall attract to the readers, and thus the many readers will attract to come to library.

He should be a man of high moral character. Morality attracts good readers to come to the library. Soft-spoken and pleasant personality gives pleasure to the readers, whether the job completed or not. Therefore, he should be a man of soft-spoken, pleasant personality and high morality.

(e) Reticent, Disciplined, Enthusiastic and Dutiful : He should be reticent and have a command of regional, national and few international languages according to the size and standard of the readers coming to the library. He should be a disciplined person to render services to the readers in a controlled way.

2. Professional and Academic Qualifications

The reference librarian should have the following qualifications:

(a) Trained in Library Science : He should be having trained by formal education and degree of B. Lib. Sc.; M. Lib. Sc. or Documentation etc. He should be well versed with the devices, techniques used in the library. He should know the every aspect of the organization and administration of library.

(b) The Reference Books and its Use : He should be well known about the collected reference books, encyclopedias and other forms of reading material and techniques of how to use them.

(c) Knowledge of Modern Techniques : He should be trained for computer, Internet; etc. It is only possible when his paper bio-data is having some specialized degree of library science along knowledge of IT.

(d) Qualification According to the Business : He should well versed with the various schemes of classification in general and particular scheme in detail, which will enable him to avail the facility of providing textbooks.

(e) Knowledge of Additional Language and Script : He should know the regional language and at least one or two of foreign languages, so that he can fulfill the demand of translation by the readers.

(f) High Education : He is regarded an academician. He is supposed to be the trained in profession as well as at least having another Master Degree, preferably Doctorate in a subject studious. He must have the capacity to adopt and learn any new method and be able to control and take any challenging task.

The role of Reference Librarian as Information Officer changes with a change in the need of society. An information officer should be able to adopt himself to modern techniques with broad humanism. Impact of computers on library and information science is growing as a result of advances in communication technology. Computers are essential for information handling as the services at the reference desk in libraries in these days are more for the advice regarding the use of computer facilities rather than the traditional references services so a Reference Librarian or Information officer should also have the ability of handling computers.

3. Administrative and Organizational Qualities

The Reference Librarian or Information Officer is a person of multidimensional personality. He is a teacher, guide, friend, guardian of the reader. But his most difficult role is as an Administrator or a Manager of the library as well as of the team.

He is expected to be an efficient administrator. He should understand the psychology of a man and human relations.

The following qualities are required to be a successful Reference Librarian/Information Officer.

1. He should be able to settle the administrative problems with all courage and spirit.

2. He should be able to coordinate and organize.
3. He should be a justified person having cordial relations with his subordinates. He should be a good listener. He should be ready to solve the problem logically.
4. He should be capable to understand and evaluate the work done by the subordinates and instruct them as per need to run library smoothly.

Thus, a Reference Librarian or Information officer having above-mentioned quality will be a successful librarian.

Q. : What is a 'Reference Query'? Discuss types of reference queries and types of reference books suitable for them?

or

Define 'Reference Question', 'Reference Interview' and 'Reference Process'. Explain the steps of reference interview.

or

What are different types of reference queries? How will you hand the reference queries?

or

Write an essay on techniques of answering reference questions with the help of flow chart.

Ans. : "Reference question" is a request of a reader in a particular and definite nature, with an hope to get it from the help of published material or other and which can be retrieved from the sources without any delay, is reference question.

Reference questions are of the following categories:

(i) Directional question
(ii) Factual question
(iii) Question related to special search
(iv) Research question

But generally, following types of questions are asked.

Class of questions about	*Types of questions concerning*
Language	Definition, spelling, pronunciation, abbreviations, usage of terms, foreign terms, synonyms, antonyms, homonyms, signs, symbols, slang, dialect.
Background	General information, self education, all about something, something about, something on.
People	Leading personalities, specialists, professionals, authors, less-known persons.
Trend	Current events, significant developments of the past year, trends in a particular field of activity or study.
Places	Location, description, distances, indentification.
Organizations including societies, Institutions	Addresses, aims, membership, publications, history, structure, names of chief officers.
Facts and activities	Events, statics, formulas, curiosities about traditions, customs, superstitions, etc. Allusions, identification of plots and characters, quotations, record of activities, how to do or how to make or how to conduct or how to perform.
List of documents	Best books, documents on a subject, literature published in a country, reviews, location of a document, bibliographical details of a document.
Illustrations	Diagrams, pictures, photographs, cartoons, slides, films, recordings.

Ways of Receiving Reference Questions

The questions shall be asked in following ways:

1. Direct Approach by a User

When reader needs any information he puts his query with the reference librarian. If this question is asked personally, the reference takes the form or interview.

2. By Telephone

The Query can also be made by phone. But this system lacks the personal contact with the reference librarian.

3. Telex or Fax

The latest technological devices makes library reference services more easy. In the libraries which are connected with the telex or fax, the query can also be solved with this method too.

4. Through Post

Though in this process too, there is no contact between reader and the reference staff, the reader can ask his questions by post.

5. Offer by Reference Librarian

Some times efforts are made by the reference librarian to contact and attract the readers by various means like advertisements, newspapers publicity or so. Sometimes few readers are of shy nature. These readers are welcome by the reference librarian by personal contact and ask his curiosity and answers those.

6. Through Messenger

Sometimes user may not find time to visit reference desk or gone out of station. He may send messenger to collect information. Messenger, being a mediator for carrying out information, may not be able to explain the actual requirement of the end user. There may be a chance for communication gap which can affect the relevance factor.

7. On E-mail

In case library and user both have computer connection and E-mail facility, then user may ask question through e-mail. Now a days, this mode has become much popular and cost effective information in electronic from can be disseminated very fast through this mode.

Where as, the reference query is a request of a reader, of a particular definite nature, type and shape, for which he hopes to get answer from the help of available published collection of the library, which is not readily available and traced from the library is reference question query.

Here 'a particular definite nature' word is used. As a matter of fact the certainty of a query is quite difficult, because the answers asked by the reader are not clearly explained. The reader himself is not aware with this certainty or the question to be asked or the clarifications of information he needs.

The main objective and step of reference service is to answer the queries asked. Various authors have defined the reference service from different angles and point of view.

Generally speaking - queries asked by the readers is answered with the help of reference books is reference. But it is not sufficient, because the queries are not answered from the reference books but from all the collections. Therefore the answers of those questions which are solved and directed with the help of published or unpublished books or personal assistance, are included in reference service.

Types of Reference Queries

The reference queries are made by the readers. These queries are divided according to the information or on the basis of information resources, or on the subject, according to the nature of the readers.

William Katz categorized into following four divisions:

1. Directional query
2. Factual query
3. Query related with specific research, and
4. Research query.

1. Directional Query

These are such questions by which the readers are given direction or guidance. In this process, a reader knows himself very clearly that what does he wants? To answer or solve this, a reference librarian is expected to direct the source of reference book where it can be found. The reader consults these sources at his own level and try to get his answer from the help of these resources. It takes less time to search the information. For an example these may be of following types:

— Where the catalogue cabinet is in the library?

— At which Story and at where the encyclopedias are arranged and kept?

— Where the works of Shakespear is kept?

2. Factual Query

These are the questions which are directly related with the facts and figures. These can be answered in a shorter time by consulting reference sources. For example:

— What is the height of Mt. Averest?

— When Rajeev Gandhi died?

— Who was the first President or who is now the President of India?

These questions can be answered by the help of biographical dictionaries, who's who? Geographical dictionaries, year books, etc. How much time shall be consumed in answering of these questions? It depends on the collected reference sources as well as on the efficiency of reference librarian or professional staff.

3. Query related to Specific Research

The readers need a concise but automatic information while asking questions of this category. To answer this type of questions, the related sources of reference source is consulted and search the desired information. Sometimes, the readers are provided a bibliography too. These query may be as follows:

— What were the main characteristics of IXth five year plan of India?

— What is the contribution of Dr. S.R.Ranganathan in the field of library science?

— What are the manifestos of Joint Front Government?

— What are the relations of multinational companies with the Government of India?

— What is *'Havala Kand'* (Reference incident)?

— What is Uria Kand?

4. Research Query

This type of queries and related questions are asked particularly by the subject experts, for intensive research and findings. The answer of these questions are given with the help of various documents available in the library. These includes books, periodicals essays and articles published in magazines manuscripts, research dissertations etc., which answers research query. Sometimes the query asked by the readers may not be available in the library, in that case it is to be acquired from other library as an help. For example:

— Colon classification scheme is more scientific than Dewey Decimal Classification Why?

— Why the male suffers from cancer more than the women?

While answering this type of questions, various literary search method are being used. In this system a reader is asked to submit a short report or by verbal short interview, of his need and then the answer is searched from the help of related reference book. The readers are provided the list of information and documents and the reader himself searches answers.

Besides, on the basis of subjects and information sources used for answering, the queries may be sub-divided as follows:-

1. On the Basis of Subject

These types of questions are analyzed first and then divided subjectwise; for example: Economics, Library Science, Political Science etc. By the nature and scope of these questions, the taste of the reader is also known, and gets help in selection of books. Acquisition list can be prepared having after knowing that what are the books required in the library which is not already available.

2. On the Basis of Information Source

In these types of questions the information is provided for the available resources particularly from primary sources-periodicals, research dissertation, patent etc., and secondary-books, encyclopedias and tertiary documents.

Techniques of Answering Reference Question

While searching the answer of reference questions the following steps are taken:

Step I — To put up question.

Step II — To answer temporarily.

Step III — To talk with the reader to know the question and actual need

Step IV — To analyse the question.

Step V — To decide about the policy of research.

Step VI — To continue the research.

Step VII — Reference Librarian decides whether the selected material is appropriate or not for the point of view of the reader.

Thus, to solve the reference queries the above steps are taken as help.

FLOW-CHART FOR ANSWERING QUERIES

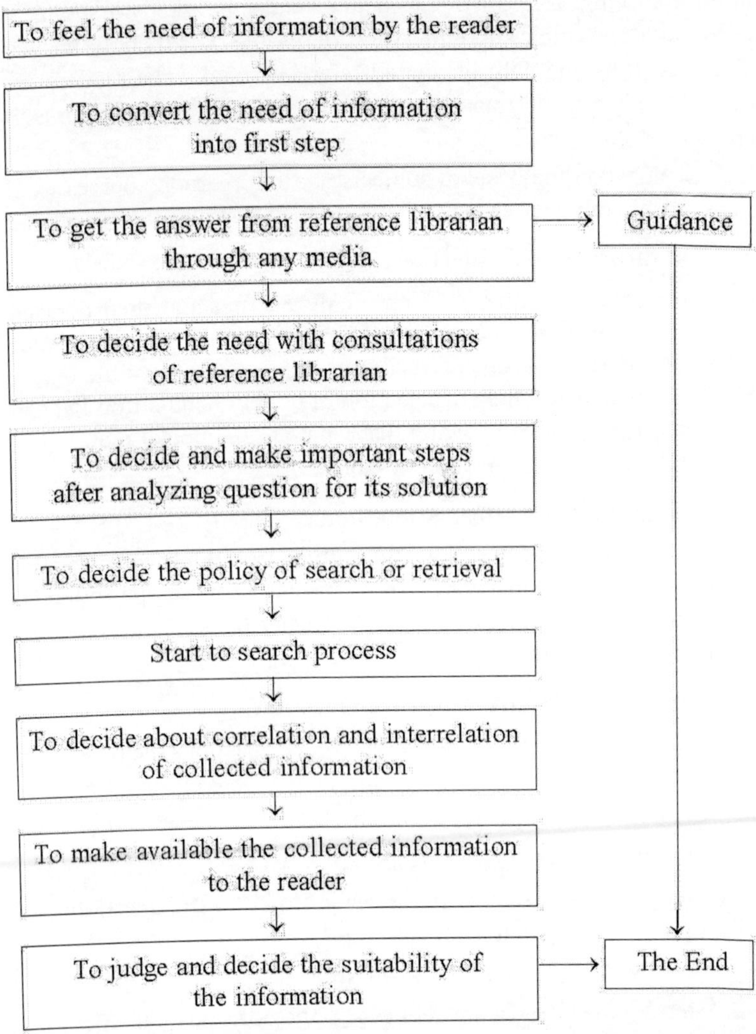

Reference Interview

Reference interview is the interview, a reader's talk with the reference librarian, to clarify the questions asked. This is an undoubtedly truth that a librarian's duty is to retrieve the information himself or to provide help. In other words, we can say that the utility of the library is proved for satisfaction of the readers.

The reference interview meets the challenge on a 'one-to-one basis' and may determine the success or failure of the reference process. It provides an opportunity to ascertain whether or not the question being posed expresses the user's need clearly and completely. "In a reference query it is presumed that half of the battle is won if we can know the actual need of the questioner. This can be done by reference interview."

Thus to answer the question of readers the reference interview is quite necessary. After interview, the need of the reader can be ascertain and only then the material can be searched.

Steps Involve in Reference Interview

The following steps are taken in reference interview:

1. Service demand slip : First of all the reader is asked to fill in a demand form and produce it to the reference librarian. This form is kept very carefully so that it can be used in future on demand or needed.

2. Determine exact requirement of the user : The main problem is to approach and determine the correct problem of the reader. Sometimes the service demand slip can not clear the exact problem. For example, somebody demanded that he requires the information about chemistry. Little later it was cleared that his particular interest is in organic chemistry. Thus after taking demand slip or form, further efforts are quite needed to pin-point the subject need. If it could not be done then the entire material of chemistry, as broads heading could be given as information which would waste the time of the reader.

3. To know the maximum information about the reader : The following information can be taken by the reference interview:

(a) What is his subject taste (Particular or general)?

(b) Scope of the answer (Short or detailed)?

(c) In which language he needs the answer?

(d) What form of literature material is needed i.e. Book, Periodical, articles, Publications of time etc?

(e) What time to take for answering?

(f) Educational qualifications.

(g) Post held, address with telephone, fax no. etc.

4. Try to understand the user : By reference interview, librarian should try to read the psychology of the reader, and actually what does he wants? Sometimes, reader may be of shy nature and can not ask his query in an effective way or approach. Therefore he should be asked in a sympathetic mood to satisfy his needs.

After completing the reference interview the following decision should be think for further consideration in the matter.

(i) Nature of the question is answering, sufficient or merely guidance?

(ii) Can answer be given immediately or takes time?

(iii) Is answering needs a further search in detail? If so, the clientele may be asked to come again.

Q. : Write Short note on Search-process.

Ans. : Search process means to find out the reading required material. The most important aspect is to get the published material, no matter how and by which method it is searched.

In search process, the outline of the assignment is made first which depends on the points like-nature of the query, available reading material in the library, the qualification and experience of the reference librarian, their taste and time devotion in reading material.

The following are the necessary steps of search process:

1. Analysis of questions: First of all the questions are analyzed to know its subject, subheading, headings. To perform this job assistance can be taken by mechanical device of computer or classification scheme, so that the facet of the subject can be find out. Thus, the librarian decides the class facets of the subject in his mind so that the reading material can be searched without loss of time.

2. Classification of questions: In this step, various sources of information are estimated keeping in view the various aspects of the questions, and a bibliography and list of resources is prepared on the priority basis.

3. Search of information : In this step, it is decided as to how the search can start. Though reference librarian may not be expert of the subject or fully unaware but he should get the primary information having after studying encyclopedias. Then he can search from library catalogue, indexing & abstracting and contemporaries articles. If he knows the actual subject of the question, librarian shall get the literature by the help of devices of library used therein. Thus, the search process much depends on the knowledge of the reference librarian.

Generally the following points should be taken into consideration while searching the information from the sources:

(i) Approach for search of information must be from general to specific.

(ii) Bibliography must be seen so that it may be clear that how many books are already published in the subject. It should be consulted first manuscripts and then subject bibliography.

(iii) Published articles in the periodicals as well as indexing and abstracting information is collected.

(iv) The bibliography of local, national and international level must be used.

(v) Listed text book at the end of published articles in periodicals.

(vi) Clipping of newspapers.

(vii) To contact with the other institutions like libraries and documentation centers etc.

(viii) Treatise of various learned persons and subject experts.

(ix) While searching questions, he should be provided the reading material of his needs.

Even after this, there may be some questions for which no relevant answers were provided to the user. The reasons may be (i) reference librarian may overlook the answer in an available source (ii) the answer may not be available in the in-house collection, and (iii) the question may not have definite answer. If the unanswerable questions of a similar type seems to be recurring, reference librarian should try to fill the gap in the reference collection through acquisition department. Even the question remains unanswered, the approach during the reference interview can build goodwill and confidence. If the desired information can not be located from in-house collection, the same may be tried through cooperative or networking arrangement. There are other agencies which have specialization in certain type of information services and products. These agencies may be contacted for such type of questions.

Q. : Define 'Documentation' and discuss its purpose.

or

What do you mean by Documentation. Write briefly about growth and development of documentation and Information centres in India.

or

Discuss the growth and development of documentation and information centres in India.

Ans. : The word 'documentation' came into existence with the beginning of 20th century. It actually means much more than building bibliography of micro-thoughts. It surpasses the technique of providing bibliographical and reference service. Its main importance lies in the retrieval of information for the scientists and research scholar.

It is variously defined by different scientists as under:

P.N. Gaur has defined documentation as "Collecting, classifying and making readily accessible all kinds of recorded knowledge."

According to *Bradford* "The process of collecting and subject classifying all the records of new observations and making them available, at need, to the discover or inventor."

ASLIB'S definition in the 'Journal of Documentation' described it as 'Recording, organizing and dissemination of specialized knowledge or in other words documentation means collecting, organizing and providing micro-thought to the scientist and research scholars."

According to *Land Encyclopedia* "Documentation does, in fact, embrace the whole gamut of operations from the discovery or creation of new knowledge, through its publication, analysis, classification and arrangement to its arrival at the user, that is to say, report writing, publication, abstracting, classifications, indexing reassembly, presentation and dissemination."

Thus, "Documentation is the complex of processes involved in pin-pointed, exhaustive and expeditious services of nascent thought to specialists."

Need of Documentation

Documentation is needed because of following reasons:

1. For Research Work : To satisfy the need of human being, research works and projects were started by the government as well as private institutions, as a result scientists felt a need of different types of documents. Apart from satisfaction of needs of the scientists, the projects result too delivered upto the public.

In the changing time of research needs, the emphasis has been given to start on practical research instead of basic research and also group research instead of personal research. As a result there is explosion of literature and other problems raised. These all problems can be solved by documentation only.

2. Social Needs: Dr. S.R.Ranganathan, the father of library science in India, has stated that the need of documentation is due to social need. Earlier research work was depended on the need of researcher but not it is due to social needs. Increasing population and to satisfy the growing need documentation is quite necessary. At present, industrial productivity and research project depend upon documentation. Researchers of one country should exchange ideas from other countries too, which depends upon documentation.

3. Problems of Communication: In the ancient period, the research work was in very small in numbers, and users were very less hence there was no problem in communication. Now there is rapid growth in literature explosion at one side and increased in research work at the other, raised difficulty in communication. Documentation service is the bridging channel between reader and the communication.

4. Literature Explosion: In the ancient period, books were in handwritten form i.e. manuscript form, and quantitatively very few, but due to invention of printing press, and developments in printing technology, a sudden rise took place in publishing world. Today there is an explosion in book publishing and very difficult to search the need of a researcher and scientist. To get the required documents from the huge collection of publications, few technical devices and other mechanical systems including computerized services like, abstracting, indexing, photocopying and microfilming came into existence, which is called documentation.

5. Economic Problems: Today no library in the world can claim self dependent in economic and financial budget. Every library has its limited resources and cannot purchase all the publications.

Under the situation, researchers and scientists will get difficulty in completing research projects which can be solved by adopting the documentation techniques.

6. Language Barrier: Today the world literature is published almost in 50 script languages while any scientists or user knows not more than two or three languages. Under the circumstances how they will get and use their desired document. To avoid this situation the techniques of documentation can be adopted.

7. Organization of Literature: Trade, commerce and industry, research organizations give importance to specific and research literature instead of traditional literature. To collect, organize and to make available the latest developments of subject to the employees, executives, documentation is required.

8. Industrial Needs: Industrial development is taking place with a fast rate. To get the productivity and profit and to economise, cost factor at one side and to increase productions on the other, every day new techniques, mechanized devices are being used. Continuous research projects are in progress. To do this jobs easily, library services to industry has become necessity, libraries are providing documentation services in these industries.

Purpose of Documentation

Documentation has vital role in the present age of scientific and technological for its R & D (Research and development) sections. The credit goes to documentation for getting the desired information easily out of bulk publications.

The following are the main objectives of documentation:-

1. Scientists and researchers cannot search as well as specialize the literature both at a time but documentation them to search their need promptly.
2. There is high speed in literature explosion which cannot be controlled without help of documentation.
3. Updateness of intellectual awareness cannot be controlled without documentation.
4. In order to increase production which is a direct need of industry and commerce is not possible without documentation.
5. It is very essential to collect, classified and distribute all types of documents related with the human activities of all fields.

6. To collect, organize and distribution of the micro thought of the scientist and researchers.
7. Book selection, receipts, accession, classification, cataloguing, circulation of books are the main activities of libraries which can be easily done with the help of documentation.

Growth and development of Documentation and Information Centres in India

Documentation and information centers are intermediary information sources between the generators and the users of information. They constitute the information resource of a country. By developing a strong information resource base and a suitable information infrastructure, a country is able to improve its capability in information handling, service and utilization. In actual, the growth and development of documentation and information centers can be studied after independence of the country because only post-independence period of India (1947) withnessed the establishment of many bibliographical information centers and systems, in response to the need for information support in diverse national endeavours. The successive Five-Year Plans of the country supported development of a vast infrastructure for science and technology. The Government was committed to the policy that science and technology are to be used as instruments of national development and progress. There has been a vast expansion in facilities for higher education, particularly in technical disciplines. The industrial growth has also been phenomenal. To documentation and support became imperative and creation of necessary infrastructure, therefore, has been attended to continuously. The overall growth and development of Documentation and Information Centres in India can be studied under following heads :

(i) Government's Encouragement and Support : The government policy declarations in many fields advocate explicitly or implicitly, the development of facilities for library and information support. The Scientific Policy Resolution (1958), the Technology Policy Statement (1983), the National Policy on Education (1986), and the recommendations of the Science Advisory Council to the Prime Minister have all stressed the importance of information in national development.

The Five-Year Plans of the country have laid a good deal of emphasis on the planned development of library and information facilities. NISSAT came to be established as a project under the SandT

Plan of the Fifth Five-Year Plan. A Seventh Plan Working Group (1985-1990) outlined detailed proposals for modernization of libraries and informatics. The Eighth Plan (1990-95) Working Group on Libraries reiterated the same action. The Ninth Plan Working Group on Libraries and Informatics (1997-2002) also emphasized modernization of library and information facilities in the country for optimum use of the information resources and for sharing of these resources. In addition, the Planning Commission appointed a high-level core Task Group with Dr. .P.J Abdul Kalam, Scientific Adviser to Defence Minister as the Chairman and Dr. N.Seshagiri, Director-General, NIC as member-Secretary, to advise on the use of information and communication technologies for resource sharing among libraries and information centers. The recommendations of this Task Force are being duly considered by the Planning Commission for incorporation in the Ninth Plan document. Thus, in all the planned endeavours, the emphasis is on modernization and introduction of computer-oriented information handling.

(ii) Progress during the 1950s and 1960s : As a support to the growing RandD activities in the country, the special libraries attached to various scientific institutions initially began to assume the functions of information centers and have been offering services at the local level. At about that time international organizations like UNESCO and the FID were interested in promoting national systems of information facilities. The establishment of INSDOC (now NISCAIR) in 1952, with technical assistance from UNESCO, is a landmark in the development of documentation facilities in the country. Later, DESIDOC came into existence in 1967. The Library and Information Services Division of the Bhabha Atomic Research Centre at Mumbai was also established as a central facility in 1968 and this Division took active part in the INIS programme. The Library of the Directorate General of Health Services assumed the role of National Medical Library in 1966 to offer nation-wide service on heath science literature. The creation of such national level information centers gave an impetus to many RandD institutions under the Council of Scientific and Industrial Research (CSIR), Indian Council of Agricultural Research (ICAR), Indian Council for Medical Research (ICMR), and Defence Research and Development Organization (DRDO) to develop their information infrastructure by upgrading and strengthening their libraries.

(iii) Progress during the 1970s : There was a spurt in expansion of documentation and information facilities during the seventies. At the national level, the National Social Sciences Documentation Centre (NASSDOC, 1970), the National Informatics Centre (NIC, 1975), the National Documentation Centre for Health and Family Welfare (1975) and the Agricultural Research Information Centre came up. An important development was the evolution of sectoral information System under the NISSAT programme and other agencies like the Biotechnology Information System (BTIS), and Environmental Information System (ENVIS). These sectoral centers came up around the information centers already having well developed facilities and expertise. They are able to offer specialized services devoted to specific disciplines and missions.

There would be more than 2,000 special libraries, and information centers attached to RandD institutions, academic institutions, industrial undertakings, government departments, etc. They endeavour to take care of information needs at the local level. There has been realization lately that their resources and facilities need to be co-ordinated towards optimum utilization and elimination of unnecessary duplication. There has also been a need to follow uniform techniques, methods and practices towards facilitating exchange of information among the individual centers. In order to achieve these, information systems are being developed around the existing infrastructure. The action programme in this regard envisages interlinking and co-ordinating a large number of resources, services and centers to form versatile, articulated and integrated information systems. A trend in this direction has been set by evolving the National Information System for Science and Technology (NISSAT) in 1977. NISSAT is a major programme in the information field in the country and is expected to contribute substantially to the development of modern and effective information systems and services.

(iv) Progress during the 1980s - 2000 : The expansion of the information infrastructure continued in the eighties and nineties but began moving in new directions. There has been technological revolution in information handling and service. Every sector is moving for possession of knowledge and information. It is said that we are now an information-intensive society. In this context, the dominant role of information is to be perceived. Apart from increase in number, the documentation and information centers have been strengthening their resources and facilities and modernizing their operations and services. The present emphasis is on computerization of information activities and services and networking of libraries and information centers. Conditions are quite favourable now for the country to make rapid progress in building and strengthening the information systems and services along modern lines.

During the eighties, NISSAT added six more sectoral centers devoted to crystallography, chemical sciences, textile technology, bibliometrics, ceramics and CD-ROM database collection. Earlier, four sectoral centers had already been established in drugs and pharmaceuticals, food science and technology, leather technology and machine tools. The UGC has established the National Centre for Science Information (NCSI), at the Indian Institute of Science, Bangalore and two others for social science disciplines at SNDT University, Bombay and MS University, Baroda. The Environmental Information System (EIS) are operational now and they take care of three important areas for information support. A few more national level information systems are in the pipeline, Parallely, the present decade saw the emergence of networks. The biggest of these, after that of National Informatics Centre (NICNET), is INFLIBNET that had linked all the university and major research libraries in the country to form a single information system.

(v) Future Direction : The present first decade of the twenty-first century will see a number of major milestones in the services provided by the libraries and information centers. There centers will have more and more of electronic publications in the form of floppies, tapes and CD-ROMs. Also, libraries in the academic and RandD institutions will be subscribing to online journals also, in addition to journals in paper format. More and more libraries will have online catalogues in place of card catalogues, use Internet and other public data networks extensively for collection and dissemination of information.

Traditional Librarians and Documentalists will play a new role as Information Managers and Database Administrators. Information services will be provided to users usually online who can receive the information right from their homes or work places.

3
Source of Information

Q. : What do you mean by a 'Document'? Discuss various kinds of documents as enunciated by Dr. Ranganathan.

Ans. : Human desire to preserve the knowledge gained and to transmit it for next coming generations gave rise to the concept document. This desire made another effort and shaped it in script language of written form with a view to preserve for future generation.

Dr. S.R.Ranganathan defined the document as below:-

"Any embodied micro-or macro thought, whether exclusive to one work or shared by more than one work."

Glossary-Library Science Technical terms by *P.N.Gaur* has defined, a document as follows :

— A record of mental thought expressed in language, written on paper.

or

— Any material containing recorded information. It is sometimes used for 'Book' or any other form of record.

or

— Any written, printed or otherwise recorded item that may serve as evidence of a transaction.

Types of Documents

Today libraries acquire the different types of documents for use. Various learned persons have tried to categories these documents on the basis of characteristics. *Dr. S. R. Ranganathan* has divided these documents into four categories which can be explained and understand with the help of following diagram:

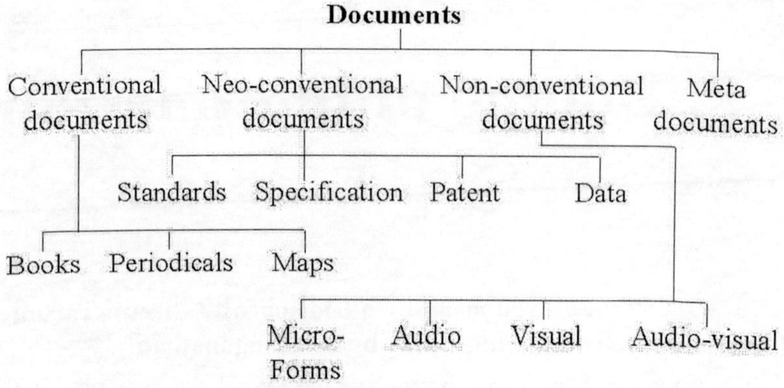

1. Conventional Documents

Conventional documents are in use since ancient times. Before the inventions of paper and printing press, it were in the form of leather card cloth piece, bark of tree, and clay tablets.

According to Dr. S. R. Ranganathan, conventional documents are of three types, as follows :

(A) Books: It is the most popular kind of document. It has continuity in thoughts and a collection of a particular subject of a particular author. The books further may be subsdivided into following three categories:-

(i) Multi-volumed book

(ii) Supplement book

(iii) Composite book

(iv) Simple book

(B) Periodicals: Another most useful and popular documents of the day, are known as periodicals or journals. New ideas and thoughts, research and invention reports are being carried to the readers within a short span of time with the help of periodicals.

(C) Maps : Dr. Ranganathan has put maps in an ordinary category as these are available in ordinary size as well as small quantity of circulation.

2. Neo-Conventional Document

Natural and physical science and its related standards, patents, clippings of newspapers in social science, formulaes of chemistry and chemical calculations, are included in neo-conventional documents. Ranganathan has divided further these into following four categories:-

(i) Standards

(ii) Specifications

(iii) Patents, and

(iv) Data.

3. Non-Conventional Documents

Such documents are quite different from conventional and neo-conventional. The thought contents of these documents are on the basis scientific methods. Dr. Ranganathan divides these further into four categories as follows:-

(i) Microcopy: Due to printing technology, need of space for storing documents became a problem. To solve this problem, the techniques of microfilming and photocopying developed. With the help of these devices more information can be stored in a very little space.

(ii) Audio document: In ancient period 'Sound' documents were used for music and entertainment only, while these are used as an information retrieval tool, today.

(iii) Visual document: With a view to maximum use of information, visual documents are used, particularly for providing library services to illiterate people.

(iv) Audio-Visual document: After 2nd world war, the use of audio-visual, photographs, increased. These documents are quite popular and are used not only for illiterate but to literate also. These documents are very attractive and a source of increasing memory and to sharpen the mind. These are available in macro and micro size both.

4. Meta Document

Meta document are made with a fast speed and without any contribution of human mind directly and scene happening is without human mind. For example: Mechanized technology, photography, radar etc. These documents are important as these makes fixed documentation of a document and thus are errorless.

Q. : What are different types of reference sources and their importance in libraries?

or

Distinguish the difference between information sources and reference books. Discuss with suitable examples, the utility of Primary, Secondary and Tertiary sources of information.

or

State the kinds and characteristics of 'Primary sources of information'. Discuss their role in the advancement of research.

or

Explain the difference between 'Primary' and Secondary' sources of information. Describe the main features of any two secondary sources in the field of library and information science.

or

Describe various categories of documents with examples. Discuss different types of primary documents with their specific function.

Ans. Traditionally speaking, information sources would include primarily books, periodicals, and newspapers. However, the number and forms of sources are continuously increasing. Even unpublished sources are becoming increasingly important to scholars. Occasions will arise, especially in a special library or a university library, when information would be required by a user without pre-condition about the form of document. In such a situation, what matters is the finding of information not the sources of information.

We may recognize the following kinds of sources of information: *Documentary sources.* Primary, secondary and tertiary sources-(The primary sources are the first to appear. Secondary sources come out next. The tertiary sources are the last to appear). *Non-documentary sources*-Formal and Informal.

A. Documentary Sources

These are generally published or recorded documents of knowledge.

Documentary sources may be divided into primary secondary and tertiary sources as under :

INFORMATION SOURCES

Primary		*Secondary*		*Tertiary*
Periodicals	Condensation & Repackaging	Indexing Services	Keys and Aids to Search	Yearbooks and Directories
Research Reports		Abstracting Services		Bibliographies
Conference Proceedings		Review of Progress		Location Lists of Periodicals
Patents		Reference Works		Lists of Abstracting and Indexing Services
Standards		Treatises		Guides
Trade Literature		Monographs		Lists of Research in Progress
Theses		Text Books		Guides to Professional Organizations

I. Primary Sources

Primary sources of information are the first published records of original research and development or description of new application or new interpreation of an old theme or idea. These are original documents representing unfiltered original ideas. These constitute the latest available information. A researcher producing new information can make it available to the particular community through the primary sources. Often, it may be the only source of information in existence.

Primary sources are unorganized sources, which are rather difficult to use by themselves, the secondary sources help us to use these. These are important sources of information. A subject becomes a discipline in its own right when independent primary sources begin to be produced in that area. The rate of growth of a discipline to a large extent depends upon the amount of literature being produced in the form of primary sources reporting developments in the concerned field.

These aid the researchers to:

(a) keep themselves up-to-date and well informed of the new developments,

(b) avoid duplication in research, and

(c) help others to build on this by means of further work and thus generate more information.

Kind's of Primary Sources

1. Periodicals : Periodical is a social publication, which is the most important and useful source. Generally its publication's periodicity is weekly, fortnightly, monthly, quarterly, half yearly or annual. Periodical includes, journals, bulletins, transactions, proceedings or similar works, which appear regularly and continuously in numbered sequence. Information published in the periodicals is almost invariably more uptodate than the appearing in books.

The each volume of the periodical is free from subject limits, but generally the subject periodical is related with any part of a particular subject. It's authors are many and more than one. It is published in volumes.

Generally speaking it is assumed that periodical/magazine is the child of book or say that today's magazine is tomorrow's book. Practically it shows that most of the material reported in periodicals is never published in books.

Examples :

Historical Journal, 1958, New York, Cambridge University Press, Quarterly,

Nature,1899-,London, Macmillan, Weekly.

Physics of Fluids, 1958-,New York, American Institute of Physics, Monthly.

Photochemistry: an International Journal of Plant Biochemistry. 1962-Oxford, Pergamon Press, Monthly.

2. Research Reports : Now a days the research reports are more usable instead of periodicals or journals. Primarily in first decade these reports were calculated 10% of the total publications. Thus, these reports were used as most effective source of scientific communication. The main reason of using was due to lack of limited paper distribution, much time to require in publication. It was decided to develop such a media which was economically in paper consumption and rather useful.

The information containing in research reports are of original nature. Sometimes these are available in the form of typing. Some reports provide unorganized information in the initial while other provides some standard and detailed information. The government reports of various projects which are published form these, categories in the following subjects as example: Sociology. Education, Economics etc. These publications are not a regular but uncertain. When any research scholar takes his project then only it is declared.

NASSDOC, and ICSSR, the centres have a great collection of these types of documents and publish their regular report.

Example :

Scientific and Technical Aerospace Reports, National Aeronautics and Space Administration (NASA).

3. Patents : A patent is a facility grant to the new invention for a particular time for its use in public clientele. A patent thus, becomes the form of an official document having the seal of government related with it, which decides an exclusive privilege or right over a period of time to the proceeds of an invention. In every country, there is one publishing agency and these are serially numbered. In India-Indian patent office is responsible for granting patents.

The patents are listed in official patent office bibliographical tools. Besides, regular indexing and abstracting services also cover patents.

A patent covers the following information:

(i) Heading as title in which name of the patentee, address, his nominee with address, date of application, title of the inventions.

(ii) Nature and scope of the invention.

(iii) Details of the linear pictures.

(iv) The detailed statement of the characteristics of the invention.

(v) Claimant of the patent and his patentee's clarification.

Examples:

Chemical Abstracts, 1907-,Easton, Pa., American Chemical Society, 1907-, Vol. 1-, Weekly.

Indian Science Abstracts, Delhi, Indian National Scientific Documentation Centre, Vol.1-, 1965-, Monthly.

Physics Abstracts: Science Abstracts Aeries. London, Institution of Electrical Engineers, 1898-, Fortnightly,

World Patents Index Abstracts Journal (19 different editions are published), 1975-, London, Derwent Publications, Weekly (exclusively devoted to patents).

World Patents Index Gazette Section-Ch: Chemical, 1975-,

London, Derwent Publications, Weekly (There are three such other indexes).

4. Conference Proceedings : The papes submitted in the conference, seminars organized at national and international level, are very useful source. These papers which are read in these conferences, are used in new inventions or research. The questions and answeres asked in the seminar by the various participants are also published. Conference proceedings can be divided into following three categories:

(i) Pre-Conference Literature

(ii) During Conference Literature

(iii) Post-Conference Literature

In short the papers to be read are included in pre-conference literature. The papers are read actually comes into middle category and at the end of conference these all ideas, discussions, approved literature are published in the form of periodical magazine, books, records etc.

5. Standards : Standardization of publications is the good source of maintaining uniformity. This given uniformity, as a result of the use and action of the commodity increase its quality. Repaid growth and continuing increase in publications create the need of standardization. Therefore, public corporations, government or registered body decides the standard of a commodity in size, quantity, quality and use and thus a product is standardized. The consumer's faith in commodity increase. The things which are not standardized, disappear form the market after a certain period.

A typical standard is a pamphlet covering definitions, methods, properties, measurements, etc. It may be illustrated with tables and diagrams. In India, Indian Standards Institution is a major organization issuing standards, which brings out about 300 standards annually.

Examples:

International Standards Organization, *Guidelines for the establishment and development of monolingual thesauri for information retrieval,* First draft proposal (IDO/TC46/TG (Paris 1971-1) 1034E, revised 3rd August, 1971)

British Standards Institution, *Microfiche,* BS 4187: 1976.

6. Industrial and Trade Literature : Business houses and industries are the main source to provide the qualitative and quantitative information of a product to which these firms are directly related, whenever such types of information is required from these business and trade houses. The main objective of these houses is to increase their sale of product and to consume it in the market by gaining credit or goodwill. Thus, business literature provides the detailed information of the products, its quality. These informations are given by the dealers or producers.

These literature include technical bulletin, price lists, data sheets, business directories and institutional publications. Generally the publishers do not purchase these literature and publications, as a result these publications are not having its entity as a collection.

7. Dissertation or Thesis : In all the leading universitites, and specialised institutions of national repute, the research and development projects are maintained. It is assumed that these research and development projects are completed by the learned research scholars giving the original ideas for the given subject. Moreover, these projects are completed under the supervision and able guidance of the learned scholars and experts of the subject. The main objective of these projects is to examine the qualifications and knolwdge of the scholar in depth of the related subjects.

These research projects enunciates new techniques, system or principle. These are not the publications of public hence it is difficult to get information from these sources. In order to solve this problem measures were adopted. Certain government agencies and department started to collect these research projects and published bibliographies of dissertations submitted.

'NASSDOC' has done a remarkable work in this regard. Approximately more than 2000 project's list are published. A classified list of such publications is also published by ICSSR (Indian Council of Social Science Research), New Delhi in the country. In the same way the U.S.A. Microfilm University has also published 'Dissertation Abstract International'. Thus, the Dissertations and its importance is increased as a primary source.

8. Manuscripts : As regrads the oriental subjects few information for research is coins, ancient monuments, family chronology, which may form the important source and tool. Besides hand written books, manuscripts, unpublished books, archives, memoirs etc. are also important source of primary sources.

In our country National Library, Kolkata, Archieve Gallery, Delhi; Oriental Research Library, Poone; Khuda Baksh Oriental Public Library, Patna; Government Manuscript Library, Chennai are also involved in collecting manuscripts

9. Unpublished Sources : There are certain primary sources of information, which remain unpublished. Very often these may be consulted for historical interest. In some of the subjects as social sciences, their percentage is high.

Examples:

(i) Laboratory Notebooks

(ii) Memoranda

(iv) Diaries (A diary is a personal record of what interested the diarist, usually it is kept from day-today)

(v) Letters to or from a particular Individual

(vi) Company Files

(vii) Internal Research Reports

(viii) State Papers

(ix) Inscriptions on Tombstones

(x) Portraits

(xi) Oral history (Oral history memoirs are records of interview. It consists of a systematic attempt to obtain from the lips of living persons, who led significant lives, a fullest record of their contribution to the political, economic and cultural life of their nation. It can be both detailed and as intimate as any private correspondence and often more reflective in nature. The interviewer and the subject can also verify the transcript).

(xii) Coins, etc.

II. Secondary Sources

Secondary sources of information are those which are either compiled from or refer to primary sources of information. These contain information regarding primary or original information. The original information having been usually modified, selected or reorganized so as to serve a definite purpose or group of users. Such sources contain information arranged and organized on the basis of some definite plan. These contain organized repackaged knowledge rather than new knowledge. Information given in primary sources is made available in a more convenient form. Due to their very nature, secondary sources are more easily and widely available than primary sources. These not only provide digested information but also serve as bibliographical key to primary sources of information. The primary sources are the first to appear, these are followed by secondary sources. It is difficult to find information from primary sources directly. Therefore, one should consult the secondary sources in the first instance, which will lead one to specific primary sources.

Kinds of Secondary Sources

'*Bonn*' has divided the secondary sources into three types which are as below:

1. Index Type:
   - (a) Index
   - (b) Bibliography
   - (c) Indexing Periodicals
   - (d) Abstracting Periodicals

(2) Survey Type:
   - (a) Review
   - (b) Treatise
   - (c) Monograph

(3) Reference type:
   - (a) Encyclopedia
   - (b) Dictionary
   - (c) Handbook, Manual
   - (d) Critical Tables

Important ones are discussed below :

1. Abstracting and Indexing Periodicals : Abstract appear in different format. One of the best form of abstracting service is periodical. An abstracting periodical is a regularly issued compilation of concise summaries of significant article and of important new research monographs, reports, patents and other primary sources publication of that field.

An index to a publication contains an alphabetical list of names, topics, places, formulate, titles of any significatnt items referring to material presented in the main part of the work. These items are arranged chronologically, geographically or in some other way. An indexing periodical is a regularly issued compilation of titles of articles that appear in current primary sources journals, generally titles of new books, pamphlets are also included.

These periodicals are helpful to get the information of a particular time, particular subject, to trace. Now, CAS-Current Awarencess Service has started, as a result time of the reader is saved and facility of speedy retrieval of information is available.

Examples :

American Economic Association, *Index of Economic Journals*, Homewood, III., Irwin, 1961-62,5.

New Scientist, edited by Bernard Dixon, London, IPC Magazines, 1956-, Weekly.

New Society, London, New Science Publications, 1962-, Weekly.

2. Reviews of Progress : A review provides background information to a new problem in a suitable form and serves as a key to literature. List of reference given in a review can serve as a first rate bibliography of the concerned subject for a period covered by it. Dr. Ranganathan has given the name of descriptive bibliography to these reviews. These reviews evaluate, analyze and arrange the information in its related subject field as reference.

Examples :

Advance in Nuclear Science and Technology, 1962-, New York Academic Press, Irregular.

Annual Review of Information Science and Technology, 1966-, Vol. 1-, Washington, D.C. American Society for Information, Annual.

3. Reference books : These sources of information, represents in the best way having after collecting the information from primary sources. "Reference book is such a source which is used by the researcher as and when needed. Normally speaking a reference book is that which helps to locate a subject, and its clarification, clarity of the answer, as a ready reference."

Reference book can be divided into following categories:

(A) Dictionary

(B) Encyclopedia

(C) Handbook, Manual, and

(D) Tables etc.

(A) Dictionary : It is one of most important source of reference book."A dictionary is a book, which deals with words of a language or of some special subjects, author, etc. Thus a dictionary is a word book. Although a dictionary is supposed to deal with words but often it may go beyond this.

Example :

Websters Third New International Dictionary of English Language.

(B) Encyclopedia: An encyclopedia is a storehouse of knowledge giving all information of significance. An encyclopaedia is a book giving information on all branches of knowledge or particular subject. It is an ideal book, which deals with depth of knowledge. However, it is best used for finding answers to background questions related to general information and self education. Generally it is consulted for everyday information and the past knowledge.

Example :

Encyclopedia Britannica, Encyclopedia Americana, Encyclopedia of Social Science, Encyclopedia of Library and Information Science.

(C) Hand Book: It's a small book having a compilation of miscellaneous information in a compact and handy form. It contains data, procedures, principles, etc. Tables, graphs, diagrams and illustrations are also provided. Scientists and Technologists use mini handbooks in their field work and duty.

Hand books are of two types : (i) General hand book (ii) Subject hand book

Example :

Handbook of Chemistry and Physics, N.Y. Chemical Rubber Co.

(D) Subject books: These books are the books of information, some of which provide the detailed study of a subject in an organized way. These enable to provide the basic fundamentals of a subject in depth. It's primary aim is not to import information about a specific but to enable one to develop proper understanding of the subject. A good subject book takes into consideration the method of teaching and level of readership. These are of three types:

(i) Treatise (ii) Monograph (iii) Text book

(i) *Treatise* : This is a comprehensive compilation or summary of a subject. A treatise on a subject provides enough information like encyclopedia. Generally its arrangement is subjectwise,

Example :

Treatise on the Calculus of Finite Differences, 4th ed., New York, Chelsea, 1960.

Treatise on Inorganic Chemistry, by H. Remy, edited by J. Klein berg, New York, American Elsevier, 1956, 2 vols.

(ii) *Monograph* : It gives the emphasis on newly part of a subject. Treatise and monograph have little difference in each other of explaining subject. The scope of treatise is wide while the monograph is small. Thus, a monograph is short treatise of a particular subject. Sometime a monograph may be brought out as a part of a series.

Example:

Study in the History of Ideas by E-Baldwin, N.J.Princeton University Press, 1971.

(iii) *Text Book* : It has a part of principle of a subject. It gives instructions of study.

Examples :

Textbook of Crop Production, by P.C.Raheja, etc., Bombay, Asia, 1973.

Textbook of Cytology by Walter V. Brown and Eldridge M., 2nd ed. Bertke, St. Louis, Mosby, 1974.

Theory of Cataloguing, by Girja Kumar and Krishan Kumar, 5th ed, Delhi, Vikas, 1986.

Cataloguing of Non-book Materials, by Anil Kr. Dhiman, Ess Ess Publications, New Delhi.

Besides, Translations are also the important part of secondary sources. Their charcteristics are the same as those of primary or secondary or tertiary sources from which these are translated. Many of the authors of research papers prefer to cite original sources rather than translations.

III. Tertiary Sources

Tertiary sources of information contain information distilled and whereas collected from primary and secondary sources. The primary function of tertiary sources of information is to give assistance to the researcher so as to make enable them to use of primary and secondary sources of information. Due to heavy increase in publications, tertiary sources are becoming increasingly important. Tertiary sources are the last to appear out of all other sources of information.

Kinds of Tertiary Sources : These sources are as follows:

1. Bibliography of Bibliographies
2. Directories and Yearbooks
3. Guide to Literature
4. List of Research in Progress

1. Bibliography of Bibliographies: When secondary sources indexes the list of books, it becomes tertiary source of information. This is called bibliography of bibliographies:

Examples:

Bibliographic Index: Comulative Bibliography of Bibliographies, 1937-, New York, Wilson, 1938-.

Index Bibliographicus, 4th edition, The Hague, Federation International de Documentation, 1959 to date.

A World Bibliography of Bibliographies and of Bibliographical Catalogues, Calendars, Abstracts, Digests, Indexes and the like, by Theodore Besterman, 4th Ed., Geneva, Societas Bibliographica 1965-67, 5 vols.

2. Directories and Yearbooks: A directory is a list of names and addresses of persons, organizations, manufacturers, or periodicals. It may list information in a way which best serves the requirements of its users so as to enable them to get the required information readily. The word directory may or may not appear in the title.

Examples :

World Directory of Mathematicians, 4th ed. Stockholm, Almquist and Wiksell, 1970.

World of Learning, 1947-, London, Europa, 1947-, Annual.

Ulrich's International Periodicals Directory: a Classified Guide to Current Periodicals, Foreign and Domestic, 40th ed., 2002, New York, Bowker.

Whereas, a Yearbook indicates such publications which publishes in a particular period and once in a year, giving the particulars of incidents, tables etc. of great importance. Some of them are published with a view to update them.

Example:

Mcgraw Hill Yearbook of Science and Technology; Manorma Year Book etc.

3. Guide to Literature: A guide to literature assists a user to make use literature of a specific subject. It helps to evaluate and introduce literature. It gives emphasis on literature instead of the content of a specific subject.

Examples :

A Guide to the Literature of Chemistry by E.J.Crame and others.

Guide to Indian Periodical Literature. Indian Documentation Centre, Gurgoan (India).

4. List of Research in Progress : It is quite essential to publish a list of research done in the various field so as to avoid duplication. To achieve this and to get objective, these sources are prepared.

Some of the institutions which are responsible for the development of research and provides assistance as grant in aid, makes publish of these lists to maintain a record.

Examples:

INSDOC, New Delhi

CSIR, New Delhi

Directory of Scientific Research in Indian Universities, 1974

B. Non-Documentary Sources

Non-documentary sources of information form a substantial part of communication especially in science and technology. User's studies have underlined importance of such sources. These sources provide information which other sources do not.

Kinds of Non-Documentary sources

These are of following types:

1. Invisible College : Informal communication or personal communication may occur among scientists working in the same institution or among scientists in different institutions working in the same field, thus an informal, personal information network develops where by a one way or two-way communication takes place.

Common research interests, institutional ties or formal associations being them together. They may discuss current work in correspondence or at a conference and possible collaborating on various joint projects. This invisible college' as described is a personal network that tends to comprise an elite, influential and cohesive group of workers engaged in research at the forefront of their field. These are often vary important as it helps to propagate nascent thought quickly as the communication is direct.

2. Research Associations: Research Associations may establish cooperative information centres. They collect and provide information service to all members. The member firms are known to each other. They are aware of their problems. There is the possibility of person-to-person; firm-to-firm discussions and exchange of data or/and documents. Results of the cooperative research projects are normally limited to its members. Thus, there is much informal exchanges between the members of an association.

3. Industrial Liaison Officers: These are among the most useful of the widely available sources of technical information. These officers provide particularly the preliminary information needed to put a firm on the right track and for information which needs to be given personally and supported by practical advice in order to be fully effective. They visit firms, explore their needs and problems and help them to find solutions, some times directly on the spot, more often by putting them in touch with specialized sources of information and assistance, or refer to some other specialists.

4. Public and Semi-Public Research Establishments: Government departments, their research establishments, public undertakings, etc. possess a wealth of specialized information. However, this information is available with some institution. Some actively promote the outward flow of information, whereas some not.

5. Technical Specialists of Development Boards/Associations: Governmental, quasi-governmental agencies are establishing development boards for various industries. Industries are also establishing development associations. These agencies provide technical assistance and advisory services, often free of charge.

6. Learned Societies and Professional Institutions: The members of these bodies comprise the core of a discipline or profession. The headquarters staff help members personally on many professional matters. They may direct the queries sometime to the expert members of the body.

7. Technical Faculty of Universities/Institutes: The science and technology faculty of the universities and institutions constitute a considerable percentage of research scientists and technologists of a country. They often take-up consultancy and advisory work.

8. Private Consultants: Senior scientists often start consultancy services either after retirement from active service or by quitting their job after having gained expertise and knowledge. These people equip themselves with uptodate information.

9. Scientific Attaches of Overseas Mission: It may take a longer time to acquire information via such intermediaries, but there may be no feasible alternative when the information sought is not published and necessitates personal approach by some one in the country.

10. Consultants of Industrial Organizations and Inter-governmental Agreements: International organizations may depute or provide expert assistance for technical advice. Experts are provided by a nation by inter-governmental agreements as well. These also provide information.

4

Reference Sources and their Evaluation

Q. : What do you mean by encyclopaedia? Discuss its various types with suitable examples.

or

Evalute followings:

— **Encyclopaedia Britannica**

— **Encyclopaedia Americana**

— **Encyclopaedia of Religion & ethics**

or

Evaluate any two standard encyclopaedias-one from general type and another from special type.

Ans. An encyclopaedia is a systematic summary of the knowledge that is most significant to mankind. It is a work containing information on all subjects or limited to a special field or subject, arranged in systematic usually in alphabetical order. Encyclopaedias may be in one volume, in which very brief information will be given, or they may be in many volumes in which the various kinds of matter will be comprehensive. Encyclopaedias are usually written by experts, and sometimes contain bibliographies and illustrations. These are different from dictionaries in the sense that dictionary tells "what", about a word whereas encyclopaedias tell "what", "when", "how", "where", and "why" of an idea, a person, a place, an event or thing.

The first known encyclopaedia was written by Aristotle, the ancient Greek philosopher, which resulted from his assembled treatises. That is why Aristotle is referred to as the father of encyclopaedias although he never intended to write one. The first encyclopaedia to be published in English was John Harris's *Laxion Technicum,* or, *An*

Universal English Dictionary of the Arts and Sciences, London, 1704. One of the earliest encyclopaedia was the Spanish Archbishop Isidore of Seville's *Etymologiarum Sive orginum Libri XX* which was completed in 623 A.D.More than a thousand manuscripts of this survived, and in printed form it had an undiminished appeal as late as the 17th century.

Types of Encyclopaedia

Based on the subject converage, encyclopaedias are divided into:

(i) General Encyclopaedias: The popular general encyclopaedias are most impressive by their size and number of volumes. The famous adult encyclopaedia are remembered as the ABC's-that is *Americana, Britannica* and *Collier's.* These encyclopaedias are very useful for comprehensive coverage of various topics. For example, if one wants to know all about aeroplanes or butterflies, a general encyclopaedia would be a good starting point. For any American topic, say some historical aspect or geography of some place, the *Encyclopedia Americana* would be particularly useful.

Examples : *Collier's Encyclopaedia.* 24 volumes. Annual Revision. First Published 1949-51.

Encyclopaedia Americana. 30 volumes, Annual Revision, First Published 1929-23.

The New Encyclopaedia Britannica. 15th Edition. 32 Volumes. Annual Revision. First Published as *The New Encyclopaedia Britannica.* Since 1974, published earlier as *Encyclopaedia Britannica* since 1768-71, first edition.

(ii) Subject Encyclopaedias: The increased specialization in various subjects has resulted in users requiring more information in narrow fields. This has led to publication of subject encyclopaedias in various subjects. The subject encyclopaedias provide in a single volume much more detailed overview of a subject than that could be found in single article in a multi-volume general encyclopaedia. However, subject encyclopaedias also exists in multi-volume.

Examples : *McGraw-Hill Encyclopaedia of Science and Technology.* 6th ed. New York: McGraw-Hill Book Company, 1987, 19 Volumes and Index.

Encyclopaedia of Library and Information Science. 1968-. 35 vols. Supplements 1- starts from volume 37 onwards, by 2003 total 73 volumes published.

Difference between General and Special Encyclopaedias

General Encyclopaedias	*Special Encyclopaedias*
(a) It contains a collections of articles providing essential information about branches of knowledge.	(a) It is a collection of articles limited to a specific field of area.
(b) They are arranged usually in alphabetical order.	(b) They are arranged usually in alphabetical or classified order.
(c) They are intended for general readers.	(c) They are designed to satisfy the needs of the subject specialists.
(d) They are occasionally revised to bring new editions. Annuals or supplements are brought out to keep them up-to-date.	(d) They are published in abundance in all subjects to satisfy the user's demands due to knowledge explosion in all fields.
(e) It is a huge and expensive task to produce an authoritative general encyclopaedia.	(e) The cost of publishing is com - paratively less due to its limited scope and coverage.

Criteria for Evaluation

A good and useful collection of general and sepcial encyclopaedias form the backbone for the reference work in any library. The strong collection of general and special encyclopaedias in English and other languages ensure efficient reference service in a library.

In order to make the best use of encyclopaedias, it is essential to acquire a thorough understanding of them. This can be achieved to a large extent by evaluating these and laying down criteria for their evaluation. The checklist for the evaluation of an encyclopaedia for the purpose of its study should consist of the following:

(i) Authoriy: The work should be authoritative. The authoritativeness of an encyclopaedia can usually be judged on the basis of the qualifications, experience, reputation and responsibility of the sponsoring body (if any), publisher, distributor, authors, editors. The knowledge regarding the subject, and academic qualifications of the authors and editors are extremely important in this context.

(ii) Scope and Purpose : Editors usually state the scope and purpose of the encyclopaedia in the preface and introduction. After proper scanning, the buyers should check a few items in the volumes to verify whether the promises are carried out or not. The scope of an encyclopaedia covers plan, range and selection.

(a) **Plan :** The encyclopaedia work should have a definite plan. The articles should be even in length and content and continuous editorial supervision should ensure that the plan is followed consistently.

(b) **Coverage :** The topics should be complete in coverage. It varies according to the needs of the users. The facts provided in the encyclopaedia should be accurate and reliable.

(c) **Selection :** There should be balance in the selection of topics and dealing with different periodical events, subjects, countries, etc.

(iii) Treatment : Readability, objectivity and style are the three important criteria of topics in encyclopaedias.

(a) **Readability :** The topics covered by the encyclopaedia should be readable and easily understandable. The information should make the unfamiliar subject clear to the user. The standard and the quality of the articles should be in tune with the readers' need and should be comprehensible both for the scholars and laymen.

(b) **Objectivity:** The articles should be objective without having any national, political or religious bias. National encyclopaedias may deal extensively with the national topics but there should not be exaggeration. As far as possible, they should be neutral and not prejudiced.

(c) **Style:** As encyclopaedias are meant for the varied audience of different age group and coverage, they have different style. The scholarly style is for the learned scholars, popular style for the common men and the college students, while easy, lucid and simple style is for children. Hence, the reference librarian should be conscious in selecting encyclopaedias to suit the needs of the readers.

(iv) Arrangement: Arangement is of utmost importance. It is essential that one should be able to locate information easily and quickly. This will add to the value of an encyclopaedia.

The arrangement of main text can be alphabetical (by large subject or small topic) or classified or some other. The kind of arrangement used should have a sound basis.

(v) Format: The value of the format can be determined by verifying the following aspects.

(a) **Typography:** The size and style of the type faces should be clear and legible. The proper spacing between the letters, words and lines and layout of the columns improve the readability of the sources. The distinct difference between the headings and sub-headings by using the bold letters or different sizes of the letters facilitate the usability of the sources.

(b) **Paper:** Good quality papers should be used for durability. Thin and opaque papers reduce the weight and make the size of the source handy.

(c) **Binding:** Binding should be of leather, rexin or calico cover and should be light but strong enough to withstand heavy and rough use.

(d) **Physical Appearance:** The physical get up and appearance should be appealing, functional and pleasing with golen or ink print lettering.

(vi) Special Features : The special features include those features which distinguish one encyclopaedia from other encyclopaedias, like:

— Does it include supplementary lists or appendices?

— Are the bibliographies up-to-date and useful?

— What are the supplementary devices used to keep it up-to-date (issuing of a supplement or year book on annual basis or loose leaf insertions)?

— What is the policy of revision (periodical revision or continuous revision)? Is it satisfactory?

(vii) Indexes : The whole purpose of encyclopaedia is defeated, if the user is not able to locate the required information easily and quickly. Thus, it is necessary to have detailed, exhaustive indexes - chronological, alphabetical, classified and geographical having cross reference of '*see*' and '*see also*' and additional keys or citations. These will provide guidance to interested readers to locate the information and also assist them to refer the primary sources if they want more details.

(viii) Bibliographies: The references and bibliographies given at the end of the articles are very useful to the subject specialists for further reference. As they are secondary or sometimes even tertiary sources, the references will help them to refer to the primary sources for more information and authoritative data.

The above checkpoints are very useful to judge the value of any encyclopaedia before adding it to the collection. The thorough scrutinization of these tools in the light of the above guidelines makes the reference librarian familiar with the sources and information available in them.

(ix) Conclusion: Conclusion should provide overall judgement about the encyclopaedia. Should it be recommended for a library or not? If so, indicate the kind of library which will benefit most.

Uses of Encyclopaedias

As already been stated, encyclopaedia is a store house of knowledge and provides information on all subjects. They form the backbone of the reference work in a library. Most of the users consider reference book as encyclopaedia without differentiating them with each other. Even though number of reference books are available in the library, librarian first turns to encyclopaedia for tracing information. In olden days, encyclopaedias were referred only by elite but now, they are used by all the common people. They are very popular among students and research scholars because of following reasons.

(i) Encyclopaedias are looked for concise, digested and in some cases simplified account on a topic on which otherwise there may be abundance of available literature.

(ii) Encyclopaedias also help us in such cases where the topic of enquiry is very restricted in scope and the library has no book on the topic.

(iii) Encyclopaedias generally present information in an impartial manner, giving all the view points on a subject.

(iv) They attempt to provide essential historical background to the topic of enquiry.

(v) References generally listed at the end of a brief or detailed description are selective and provide important help for further study of the topic.

(vi) Very often encyclopaedias are the only source for biographical information on an other wise minor figure not covered in standard biographical dictionaries.

(vii) The earlier editions of encyclopaedias have their own value. They are a rich source for an account of state of knowledge at a given time on any topic that may be omitted from subsequent writings on the subject. Encyclopaedia Britannica 9th and 11th editions are often cited as examples for their scholarly articles.

(viii) The index is the most valuable part for accessing information on topic not featured in the main body of an encyclopaedia.

(ix) The role of illustrations in making a subject more comprehensible can be hardly overemphasized. Colour plates, black and white photographs and line drawings in encyclopaedias not only add to their aesthetics but are of great help in clarifyuing descriptions.

(x) Scholarly treatment of subject is one point on which editors of encyclopaedias lay special emphasis. Without denying the truth in the statement "Do not rely on encyclopaedia work, suspect every statement and do your best to verify it". "General encyclopaedia can serve as a gateway to understand the most profound or intricate knowledge human beings have yet produced". As Grogan has rightly pointed out, New Britannica availed the services of 4300 scholars including Nobel Laureates, Milton Friedman and Linus Pauling, etc., in preparing the set.

A few leading general encyclopaedias are described below:

1. New Encyclopaedia Britannica, 15th ed., Chicago, Encyclopaedia Britannica, 1985, 32 Vols.

The first edition of *Encyclopaedia Britannica* in 3 volumes was completed in 1768 and it published between 1768 and 1771. The articles were brief. The first eight editions are mainly of historical interest. The 9th, 11th, 14th editions and their supplements are still useful in certain ways. Ninth and the eleventh editions are landmarks being works of great scholarship. *Encyclopaedia Britannica* completed 200 years in 1968. In 1974, the fifteenth edition was published as the "*New Encyclopaedia Britannica*" consisting of thirty volumes. It has three parts.

(i) Propaedia - 1 volume

(ii) Micropaedia - 10 volumes

(iii) Macropaeida - 19 volumes

(i) Propaedia, a guide to the set, gives outline of knowledge and is a schematic introduction to articles in Macropaedia.

(ii) Micropaedia, a study guide contains brief information for ready reference and acts as a detailed index to the set by giving volume and page reference to articles in the Macropaedia. Cross references are freely given throughout the 10 volumes. Users needing broader details can refer to Micropaedia and save time whereas those who want minute facts can refer to Macropaeida to get elaborate information.

(iii) Macropaedia containing knowledge in depth has lengthy articles. It covers major topics of human interest and is intended to educate the serious readers. They are written by well-known experts and include selective and annotated bibliographies. It has international approach and universal coverage. Since 1938, every year '*Britannica Book of the Year*' is published to update the information which also follows policy of continuous revision.

The new edition was criticized for not providing an index to the set, hence in 1985 print, a two-volume index was also published making it a set of 32 volume. The Encyclopaedia volumes were also re-numbered as:

Propaedia	-	1 volume
Micropaedia	-	12 volumes
Macropaedia	-	17 volumes
Index	-	2 volumes

Britannica book of the year has been brought out on yearly basis since 1938. This work serves as a supplement to *New Encyclopaedia.* It updates the set and also points out to the more extensive treatment provided in *New Encyclopaedia* by means of a code.

Now-a-days, Encyclopaedia is also available in digital form. This is available online as well as on CD-ROM. Encyclopaedia Britannica 1998 to date can be consulted online free of cost from its website (www.eb.com). The encyclopaedia from 1994 to date is available on charges basis on the site http://britannica.com

2. Encyclopedia Americana, New York, Groher, 1984, 30 vols.

This encyclopaedia is based on the seventh edition of the German encyclopaedia *Brockhaus Konversations-Lexikon* published during

1827-29. It was first published between 1829 and 1833 containing articles translated from the German work. The first edition as a new work appeared in 1903-1904. This was followed by several partial revisions. One edition came out in 1912 under the title *The Americana.* Its 1980-20 edition was a completely revised edition. This has formed the basis of later editions.

Editors, consultants, and contributors are well chosen, which lend authority to this work. There are about 6000 contributors to the 1973 edition. Normally, the contributors are scholars and authorities in their field. Most of them have an academic affiliation of one kind or other.

Americana is a general encyclopaedia, which aims to serve a wide range of readers. The contributions are written to serve the needs of nonspecialized readers. The contributors are instructed to present facts and interpretations in an orderly manner, using direct style. The emphasis is being on readability. However, it may be added that scholarship has not been abandoned for the sake of readability. Over the years, the ratio of signed to unsigned articles is increasing. This is a good sign.

Since the early 1960's, *Americana* has been following a continuous revision policy. Under this policy, the following two approaches have been practiced simultaneously.

(i) At the time of each printing, changes are incorporated and updating is put into practice throughout the set;

(ii) Besides the above, selected entire volumes are completely reset each year. In these volumes major changes are incorporated such as new articles, deletions, new subjects etc. For example, volumes 7, 8, 9 and 15 were completely reset in 1969. Changes in volumes not reset are usually of minor nature.

As a result of year to year revision, sometimes require adding pages and in some instances, dropping pages.

Americana annual has been brought out sine 1923. It records the major developments taking place each year. This helps to keep the basic work up-to-date.

Americana contains a series of historical essays covering each of the century. Glossaries defining technical or difficult terms are given in many of the concerned articles. A full list of glossaries has been indexed under the terms *glossary*. There are separate articles on important works of literature, philosophy and economics and on major operas. Similarly, there are articles to be found on the books of the Bible and on significant historical documents. Summaries, resembling a table of contents given in the beginning of multiple page articles.

Generally bibliographies have been provided for major articles. In many cases bibliographies have been appended on minor subjects. Often, these are not up-to-date. Bibliographies have been give to identify the sources forming basis of the articles and to assist the readers to go beyond the articles to get additional information.

There are about 24,000 illustrations out of which 10 per cent are in colour. Maps are detailed and easy to understand.

The index is detailed and analytical one. Its 1984 edition contains 350,000 entries. The index volume contains a clearly written guide to the use of the index. The typeface is attractive and highly legible one.

This encyclopaedia is strong about subjects of American interest such as American history, geography and biography. The fields of science and technology seem to be well covered and articles in these areas are readable, accurate and fairly up-to-date. It is extremely useful for little known information about the United States. In general, the *Americana* is weaker in music, fine arts and architecture.

Americana lays emphasis on popular treatment of articles to the extent that even complex topics or ideas have been dealt in such a way that even a average educated layman can follow these to an appreciable degree. *American* is generally reliable and extremely useful for ready reference work, which undergone significant revision over the years. But there is a need for complete revision similar to that of *Britannica.*

The Encyclopaedia Americana is also available in electronic form. It is the electronic version of the full 30 volume print set, although with considerably fewer illustrations (about 2000 on CD-ROM as compared to 23000 in print). What is missing from it is the low price, no sound, and not for the one looking for data spiced with entertaining sound or sight bites. The unique features of CD-ROM are the Merriam-Webster Collegiate. Dictionary; a Chronology of World History; and a Dictionary of Science and Technology.

Encyclopaedia Americana from 1997 to date is also available on the Internet under the umbrella title "Grolier Online". The address is http:// ea.grolier.com. The Americana online includes all of the 45000 articles found in the print and CD-ROM version. Its updates are highly selective. Still this keeps the online encyclopaedia ahead of the CD-ROM and print. On the net there are few of the illustrations that are found in the standard volumes. The charges for access vary.

3. Encyclopaedia of Library and Information Science, New York, Dekker, 1968-, volume 1-. (So far 73 volumes have been published).

This encyclopaedia contains signed articles by qualified contributors. The articles vary in length from few pages to long monographs. The topics dealt with include articles on literature of individual fields, library service in various countries, biographies of leading figures in library science and related areas, types of libraries, etc. The articles are generally well written and illustrated, and data in the form of tables have been provided wherever needed. There is a great stress on providing information of historical interest.

The list of contributions to a particular volume is given in the beginning of each volume.

Cross references have been given, where necessary. Most articles have been provided with extensive list of references/bibliographies.

The composition of the advisory board as well as the names of authors clearly underline the American orientation of the publication. This is also indicated by the topics covered and the information provided in the articles.

By 2003, its 73 volumes including 37 supplements from 1983 have been published.

The work is claimed to be the first complete and authoritative work on library an information science. This encyclopaedia is certainly an important landmark in the history of library science and information science. It should be of immense value to librarians, information scientists and computer scientists.

4. Encyclopaedia of Religion and Ethics, edited by James Hastings, etc. Edinburgh, Clark, 1908-27,12 vol. and index.

The work is edited by James Hastings, who is considered an authority. The articles are all by specialists and are signed.

This is a special encyclopaedia, which is comprehensive in the concerned fields. The fields covered include, "all religions of the world, ethical systems and movements, every religious beliefs and customs, prilosophical ideas, moral practices, related subjects in anthropology, mythology, folklore, biology, psychology, economics and sociology, and names of persons and places connected with any of these subjects."

The treatment is scholarly in nature but readable. "Every subject has been described comprehensively in one general article, then one or more particular topics touched by the general article, have been dealt separately and fully described." There are a number of comparative articles on certain topics.

13th volume is an index volume consisting of subject index, index of foreign words and of scripture passages and complete list of contributors. The subject index covers a wide range of subjects. An attempt has been made to bring together related topics under important headings.

This is the most useful and comprehensive work in the fields of religion and ethics.

5. McGraw Hill Encyclopaedia of Science And Technology. Ed. 7th New York: McGraw Hill. 1992. 20 volumes.

It was first issued in 1960 and since then it has been continually revised. The sixth edition of this widely used science reference source is a revised and updated revision of the earlier editions of 1960, 1966, 1971, 1977 and 1982.

Editor in chief and consulting editors are well-known authorities. Almost 3500 scientists and engineers have contributed to the encyclopaedia, including a number of Nobel Prize Winners.

It is basically a work of science and technology, not about it. Thus, it does not cover articles of historical, philosophical and biographical interest unless these are essential to the presentation in an article. Thus, historical and biographical references are rather brief if any. McGraw-Hill brings out two-volume companion set, *Modern men of science* for additional biographical information. There are about 7,700 articles including broad survey type articles and special short entries for specialized topics, varying from a few paragraphs to more than a dozen pages each.

The quality of writing is high. An article usually begins with a definition of the subject and then goes on to provide sufficient background information and further lead the reader into the more detailed body of the article. College undergraduates in science and engineering will be able to understand most of the articles or at least their introductory parts as articles have been written so as to be understandable to non-specialists. The language is clear and readable. The level of writing depends upon the 'nature and degree of complexity of the subject.'

The articles are signed by their contributors. The bibliographies to the literature are also given at the end of the majority of articles. This work is periodically revised and kept updated by the *McGraw-Hill Year book of Science and Technology* which 'reports and analyzes the past year's significant developments and serves as a concise guide to ongoing scientific and technological activities'. There are large number of graphs and charts and few full-page maps. However, numerous smaller maps are spread throughout the text in the fields of geology, agriculture and meteorology. The index volume contains two kinds of indexes, namely analytical index and topical index. Analytical index contains 150,000 entries, indexing in depth the articles of the main text. These entries are arranged on word-by-word basis. The topical index groups 7,700 article titles into 77 major subjects areas of science and technology. It enables one to identify all articles on a broad subject.

"Scientific notation in the encyclopedia" is a special feature of the 20th volume. It aims to clarify usage of symbols, abbreviations, and nomenclature and also helps in conversions between the international system, US customary and metric measurements.

There are a large number of subheading given in bold type in each article. Cross references are given at the end of subheadings. There are 15000 llustrations, clear and well presented.

This edition explores all important developments and achievements since 1982 which have been thoroughly revised. Major overhaul of 28 of the 77 major subject areas have been carried out. Many of the brief, definitional articles have been deleted to provide more space for more comprehensive treatment of particular subjects. As a result there is"less fragmentation and more integration", 500 former entries have been deleted and 450 new entries added, 1600 entries are extensively revised. It is claimed that all bibliographies have been reviewed and revised, where required. There are 50,000 cross references.

Its sixth edition presents accurate and up-to-date information in a "more attractive, more convenient and better-organized format" than the previous edition. It has also been expanded from 15 to 20 volumes.

The seventh edition explores all important developments and achievements since 1987. To overhaul the major subjects, a number of brief, definitional articles have been deleted so that more space can be provided for more comprehensive treatment of these subjects. This edition presents accurate and up-to-date information. The encyclopaedia will appeal to above average layman, scientists, teachers and students research as well as ready reference questions, especially for brief definitions of terms. The quality of writing is high. Although the cost of the encyclopaedia is high, but it can be recommended for every type of library, which can afford it.

Keeping in view the level of the users, it can be concluded that encyclopaedias have been brought out in great variety. Multi-volume encyclopaedias give brief treatment to topics. The brief encyclopaedias are more useful for ready reference service, on the other hand large encyclopaedias are useful for detailed knowledge of a topic. The selection of an encyclopaedia for purchasing in a library depends on the size of the library. A small library may prefer one or two volume encyclopaedia, but for a large library leading general encyclopaedas and some subject encyclopaedias such as Encyclopaedia Britannica, Encyclopaedia Americana, Encyclopaedia of Indian Literature, International Encyclopaedia of Social Sciences, McGraw Hill Encyclopaedia of Science and Technology are found indispensable.

In the era of information technology, libraries nowadays prefer to purchase encyclopaedias in digital form. These may be online or on CD-ROM. The reason being that these digital encyclopaedias occupy less space and can be shared online on computers spreaded over the campus of the parent institution through the library.

Q. : What is a dictionary? Discussing its various types, mention some important dictionaries.

or

Enumerate major types of dictionaries. Discuss the purpose and importance of such tools for reference and information services in brief.

or

Discuss the objectives and utility of dictionaries in brief. Enumerate different types of dictionaries.

or

Evalute the following:

— **Oxford English Dictionary**

— **Webster's New International Dictionary.**

Ans. The word 'dictionary' is derived from the medieval Latin word 'Dictionarium' originating form the term 'dictio' which means word. Oxford English Dictionary defines dictionary as "a book dealing with the words of a language, so as to set forth their orthography, pronunciation, signification, and use; their synonyms, derivation and history; or at least some of these; the words are arranged in some stated order, now, usually, alphabetical, a word-book, vocabulary, lexicon. By extension, it means a book of information for reference on any subject or branch of knowledge, the items of which are arranged alphabetically; as a dictionary of architecture, biography, of the Bible, of dates, etc."

So, a dictionary is systematically arranged list of socialized linguistic forms compiled from the speech-habits of a given speech community and commented on by the author in such a way that the qualified reader understands the meaning of each separate form, and is informed of the relevant facts concerning the function of that form in its community.

Types of Dictionaries

For the purpose of organization of dictionaries in the reference collection of a library, they are usually, divided into 4 broad categories, considering their density of entries, number of languages involved, nature of entries, purpose and prospective user. All these criteria can be utilized sometimes alone and sometimes with the other for the classification of dictionaries.

(i) General dictionaries

(ii) Special dictionaries

(iii) Subject dictionaries, and

(iv) Translating dictionaries

Each group is sub-divided into several kinds. But kind number (i) and (ii) are most common in use.

(i) General Dictionaries : These are just like general encyclopaedias, where subject coverage is not limited to a particular field rather it contains the word-meanings and their uses for the general readers.

Examples:

— Webster's Third New International Dictionary of the English Language. Springfield: Merriam, 1961.

— Oxford English Dictionary or OED... A New English Dictionary on Historical Principles etc. Oxford: Clarendon Press, 1933. 13v.

— Comprehensive English-Hindi Dictionary, Compiled by Dr. Raghuvira, Nagpur: International Academy of Indian Culture, 1955.

(ii) Subject Dictionarties : The rapid development in all the fields of knowledge, has necessitated compilation of subject dictionaries, devoted to the specific subject fields, occupations and professions. Thus, dictionaries dealing with the terms of a particular subject are known as subject dictionaries. They are not usually recorded in general dictionaries. They give accurate description, definition and illustration to explain the term. In some of the subject dictionaries extra features like biographies of the specialists and addresses of the scientific institutions are also mentioned.

Examples :

Dictionary of Library & Information Science.

On the basis of number of languages covered, such dictionaries can be categorized as :

(i) Monolingual

(ii) Bilingual

(iii) Multilingual

Uses of Dictionaries

The dictionary serves a very useful purpose. These are frequently consulted by users, because of the following :

(i) To find the meanings of words and terms.

(ii) To check the pronunciation and verify spellings and syllabication of word.

(iii) To trace the origin, derivation and history of a word.

(iv) To indicate the dialect and correct usage of a word.

(v) To determine abbreviations, signs, symbols, synonyms, antonyms and homonyms, etc.

Some dictionaries provide illustrated examples, and quotations. In order to have the best use of a dictionary, one should read its introduction for its use.

Some of the important Dictionaries are evaluated below:

(i) Oxford English Dictionary, *2nd edition prepared by J A Simpson and E S C Weiner, Oxford, Clarendon Press, 1989, 20 volumes. Additional series: vol. 1 (234 pp.); vol. 2 (234pp.); vol.3(234pp.).*

The Oxford English Dictionary (OED) is the most magnificant of all the dictionaries of the English language, and it is with some justification that H L Mencken called it the "emperor of dictionaries." The purpose of the dictionary is to trace the history of the English language. This is done through definitions and quotations that illustrate the variations in the meaning and use of words. OED is considered the most authoritative, complete, scholarly and famous English language dictionary. The OED's first fascicle was published when the Irish author of Ulysses was two years old, and the last when Ulysses itself was six. Work on the great dictionary began about the middle of Victoria's and Tennyson's century.

About 616500 words have been defined in the dictionary. OED support the definitions and usage with some 2.5 million quotations. In Webster's New World Dictionary, the etymology of black takes five lines, whereas in the OED it takes twenty-three lines. The entry on "set" alone is 60,000 words long. In comparison, John Milton's Paradise Lost has just under 80,000 words. The word point in the OED consumes 18 columns and put accounts for 30 columns.

This dictionary covers "1. All common words of speech and literature, and all words that approach these in character, the limits being extended further into science and philosophy than into slang and cant; 2. In scientific and technical terminology, all words of English in form except those of which an explanation would be intelligible only to a specialist, and such words not English in form as are in general use or belong to the more familiar language of science; and 3. Dialectical words before 1500, omitting dialectical words after that date except when they continue the history of a word once in general use, illustrate the history of a literary word, or have a literary currency."

It is also available online and on CD. The online OED searching system is simplicity itself. One enters in a word for a quick search and full entry of the print dictionary appears. A number of methods are provided for narrowing or making the search wider, e.g., one may choose words from the vulgate Bible to twentieth century texts (1900-1941). It is more compact than the printed set and most important, and it gives the user access points impossible to find in print. Just what one can do with digital besides checking out the history, definition, spelling and so forth, of a single word?

(ii) Webster's 3rd New International Dictionary of the English Language, *Springfield, MA: Merriam Webster Inc. 1961.*

Today, there is only one true unabridged dictionary of the English language and this is the Webster's third New International Dictionary. It is more concerned with etymology than definitions, and is not meant to be an everyday working dictionary. Webster's International was first published in 1909 and in 1934 its second edition appeared. The third edition was published in 1961. Several dates of copyrights have been mentioned in its 1985 edition. Usually every new edition came after five years. There is so much variation between the second and third edition that it is considered advisable to have both editions in a library. In second edition there were 6,000,000 entries, which have been reduced to 450,000 in third edition. Numerous obsolete and rare words have been dropped but about 100,000 new entries have been added, including new scientific and technical terms.

The Webster's Third International Dictionary provides spelling, syllabication, part of speech, etymology, definitions, inflections, capitalization, illustrative quotations chiefly from contemporary sources, pronunciations, labels and some pictorial illustrations.

Its supplement is also published as 6000 words: a supplement to Webster's in Third New International 1976, which covers 6000 words and meanings which have become firmly established in the language since the publication of the volume in 1961. The words have been selected largely from the current vocabulary of science, mathematics and technology. The words from the subjects like music, sports, politics, etc. have also been covered. The significance of different typefaces, abbreviations and the devices used have been explained in detail in the introductory pages. The dictionary is must for every type of library.

(iii) Roget's International Thesaurus. *5th edition. Edited by Robert L. Chapman. New York: Harper Collins. 1992.*

The author of the "Treasury of Words" could hardly have thought this his name would become for ever associated with a particular book, even though he hoped that he was suggesting a unique way of utilizing the richness and flexibility of the English language most effectively. Originally, this thesaurus was compiled by Peter Mark Roget. Its fifth edition is edited by Robert L. Chapman and it was published in 1992. The thesaurus has a text of about 325,000 words and phrases, arranged in categories by their meanings, and a comprehensive index. The main part contains 1762 pages and index part contains 764-1141 pages. The words and phrases have been arranged in fifteen broad categories.

The coverage of the thesaurus can be measured from the size of words and phrases included in the thesaurus. Under the category, "THE BODY AND THE SENSES" as much as 92 sub-categories have been provided, and these are 1073 in total in this thesaurus.

The search procedure is very simple and it begins in the index. Suppose that one want a word to describe something that first occurred in the part: here the procedure what he/she has to follow is firstly to look up the word "first" in the index and pick up the subentry closest to the meaning he/ she wants. Then he/ she has to follow its category number into the text and there he/ she will find a whole paragraph of adjectives for things "previous" or "prior". The thesaurus is a device for finding specific words or phrases for general ideas. Roget's International Thesaurus is a more efficient word finder because it has a structure especially designed to stimulate thought and help one to organize his/ her ideas.

The terms with in a category are organized also by part of speech, in the following order: nouns, verbs, adjectives, adverbs, prepositions, conjunctions, and interjections. This grouping by parts of speech enhances the usefulness of this thesaurus. There is a further refinement of word arrangement. The sequence of terms within a paragraph, far from being random, is determined by close, semantic relationships. The words closest in meaning are offered in clusters or "domains" that are set off with semicolons. Cross references in the text are provided appropriately.

Concluding it can be said that a dictionary is usually the first source to be consulted for determining the definition of a word. The number of dictionaries in the collection of a library depends upon the size of a library. A small library may have a couple of dictionaries, whereas a large library may have a large variety of dictionaries. A dictionary should be purchased very cautiously due to their high costs.

Sometimes, an unscrupulous publisher may offer a reprint of an early work with hardly any revision or incompetent editors may have compiled it. Thus, librarians and information scientists should select the authoritative dictionaries.

Q. : Enumerate different categories of Geographical Sources of information. Discuss in detail the usefulness of Gazetteers as a source of information.

or

Enumerate major Geographical Sources of information. Discuss the importance of gazetteers.

or

Evaluate some of the major geographical sources.

Ans. : The geographical sources are a category of reference books that help in answering queries related to places. They provide information like description and location related to countries, states, regions, districts, cities, mountains, rivers, lakes and all places throughout the world.

Geographical sources consist primarily of graphic representations. Most of them are produced through team effort. These are meant for, to find out answers to geographical questions. For instance, location of Varanasi, distance between Delhi and Jaipur, population of Tokyo, etc. Such questions can be asked in various forms and details.

Types of Geographical Sources

Geographical information can be located in a variety of sources of information, each of which has its own usefulness. There is much duplication of information in these sources, therefore, a reference librarian should make use of wise and careful selection.

The following sources of information, are recognized which can be used for getting geographical information:

(i) Bibliographies and indexes:

(ii) Encyclopaedias;

(iii) Dictionaries;

(iv) Sources of statistics;

(v) Biographical sources; and

(vi) Geographical sources.

(i) Bibliographies and Indexes : Bibliographies are useful for locating geographical sources. Indexing and abstracting periodicals are helpful for locating articles on cities, towns, places of interest, etc. These do not contain the information itself but direct one to sources, which contain information.

(ii) Encyclopaedias : These are extremely useful sources of geographical information regarding countries, states, cities, etc. These are also good sources for maps, but for small areas and thematic maps, one should consult geographical sources. Encyclopaedias provide enough information about historical and socio-economic aspects for places covered by it. In this respect, encyclopaedias are superior to geographical sources; besides, the articles in encyclopaedias are usually more detailed and comprehensive covering many facets. On the other hand description given in a gazetteer lays emphasis on geographical details.

(iii) Dictionaries : These provide definitions of geographical terms, but also may help in the identification of large cities and towns. Very often, these provide population figures for countries, states and towns, etc.

(iv) Sources of Statistics : These provide data in tabular forms and also thematic maps. Sources of statistics, very often, give geographical data in readily accessible form.

(v) Biographical Sources : These are extremely useful for biographies of geographers and cartographers.

(vi) Geographical Sources : These are specific sources, which are specifically prepared to provide geographical information. These occur in large variety, varying in scope and form.

As geographical sources are concerned, these are divided into following sub-categories:

(I) Gazetteers,

(II) Guide books,

(III) Atlases, maps and globes.

(I) Gazetteers

A gazetteer is a geographical dictionary of places arranged alphabetically. It serves as a finding list for geographical places like towns, cities, oceans, rivers, lakes, mountains, etc., giving indication about location usually in the form of exact latitude and longitude and a brief description such as pronunciation, population, area, historical and socio-economic information, etc. It is essential that it should provide officially standardized form of spelling of place-names, along with cross-references to variant spellings. The emphasis should be on inclusiveness of entries and the information should be up-to-date.

From above, it follows that an index to any atlas can be considered a gazetteer. A gazetteer is the same as that of an atlas but the former is usually without maps. The main value of a gazetteer lies in the fact that it often helps in locating places, which may not have been covered by an index to a standard atlas. Thus, we find that a gazetteer is usually more comprehensive than the index to an atlas. As most of the gazetteers provide latitude and longitude, therefore it becomes possible to locate places on a large-scale map.

Difference between Gazetteer and Index

	Gazetteer	*Index to an Atlas*
1.	The information available about each place name in the gazetteer is much more in detail.	It gives factual details about longitude, latitude and the page number of the map on which the place name is marked.
2.	It enlists many small places of less importance.	It includes only important places. However big may be the maps, they can not accommodate all small places.
3.	It may be published in a single, handy volume or multi-volumes.	It is usually available in larger size as it contains big maps to include all important places and it is heavy as maps are printed on thick art papers.

According to the level gazetteers are of following three types:-

(i) Gazetteers of International level :

Examples :

(a) Webster's New Geographical Dictionary, 1985.
(b) Columbia Lippincott Gazetteer of the world, 1952.
(c) Chambers World Gazetteer and Geographical Dictionary, 1965.
(d) Statesman's Yearbook World Gazetteer.

(ii) Gazetteers of National level :

Examples :

(a) Imperial Gazetteer of India.

(b) Gazetteer of India

(c) Encyclopaedic District Gazetteers of India (1998), 11 Vols.

(iii) Gazetteers of Regional or Local level :

Examples :

(a) District Gazetteer of Haryana.

(b) Uttar Pradesh District Gazetteer, Vol-9 Moradabad

(c) The Himalayan Gazetteer.

(d) Orissa District Gazetteer.

Uses of Gazetters

Information about a place in a district or town is generally sought through gazetteers. The usual delay in their revision compared to atlases often renders them unsuitable as a source of recent information. As a reference source, a gazetteer provides historical, social, cultural, political, industrial, demographic and administrative details about a place in a country or about a whole country.

Evaluation of Important Gazetteers

(i) Websters New Geographical Dictionary. Springfield, Mass: Merriam- Webster, 1984.

Claimed to be a thoroughly revised edition, it is a dictionary of more than 47000 geographical names from Biblical times, ancient Greece and Rome, medieval Europe, to World War I and II. Some 15000 cross-references are provided for equivalent and alternate spellings of foreign language names and former names. It gives the usual gazetteer information and pronunciation, e.g., location, area, population, physical description, altitudes of mountains, etc., also gives geographical features, historical monuments, a concise history, and economic and historical data. It gives a short account but amount of information varies depending upon the importance of entry and probable value of such information to the user. The arrangement of entries is alphabetical. It also contains full page and smaller inset maps. List of geographical terms with language of origin and English equivalents is given in its introductory section.

(ii) Chambers World Gazetteer: *An A to Z of Geographical Information* / ed. By David Munro ed. 5. Cambridge: Cambridge Univ. Press, 1988.

The new edition of this British Gazetteer which was first published in 1895, now has 20,000 entries. Profuse with line maps (150) and full plate maps (120) which is a "World atlas", cities and towns included have been generally selected firstly for their administrative functions. Population there should for selection has varied with each country. Places of special interest from historical, religious and industrial tourist point of view, as scene of some event or having curiosity value have also been included. Its previous edition was known as Chamber's World Gazetteer and Geographical Dictionary.

(iii) Statesman's Yearbook World Gazetteer, edited by John Paxton, London, MacMillan, 1975, irregular.

This yearbook "provides absolutely up-to-date information about every place one is likely to encounter in the course of general reading." A work of this kind cannot possible cover every place in the world. Therefore, it covers places of importance or size. Some of the places have been included because these were considered of historical importance.

A basic entry has been provided for each place included in the work, usually giving the location, the size of population and the inhabitant's source of income, and provides details of recent history, its industries and population. "The essential details about countries of the world are given, but no attempt has been made to duplicate the detailed descriptions which appear in the annual volumes of *The Statesman's yearbook*". More details have been provided about each country. In case of small places, fewer details have been given, the details provided are quite up-to-date.

A separate section provides precise definitions of over 900 geographical terms. A 24-page map section and a selection of comparative statistical tables have also been given.

This publication has been brought out as a companion volume to *The Statesman's Yearbook (annual).* It contains extra information about individual places, which cannot be provided fully in the annual. This is a handy work.

(iv) Imperial Gazetteer of India

The first edition f the *Imperial Gazetteer of India* was published in 1881 in nine volumes. Between 1881 and 1907, three different editions were published. In addition, the same volumes on individual provinces were also published. The companion volume, *The Indian Empire: Its history, people and products,* appeared in 1882. The second edition of the *Imperial Gazetteer of India* came out in 1885-1887, in 14 volumes. New revised edition was issued in 1907-1909 in 26 volumes. In the new edition, in addition to the India volumes, a provincial series with the provinces as units and a district gazetteer series with the districts as units were also issued. This work is regarded as an authoritative and comprehensive study of India and its people.

(v) Gazetteer of India: Indian Union, Delhi, Publications Division, Ministry of Information and Broadcasting, Government of India, 1965-1978, 4 volumes (Ministry of Education and Social Welfare, Government of India is the publisher of volumes 2-4).

Its different volumes are titled as:-

V.I Country and People

V.II History and culture

V.III Economic Structure and Activities

V.IV Administration and Public Welfare

All the chapters in each volume have been contributed by a team of experts in the field and carry a bibliography at the end. Volumes have been reprinted from time to time.

(II) Guide Books

The ALA Glossary of Library and *Information Science* defines a book guide " as a handbook for travellers that gives information about a city, region or a country or a similar handbook about a building, museum, etc."

A guidebook is a handy book for travellers that gives information about a city, a country, a region, a religious place or about a building or a historical monument. These are usually meant for tourists and people who want to visit various places. The guide books usually provide all the information about routes, travel facilities, hotels to live in, cultural, social, religious aspects, eating places and shopping centre, etc.

Types of Guide Books

Travel guides may be placed under two categories, viz.,

(a) One-time Guides: These are the guides which are prepared to introduce an area rich in history, ecology or even of monuments.

(b) Series Guides: These are prepared for tourists to assist them plan their travel programme. The guides of the first category are generally one time publication as their contents rarely undergo changes. The guides of the second category need continuous revision and hence are published as a series.

Uses of Guide Books

Basically guides books are meant for the people who want to visit various places in their own country or other parts of the world. They help making their journey pleasant and comfortable. Almost all important travel guides contain information on historic sites, museums and other places that are worth visiting for cultural enrichment. Information about routes and travel facilities is also included. Where to live and what to buy- all these can be found by using a travel guide.

A few travel guides for India are listed below:

(i) Fodor's India, 1978, London Mckay, 1978.

This is an excellent handbook for travellers. It gives maps, illustrations. This guide is published annually.

(ii) Murray's Handbook for Travellers in India, Burma and Ceylon. 21st ed. London: Murray, 1968.

This handbook includes maps and town plans. Its introductory section provides information about history and administration. In the text, India occupies the major portion. The arrangement of material is based on the route principal. A good index is also provided.

(iii) India: Destination of the 1995. Visit India, Tourism Year 1991

It is produced by Department of Tourism, Government of India and includes Tourist Map of India, Government of India Tourist offices, Sight seeing outdoors, Sports, Fairs and Festivals Shopping, Travel data, Dining Museums and galleries.

(iii) Maps, Atlases and Globes

Maps, atlases and globes form another important sources of geographical information. These are necessary reference sources in any type of library but Indian libraries have not given enough attention to this kind of materials.

Maps: According to ALA Glossary of Library and Information Science (1983), "a map is a representation normally drawn to a scale and on a flat medium of a selection of material or abstract features on, or in relation to, the surface of the earth or another celestial body."

R.A. Skeleton, formerly Superintendent of the Map Room of the British Museum defines; "A map as a graphic document in which location, extent and direction can be more precisely defined than by the written word; and its construction is a mathematical process strictly controlled by measurement and calculation."

The Library of Congress defines maps in a broad way as "All forms of cartographic materials normally added to the collections of the library including flat maps and charts, collection of maps in atlas form, terrain models, globes, etc."

Atlas : It is more than four hundred years have passed since Mercqator first coined the term 'Atlas' to describe a collection of maps bound up in a volume. The term became popular with the sixteenth century geographers. Since then, there has been rapid progress in this direction. In the turn of the nineteenth century, the scope of atlas production was widened considerably. At present, it has become possible for the publisher to produce almost a dozen different general atlases for different sectors of the market by varying the combinations of content and style.

According to ALA Glossary, an atlas is, "a volume of maps, plates, engravings, tables etc., with or without descriptive letter press. It may be an independent publication or it may have been issued to accompany one or more volumes of text."

Types and Uses

Maps and atlases are used by common men as well as specialists both for work and pleasure. Varied uses of maps and atlases depend on their types.

(i) **A physical map** is usually referred to for visual location and identification of the world, country, region, city or town, mountain, river, lake, sea, ocean, gulf, bay, desert or any other geographical formation.

(ii) Topographic maps trace details of geological, soil, forest and other basic information and for historical, economic, political or other types of development. They are used to show land use, land ownership, various methods of communications, transportation, etc.

(iii) A route map shows roads, railroads, bridges, etc.

(iv) A political map normally limits itself to political boundaries of different countries, states, cities, towns, etc.

(v) The historical maps chart the flow of a given battle or event and its progress. They indicate adjustments of boundaries after wars and due to negotiated settlement directly between two countries (China and UK) or under the auspices of international organizations (UN trust territories).

(vi) The economic and commercial atlases record general information on business facts, agricultural facts, communication, transportation, retail trade, exports and imports, etc.

Besides, Maps and atlases on the basis of area coverage, may be grouped as under :

(i) International

(ii) National

(iii) Local

Topographic and the thematic maps are used by professional people. Central and local government staff needs them for a variety of administrative purposes, viz., town and country planning. Commercial and industrial firms require them for transport, prospecting and setting up of factories, depots and offices. Students and research workers refer them to get information related to geography, history, geology, demography, land use, archaeology and topography. They also devise their own maps for their theses and reports.

The class lecture can be supplemented by the use of maps and globes. Particularly in schools, visual demonstration of maps, atlases and globes to teach geography and history may be very effective. In libraries, they help in answering various geographical queries, advising patrons in making their travel plans and young users in enriching their general knowledge. Thus, maps and atlases which contain a wide variety of information are useful to all kinds of people in the society.

Some of the important maps and atlases are discussed below:-

(i) The Times Atlas of the World. 8th comprehensive edition, London Times Newspapers. 1990.

The revised edition of the single volume edition which was first published in 1967. The new edition has 47 pages of prefatory information; graphic size comparison of continents, oceans, river drainage basins, islands and inland water bodies; and eight pages of world thematic mapping. The scale used is 1:850,000 for Great Britain and 1:2500,000 for the rest of the world. The name index forming part 3 has about 210,000 entries.

V.1. World, Australia and East Asia

V.2. South-West Asia and Russia

V.3. Northern Europe

V.4. Southern Europe and Africa

V.5. The Americas

(ii) National Geographic Atlas of the World. 6th ed. Washington: National Geographic Society, 1990.

This Atlas shows the present countries of the world after the major changes consequent to the break up of the USSR and changes in Eastern Europe. Using the newly adopted Robinson Projection, it contains a four-fold world map and a number of spacecraft images of the earth and the planets. The number of entries in the index have increased from 125,000 to 150,000.

(iii) Britannica Atlas. Chicago, Encyclopaedia Britannica, 1977.

By means of colour maps and charts, this atlas attempts to provide the latest facts about the present-day world regarding population, location of places, land use patterns and other local features of metropolitan agglomerations, physical characteristics of countries, etc. this is an encyclopaedia-type atlas. The emphasis is on internationalism of content and complete comparability among the maps. The attempt has been made to avoid local prejudices and tastes. The stress is on truly international character of contents. First a global view of the world and of the oceans, has been provided followed by an overall survey of continents. This is followed by a closer view of all regions within continents and so on. At the back of the atlas is a 29-page section of 60 maps of world's major urban centres. These maps show land-use patterns and other local features of great metropolitan agglomerations. Other special features include provision of world information table, population of cities and towns and glossary of geographical terms.

(iv) Rand McNally Cosmopolitan World Atlas. Chicago, Rand McNally, 1981.

Rand McNally and Company is one of the best-known map makers. It brings out a variety of atlases and has a high reputation.

This atlas contains 300 maps, with a large number of map inserts. Scaleranges from 1:3,000,000 to 1:16,000,000. Maps are accurate and attractive. It also includes illustrations, diagrams, and brief articles on topics like weather, geology, oceans, etc.

There are two excellent indexes. About 85000 entries are given in the general index. It enables to locate political names and physical features. The other index, indexes facts and text material from non-map section. This is relatively inexpensive and highly accurate atlas. This follows the policy of continuous revision. It updates the maps with each printing. However, complete revision is done every six or seven years.

(v) An Atlas of India. New Delhi: Oxford University Press, 1990. (with 212 maps)

It claims to be the most comprehensive atlas of India in which each state and union territory has nine maps. All India maps cover physical, political, climate, soil, power projects, religious distribution, literacy area and population. There are five tables one each on: rainfall, population, crop production, mineral production and industrial location.

(vi) National Atlas of India. Calcutta: National Atlas and Thematic Mapping Organization, 1980. 2 Vol.

This is the most comprehensive atlas of India and contains in all 264 plates. In the first volume there are 109 plates depicting, administrative, physical, forest types, parliamentary constituencies and physiographic divisions. There are insets for major cities of the country such as Delhi, Lucknow, Calcutta, Bombay, Trivandrum, etc. The plates in the second volume begin from No.110 and cover, among other topics population, transport and tourism, posts and telecommunication, industry, foods crops, handicrafts, languages and health.

(vii) Hyderabad in Maps. Hyderabad: Bureau of Economics and Statistics, Govt. of Andhra Pradesh, 1953.

(viii) Bengal in Maps: A Geographical Analysis of Resources Distribution in West Bengal and East Pakistan. *Calcutta: Orient Longman, 1949.*

(ix) Bihar in Maps with explanatory text by P. Dayal. Patna: Kusum Prakashan, 1954.

(x) Madhya Bharat in Maps. Indore: Department of Economics Intelligence and Statistics, 1951.

(xi) Maharashtra in Maps by K.R.Dikshit; assisted by Charulata Patil. Bombay; Maharashtra State Board for Literature and Culture, 1986. 245p.

This is reference book includes 67 maps of authentic statistical information about administrative divisions, sugar factories, places of tourist interest, population, growth of urban areas and towns, employment, production in various industries, etc.

Globe: The difference between a map and a globe is the form. A map is any geographic image of the earth drawn to scale on a flat surface whereas a globe is a spherical representation of the earth's surface. It is a hollow ball of metal, bearing a world map on its surface and is mounted on an axle which permits its rotation. The term 'globe' is synonymously used for the 'World' or the earth. It is called in cartography as a scale model of the earth. The first model of the globe was made in Nuremberg in Germany in 1492.

Q. : Mention the importance of Biographical Sources of information with suitable examples from Indian Sources.

or

Enumerate the major types of Biographical Sources. Discuss in detail the scope of any one Indian Biographical Source.

Ans. : The term biography has been derived from two Greek words, 'Bios', meaning life and 'Graphein', meaning to write. To quote Louis Shores, biographical dictionary is 'essentially a dictionary of notable persons, usually arranged alphabetically by surnames, with biographical identifications that range from brief outline to extended narrative'. The definition according to Sir Harold Nicholson is 'a biography must be a history in the sense that it must be accurate and depict a person in relation to his times. It must describe an individual with all graduation of human character and not merely present a type of virtue or vice, and it must be... written in grammatical English and with an adequate feeling for style.'

These are the recorded experiences of an individual, a society or a group. They contain several details often throwing light by admirer or a close companion.

The following types of the information can be satisfied from this type of information source.

(i) Notable persons (both living and dead), which include statesmen, artists, religious leaders, scientists, athletes, soldiers, philosophers, etc.

(ii) Specialist persons, in science, social sciences, humanities; professionals from medicine, law, engineering, teaching community; persons in trade, business and industry.

(iii) Socialites, from royalty, nobility, first families, social clubs.

(iv) Persons from all walks of life, from a country, from a region, in the news recently, in advertisements, etc.

Types of Biographical Sources

Biographical dictionaries can be categorized by using any one characteristic at a time or by using period or time as a characteristic. They may be grouped as:

(i) Current biographical information sources, and

(ii) Retrospective biographical information sources

From the point of view of geographical area covered the may be classified as,

(i) Universal, and

(ii) National, regional or local or institutional biographies.

Biographical dictionaries are also grouped as : (i) General (ii) Specialized or subject (iii) By gender such as men and women and (iv) By language.

The biographical dictionaries available in libraries are often found to possess more than one of these characteristics in various combinations. Examples of current universal specialized biographical dictionaries have their counterpart in current universal general biographical dictionaries. Similar is the case with retrospective dictionaries.

Some important biographies are discussed below:

(i) International Who's Who. London: Europa, 1935-. Annual.

International Who's Who as it appears from its title is of an international level biographical source. This is continuously being published for the last 64 years. Its latest 65th edition came out in 2002. The foremost aim of this source is to answer the needs of readers seeking information on the lives of most gifted and eminent contemporaries, the persons have been chosen entirely on merit, achievements and for their importance in their respective fields. The editor of this edition is Mr. Richard Fitz Williams.

It includes those eminent persons who are noted for their contributions and achievements or their prominent role in their respective specialized fields such as in art, architecture, literature, literature, medicine, music, painting, politics, science, engineering, technology, business, cinema, fashion designing, diplomacy, journalism, photography, law etc.

This 65th edition, appeared in 2002 contains about 20,000 entries. More than 1000 new biographies have been incorporated in it.

About 350 names of entrants, whose death has been reported over the last year, have also been given under 'Obituary'.

In the preliminary pages the details of "Royal Families" of about 300 countries have been provided. In this section the information about the name of the reigning king, children, parents, marriage, name of queen, sisters of the king etc. have been provided.

The entries have been arrange alphabetically according to the surnames of the biographies. The surnames are in Capital Bold Letters and the Christian names in bold small letters.

Special Features

(i) Cross-references have been given where very pseudonyms occur in the entry.

(ii) The present edition incorporates a CD-ROM version (though it first time appeared in 1999), which may be used on up to five workstations simultaneously.

(iii) CD-ROM enables a reader to search for any aspect of the biography. It has made even every word of the entry accessible.

Overall get up such as binding, wrapper, title etc are good enough. The type faces used are attractive and modern and place no strain to the eyes. International Who's Who has gained tremendous applaud and become an indispensable ready reference source all over the world.

(ii) Chambers Biographical Dictionary

Chambers Biographical Dictionary was first published in 1897. Its various revised editions with additions and deletions were published later on. Its first revised edition came out in 1951 edited by W.M. Geddie and J.Liddell Graddie. It was further revised by J.O. Thorne. The latest revised edition was published in 1984 and then its reprints were published by W & R Chambers Ltd., Edinburg, edited by J.O. Thorne and T.C. Callocott.

It is considered as an authentic standard ready reference tool, because of the fact that it is a publication of a leading, famous and reputed agency i.e. Chambers. Both the editors - J.O. Thorne as well as T.C. Collocott are experienced, well qualified and expert in this field. In the present revised edition, every entry has been thoroughly examined and revised seriously. Many articles have been rewritten and amplified as needed.

Some outdated entries possessing no ostensible interest for the modern readers have been removed. It itself claims that fame and public esteem are constantly subject to the vagaries of fashion, and critical assessment are charged by modern approach. The persons whose great importance is today more fully recognized received more words accordingly.

The new categories of eminent persons have come up during last few decades, such as astronomers, nuclear scientists, film stares, leaders, reformers etc. who now find place in it. Those persons who could not be included in its previous edition being either established or temporary eclipsed when the earlier edition was published and now gained fame, got place in the dictionary.

All entries are arranged in alphabetical order according to the surnames. For surnames bold capital letters and for Christian names and title small bold letters have been used. When two or more similar surnames occur, they are numbered, so that the persons of the same surnames may be readily distinguished and their relationship, if any, immediately be established.

This is a retrospective cum-current type of biographical source as it contains entries on living as well as past persons of the world.

Special Features

(i) Cross-references have also been provided wherever required.

(ii) The pronunciation of difficult names is also indicated, wherever needed using simplified phonetic system, the details of phonetic system have been given in the preliminary pages.

(iii) In the end there is a subject index, which gives all eminent persons of a particular field at one place. This is very helpful to know about all the persons of importance in a field within no time.

(iv) This is paperback edition bearing attractive title page. Modern typefaces have been used of larger size to save the eyes from strain.

In the end, it may be said that the Chambers Biographical Dictionary is very useful to find out the all-necessary details about a person of repute in any field of interest.

(iii) India Who's Who. New Delhi: INFA, 1970-. Annual.

'India Who's Who' is a national level biographical source and as clear from the title it includes the biographies of eminent Indians only. The edition published in 1994 is the latest one and after this edition, it could not be revised so far.

It is the most important general biographical source material from India, which covers a wide spectrum of the people of eminence in the country. Roughly, 5000 concise biographies of people in all walks of life including government, politics, civil service, business and finance, education, art, science and technology are included in each yearly volume. Entries are arranged alphabetically under each broad subject. Its two part have seven subparts in all. These parts are as under:

PART-I (Divided into three subparts):

(a) Public Affairs : Under this heading the biographies are given as under:

Biographies of President, Vice-President and Prime Minister of India. After it the biographies of Central Ministers, according to their offices, followed by the Cabinet Secretaries, duly arranged alphabetically, are given.

Besides them, the persons in different services such as Civil Services, Defence services, Foreign services; members of Lok Sabha, Rajya Sabha, Retired Military Officers have also been included.

(b) Persons from Private Sectors: This subpart includes biographies of persons eminent in the fields of industrial management, finance, labour etc.

(c) Persons gained fame in Disciplines: The biographies of those persons who are known for their activities in Humanities such as Arts, Crafts, Design and Visual Communication, Education have been given place.

PART - II (Divided into four subparts)

In this part the persons known for their achievements in the following four fields have been included:

(d) Science: Biology, Chemistry, Earth Science, Mathematics & physics.

(e) Applied Sciences: Architecture & Town Planning, Engineering, Technology, Medical Science, Ayurveda, Homeopathy, Unani Medicine.

(f) Social Sciences & Law: Anthropology, Economics, History, Philosophy, Psychology and Law.

(g) Miscellaneous: Archaeology, Archieves, Astrology, Hotel-Travel, Library Science, Museums, Naturalists, Printing, Sports & Yoga.

Thus, in both the parts there are about 50 fields and there are about 5000 biographies of eminent persons, whose achievements in their respective fields have been included in it.

Special Features

1. In this edition more than 500 new biographies have been added.
2. There is an index duly arranged alphabetically.
3. Another alphabetical index has also been given for the advertisers.
4. An addenda has also been provided for extra information.

In the end it can be said that the India Who's is Who is most reliable and authentic biographical source.

(iv) Dictionary of National Biography ed. By S.P. Sen, Calcutta: Institute of Historical Studies, 1972-1974. 4 vol. and supplements.

It is one of the most authentic and reliable sources of biography, which is published by a reputed institution, i.e. Institute of Historical Studies. The biographies have been written by about 350 scholars known in their respective fields. The editor of the biographical dictionary is also a learned person. It is frequently being used in public and academic libraries, academic institutions, embassies, government/non-government departments etc.

It includes the biographies of those persons who are well known for their achievements in politics, religion, social upliftment, education, science, law, commerce, industry, art/fine art, literature, nation building, poetry and those persons who got some high positions etc. Besides this, such persons have been included who are of national or regional importance. There are about 1400 biographies. The words in each entry ranges from 600 to 2400. The living as well as dead persons, at that time, have been given place. A supplement, to be completed in 4 volumes is planned to provide biographical information of eminent personalities during the quarter century since 1947. Volume 1 covering the names beginning with alphabet A-D ed. By N.R. Ray was published in 1986.

Special Features

(a) At the end of each biography, a select bibliography has been given for further study of the reader.

(b) Every biography contains the name of the writer.

(c) A supplement has also been brought out in the year 1986 to keep the source up to date. It contains about 1400 biographies.

(d) The surnames have been printed in bold letters.

(e) The printing is quite visible and beautiful faces have been used.

Index Type Biographical Information Sources

There are certain biographical sources, which serve primarily as an index to major retrospective and or current biographical sources. By looking up these publication one may identify sources where detailed information is available on the biographic. Given below are a few such examples:

(i) Biography and Genealogy Master Index/ed. By Miranda C. Herbert and Bardara Mc.Neil. Detroit: Gale, 1980. 8V.

A consolidated index to more than 3,200,000 biographical sketches in over 350 current and retrospective biographical dictionaries. The publication is kept up-to-date through annual and cumulative supplements. A cut down version of the *Master Index* is available as *Biography Almanac* and microfiche edition as *Bio Base*.

(ii) Author Biography Master Index, Detroit, Gale, 1982. 2V.

It is an example of master index restricting its coverage to biographies of literary figures, *Index to Scientists of the World from Ancient to Modern Times,* (Boston: Faxon, 1962) and *Index to Women of the World from Ancient to Modern Times* by Norman Olin. Ireland (Faxon, 1970) are other examples of one time publication of master index, although some are updated by supplements.

Q. : What is 'Bibliography'? Describe its need and types.

or

Write short notes on the following:

— **National Bibliography**

— **Subject Bibliography**

— **Trade Bibliography**

— **Universal Bibliography**

or

What do you mean by 'bibliography'? List the major types of bibliographies. Describe briefly the important criteria for compiling subject bibliographies.

or

Discuss the scope, purpose and use of trade bibliographies. Briefly describe some of the important current and retrospective trade bibliographies of India.

or

Explain the wide connotation of the term 'Bibliographies' and discuss with examples the types of bibliographies that are generally recognized.

Ans. The term "Bibliography" is of Greek origin derived from two words 'Biblion' meaning book and 'Graphein' meaning to write.

Thus, initially the word bibliography denotes 'writing of books' and prior to invention of printing, the word was used in the sense of copying. Over one hundred years, there was no change in the meaning of the word. However, in 1763, the meaning changed from the 'writing of books' to 'writing about books'. Between 17th and 18th centuries the principles, concepts, practices and varieties of bibliography as are understood today were laid down. This meaning was well supported by the Encyclopaedia Britannica (1797) and also first edition of Encyclopaedia Americana.

A bibliography is a list of references to primary or other sources relating to some given subject or person; it is usually arranged chronologically or alphabetically by authors. It may be comprehensive or selective and annotated or otherwise evaluative. It may be published separately or as a part of a large work to acknowledge information sources, recommend additional reading or direct attention to more detailed treatment elsewhere. Almost always the time span and the subject coverage are well defined, so that a good bibliography represents a defined coverage of the literature within the defined limits and makes retrospective searching much easier.

It is variously defined as under:

— *Arundale Isdail:* "Bibliography is an art as well as science too".

— *Oxford Dictionary:*

   (a) "The systematic description and history of books, their authorship, printing, publishing, editions etc.

   (b) "A list of books of a particular author, printer or country, or of those dealing with any particular theme, the literature of the subject.

— *Ebert :* "The Science that deals with literary productions."

— *Shores :* "A list of written, printed or otherwise produced records of civilization, which may include books, serials, pictures, maps, films, recordings, museum objects, manuscripts and any other media of communication."

To sum up the above definitions of quoted authorities, the view of Sir Walter Gerg needs mentioning which states that "books are material means by which the literature is transmitted and so bibliography is essentially the science of the transmission of literary documents. "The term, however, has assumed different meanings through the passage of time. Identification of thought content in books, has become the prime concern of bibliography. It is in this context, bibliography means two things : (a) the art of preparing a systematic list of books, and (b) the name of the list itself.

It is different from catalogues and indexes. A catalogue is basically a list of a given collection and the index, for example, is also different from a bibliography. Although both provide access to information, the bibliography usually provides a single access point to information. Besides, in-depth subject analysis is done in indexes so that user can find specific concepts. The catalogues and indexes both serve as sources for the compilation of bibliographies, the bibiography provides single access point to information, generally the first author, an index provides multiple access points, i.e., from each of the several concepts provided in the document. Catalogues and indexes can serve as sources for compilation of bibliographies.

Need of Bibliography

Bibliography is needed due to following reasons:

1. The detailed information about a document can be ascertained with the help of bibliography.
2. Bibliography contains full details like: name of author, entry, joint author, edition, name of publisher, place, year of publication, price etc.
3. Bibliography is required to select her/his needed books for the use of text book.
4. Bibliography is needed to verify the book selection materials too.
5. With the help of bibliography the literature related with science and encyclopaedia works can be ascertained and known.
6. The price verification of the books can be examine with the bibliography-Books in Print or commercial catalogues.
7. Bibliography provides the information of the books written by various writers in any language at any country.
8. Bibliography provides information about the literature of a caste and creed of a province, state or place.
9. It gives the details of all the books/writing of an author.

10. Bibliography helps to locate of availability of a book or literature published.

Branches of Bibliography

Based on the activities, to aid the users, the following branches of bibliography can be identified:-

1. Systematic or Enumerative
2. Analytical or Critical, and
3. Historical.

1. Systematic or Enumerative Bibliographies

When the records are listed in any order-alphabetically, logically, or according to some principle or in a systematic order, they are referred to as a systematic bibliography. In other words, the concern is not mere listing of printed documents, especially published documents but with the effective listing of them so that they must be traced readily by authors, titles and subjects, and also by forms and series, wherever required. It is called enumerative bibliography which means that some sort of selection has prevailed in determining what to include.

This branch is further sub-divided as under :

(i) Universal Bibliography: It lists all documents of all kinds of materials, produced in all countries, in every language, at any time and on all themes. Eg: Bibliotheca Universal.

(ii) National Bibliography : The national bibliographies are serial publications which are current and attempt to list the publications of a particular country. Eg:

— Indian National Bibliography (INB), Calcutta: Central Reference Library, 1957- monthly.

— British National Bibliography, London: British Library Bibliographic Services Division, 1950 - weekly.

(iii) Trade Bibliography : It is a list of books and other materials which are printed and available in a country for sale, through publishers, book-sellers or trade agencies. Their chief function is to promote book trade. Eg :

— Indian Books in Print, Delhi: Indian Bureau of Bibliographies, 1955-.

— Books in Print, New York: R.R. Bowker, 1948-.

(iv) Selective Bibliography: It is a collection of books according to some specific reason. Eg :

— World's Best Books, by Ara Don Dickinson, New York, Wilson, 1953.

— Guide to Reference Material, edited by A.J.Walford, 3rd ed., London. The Library Association, 1973-77, 3 volumes.

(v) Incunabula or Book Rarities Bibliography : It lists the early printed material up to 15th century. Eg :

— Index to the Early Printed Books.... By Robert Proctor.

(vi) Subject Bibliographies : This bibliography forms the largest group of enumerative bibliographies. It is a comprehensive list of all books, periodical articles, pamphlets and other reading material in a particular subject. Eg : — *Library Literature*

It also includes indexes and abstracting services such as - Science Citation Index, Philadelphia: ISI 1961-. Current Contents: Life sciences, 1961-.

(vii) Author Bibliography: This records books, articles etc. written by an author or attributed to him and the material written about the author by others. Eg:

— Chaucer : a bibliographical manual.

(viii) List of Thesis or Dissertations : Dissertations are extremely important to research scholars, and therefore, their bibliographic control is of utmost importance. Many countries bring out bibliographies of dissertations limited to their countries. Eg:

— Indian Dissertation Abstracts.

— Dissertation Abstracts International, Vol. 1-, 1938-, Ann Arbor, Michigan, Xerox University Microfilms.

(ix) Bibliography of Anonymous and Pseudonymous Works: Eg :

— Dictionary of Anonymous and Pseudonymous Literature by S. Halkett and J.Lang.

(x) List of Periodicals : Including list of current periodicals, list of retrospective periodicals, location and finding lists. Eg :

— Ulrich's International Periodicals Directory, 1994-95, 33rd edition, New providence, New Jersey, Bowker, 1994, 5 Vol.

— Directory of Indian Scientific Periodicals, 3rd ed. New Delhi, INSDOC, 1976.

(xi) Bibliography of Bibliographies : It is a list of bibliographies recorded in a systematic and logical order. It includes all types of bibliographies in various subject, fields, separately published. Eg :

— Bibliography Index.

— A World Bibliography of Bibliographies and of Bibliographical Catalogues, Calendars, Abstracts, Digests, Indexes and the like, by Theodore Besterman.

(xii) Union Catalogue : A union catalogue is an important tool for a librarian. Eg :

— National Union Catalogue of Scientific Serials in India, New Delhi, INSDOC, 1988, 4V.

— New Serial Titles, 1950-70, New York, R.R.Bowker, 1972, 5 Volumes.

2. Analytical or Critical Bibliography

An analytical bibliography deals with the study and detailed description of documents. It examines the physical characteristics of documents, the history of the documents as physical entities. It is of two types:-

(i) **Descriptive Bibliography :** Descriptive bibliography is the record of bibliographic details of documents, which have been established during the process of analytical bibliography deals with textual variation between a manuscript and the printed book or between different editions or reprints.

(ii) **Textual Bibliography :** The textual bibliographies are those bibliographies that help to determine the effect of writing or the printing processes on the validity of the text. It helps to ascertain the variety of authorship, edition. Thus, textual bibliography deals with textual variation between a manuscript and the printed book or between different editions or reprints.

3. Historical Bibliography

This branch of bibliography deals with the history of making books. In it books are studied "as objects of art". It covers the history of writing, printing materials and binding etc.

The use of paper, printing ink and printing process and the revolution in the printing technology has many implications on the development of the writing materials. Historical bibliography, thus, deals with the history and the methods of book production - printing, binding, paper making, illustrating and publishing. It is an attempt to achieve a broad understanding of the world of books and social and cultural condition in existence at the time.

Types of Bibliography

Bibliographies are regarded as most important tools in libraries and documentation centers. The reason being that bibliographies allow free flow of bibliographic information on the published literature of all disciplines. The following types of bibliographies can be identified:

1. National Bibliography
2. Subject Bibliography
3. Trade Bibliography
4. Universal Bibliography

1. National Bibliography: In simple sense, national bibliography includes the totality of bibliographic tools relating to the output of a nation, taken together. The national bibliographies are the serial publications, which are current, and attempt to list the publications of a particular country. The national bibliographies can be used to search current as well as retrospective information. Strictly in the terms of democracy, a national bibliography is a list of publications produced in a country, in the language of that country, by the people living in that country or elsewhere within a stipulated time limit. Dr. S.R. Ranganathan has divided National Bibliography into following five categories:-

— List of entire books published in a country.

— List of entire books published on a country.

— List of entire books published by all citizens of a country.

— List of entire books published on all citizens of a country.

— Any coordination of the above category.

National bibliographies serve cultural, economic and social purposes. These are authoritative source for information about the documents produced in a country. A number of countries have their national bibliographies. Some of the important national bibliographies have been listed as under:

(i) Indian National Bibliography. Kolkata: Central Reference Library, 1957. Monthly.

(ii) British National Bibliography. London: British Library Bibliographic Services Division. 1950. Weekly.

(iii) Cumulative Book Index: A world List of Books in English Language. New York: Wilson. 1898. Monthly.

2. Subject Bibliography: This bibliography contains the specific text book of specific subject which is also very useful for researchers.

Dr.S.R.Ranganathan has defined the subject bibliography as "subject bibliography is that document bibliography whose scope is limited to a specific subject field and there is not included the entire subject".

On the basis of utility, it is observed that readers search it as per subject, not by an author. Most of researchers have a subject approach instead of all the books of an author. They use bibliography in subject approach which is represented in a bibliography.

Subject bibliography may be published in form of full book or in its part of a book, a periodical in full or in its part.

As far as the form of material, time span, sources of origin and language is concerned, subject bibliographies have usually a limited scope. These can be either selective or comprehensive. These can also be either current or retrospective. The subject bibliographies can be divided into several categories depending on their contents. Some of these are described below:

(i) Reference Bibliographies: This kind of bibliographies are those which are mostly used for reference purpose. These bibliographies are considered to be exhaustive bibliographies. It is often quite impossible to compile absolutely exhaustive bibliographies. The reason being that recording every single published document on any subject is so difficult due to mass of published literature, scattering of books and journals. The published literature available in a number of languages is also a problem for bibliographers in compiling exhaustive bibliographies. These types of publications, therefore, only aim to be exhaustive within chosen limits, which should be made clear by the bibliographers. The reference bibliographies can either be ad hoc, with occasional revisions or supplements or serial bibliographies with benefit of regular, at time frequent publications, and time saving cumulations.

(ii) Reading Lists: Large size subject bibliographies are of little use when one wishes to study a particular subject, at whatever level, rather he needs a carefully prepared select bibliography of it. Such type of bibliographies are called reading lists. The reading lists are quite common and produced by people who know or should know the literature they recommend. The teachers often prepare these for distribution among the students. The more suitable example is a list of suggested readings provided at the end of this lesson. A bibliography or a reading list supporting a research article or a review article is usually very valuable for reference purpose as lot of effort goes into preparation of such lists.

(iii) Subject Indexes and Abstracting Services: If someone has to search a document from a large number of scattered references, this is a time consuming process. To a little satisfaction, some literature can be scanned from the indexes of books and periodicals. Apart from this, there are some special services called indexing services, which include all details of the published documents in a helpful sequence. Furthermore, there are abstracting services, which provide brief summaries of the text along with bibliographical details. Current contents, Chemical abstracts, Library and Information Science Abstracts, etc. are the good examples of such type of services. There are also some sources called citation indexes. One of the best examples is Science Citation Index. Current awareness bulletins, especially prepared by special libraries also help their users by presenting the list of new periodical articles, either as subject lists or as contents lists.

(iv) Bibliographic Reviews : Bibliographic reviews perform a combined function of providing information and judgment about the items reviewed and therefore, serves as useful bibliographic contributions made to a particular subject field. The bibliographic reviews can be in the form of current advances, annual reviews or state-of-the -art on a subject area.

Examples:

— **Bibliography of Library Economy :** A classified index to the professional periodical literature in the English language relating to library economy, printing, methods of publishing, copy right, bibliography etc. from 1876-1920 by H.G.T. Conos, Chicago, American Library Association 1927, revised edition based on the 1908 edition.

— **Indian Library Literature :** An annotated bibliography by R.G. Parasher, New Delhi, Today & Tomorrow, Printers and Publishers 1971.

— **ASLIB Book List:** A monthly list of recommended Scientific and Technical Book with Annotation, London, ASLIB, Vol. 1, 1935, Monthly.

— British Scientific & Technical Book, London, Clarks, 1960.

— American Scientific Books, New York, Bowker, 1962-66 (Annual).

— Asian Social Science Bibliography, 1966. New Delhi, Vikas Publishing House.

— Cambridge Bibliography of English Literature. Edited by F.W. Bateson. Cambridge University Press, 1940-57, 5 volumes.

3. Trade Bibliography: The scope of trade bibliography is upto business associations, traders of publishing world or publishers. It is published by trade organization's for a specific country. Trade associations include book sellers, distributors and publishers. The main objective of them is to gain in business. These organizations treat a book as a commodity and prepare and publish bibliography to increase sale as an advertisement agency. Though from one angle these bibliography are of national repute but from the point of view of subject it includes non-book material too. For the larger library trade bibliographies may be of less imprtance but medium and small library can use these bibliographies for book selecting, price verification.

On the basis of information trade bibliographies can be divided into following two parts:

— Current bibliography

— Retrospective bibliography.

The important trade bibliographies are:

(i) Indian Books in Print. Delhi: Indian Bibliographies Bureau, 1955-Annual.

(ii) Books in Print. New York: R R Bowker. 1948-, Annual.

(iii) British Books in Print. London: Whitaker. 1967-, Annual.

4. Universal Bibliography: A bibliography, which includes everything, that is published, issued or processed in the field of knowledge from the beginning to the future is called a universal when it includes all published materials, whether books or part of them or periodicals or articles in them or combination of them, on all subjects, in all languages, in all forms, in all countries, at all times. Though it is very useful but there are so many practical difficulties of compilation. The whole literature can be collected but it will too much and difficult to print out.

Therefore, a via-media of the problem was thought as to give practical shape for universal bibliography and named selective universal catalogue. In place of universal bibliography which was like to make castle in the air replaced by the idea to make selective universal catalogue of a cumulative list of all the national bibliography of the world.

To get print of complete universal bibliography, there are few difficulties which may be summed up as below:-

— Most of documents are those which have no written record, as such these documents can not be included in universal bibliography.

— Some documents are recorded but at the need documents are not available.

— Arrangement and printing of collected information is very much difficult.

— Literature in the world is so scattered and in multi-languages, as to collect, understand and print out of them is a difficult task and no solution almost.

Example: Cumulative Book Index: A World List of Books in English language. 1986. New York: H.W. Wilson, 1898-.

Concluding, it can be said that the basis of all librarianship is bibliography. It is a profession, in which what is recorded, by whatsoever means historical development has permitted, is the foundation of all activity. Bibliography plays a vital role in the librarianship. The national and trade bibliographies are of immense importance for libraries and documentation centers. Hence the field of librarianship can't survive without the bibliographical tools.

Q. : What do you understand by Bibliography? How it is evaluated, evaluate any two bibliographies.

or

Explain the need for and functions of a National Bibliography and discuss some of the salient features of INB or BNB.

or

Evaluate the following:

— **INB**

— **BNB**

Ans. The word 'bibliography' has originated from the Greek terms-'Biblion' meaning a book and 'Graphien' meaning to write. Bibliography, thus, means 'writing of books' which later on changed to 'writing about books'. The term was first used by "Louis Jacob de Saint Charles" in his" Bibliographic Parisiana" (1645-50), and became popular in the eighteenth century. It is variously defined as-

According to Theodore Besterman "Bibliography is a list of books arranged according to some permanent principles."

According to Louis Shores, "It is a list written, printed or otherwise produced record of civilization, which may include books, serials, pictures, films, maps, records, manuscripts and other media of communication."

Copinger defined "Bibliography as the grammar of literary investigation".

According to Van Hoeran, "Bibliography is the art or science of correctly describing books.

Presently to a library and information professional, a bibliography means the art of preparing a systematic list of books and the name of the list itself.

Evaluation of Bibliography

When considering the relative merits of a bibliography, one applies the general criteria used for evaluation of all reference works: purpose, scope, authority, etc. Beyond the general considerations, one should evaluate a bibliography in the following manner:

1. Purpose: The bibliography should fill a real need and it should not be a repetition of another work or so mysterious that it is of little or

no value. The subject as well as the purpose of compiling a bibliography should be stated clearly in the title and well defined in the preface.

2. Scope: It is important that the bibliography should be as complete as possible within its stated purpose. For example, a bibliography of books and periodical articles about nineteenth-century Indian railroads will include contemporary magazine reports about the construction of railroads. Reliable Websites (if any), too, are likely to be listed, as are related CDs, recordings, etc. Where there are different forms, these must be clearly identified.

3. Methodology: The method of compiling the bibliography should be straightforward and should make clear that compiler has examined all material listed. The standard bibliographic style should be used for the description of items. All the basic elements of a bibliography should also be included.

4. Organization: The organization of bibliography should be clear and easy to use fashion. Appropriate indexes e.g., subject, author, geographical locations, etc. should be provided where multiple access is desirable. The material should be arranged in a logical fashion so that it is not always necessary to use the index, for example, alphabetical by author, by date, by subject, and so forth. The author must offer a clear explanation of how to use the work as well as definitions, a key to abbreviations, and the like. The bibliographies which are available in digital from are called digital bibliography. As far as digital bibliographies are concerned the software should be sophisticated enough that one may do an equal type of search with entry points where needed.

5. Annotations and Abstracts: The descriptive and critical notes used for entries should be clear, succinct, and informative.

6. Bibliographic Form: This is a standard entry with the information one needs to identify and locate the item.

7. Current: The currency of the bibliography is of utmost importance. The material included in the bibliography should be current. The great advantage of digital bibliography is that these can be updated regularly and hence these are more current than the print versions.

8. Accuracy: The accuracy of the material should be given particular attention. There should be some arrangement, it possible, for corrections to be made after publication.

National Bibliographies

A national bibliography can be defined as a list of books, documents, pamphlets, serials, thesis, dissertations or other printed material produced in a country, in the language of the country, by the people living in the country or elsewhere within a stipulated time limit. It can also be defined as a publication containing bibliographies of a nation or of one country.

As national bibliographies record the intellectual input of nations, these are an authoritative source for informing about the documents produced in a country. These serve cultural, economic and education purposes.

Uses of National Bibliography

1. It keeps the user well informed about the literary achievements of a nation.
2. It helps in the transmission of scholarship and culture to future generation.
3. It serves as a device for bibliographic control of literary output of a nation.
4. It serves as a book selection tool for librarians, scholars and others and it acts as a guide to the book trade.
5. It can form a base for other kinds of current bibliographies.

Only two National Bibliographies which are most important, are being discussed in detail.

1. Indian National Bibliography (INB)

Indian National Bibliography (INB), Quarterly. October 1957-December 1963: Monthly January 1964- Central Reference Library, Kolkata, 1959- With Annual Cummulation, the five year cummulative index to volumes for 1958-62.

After independence in India, in the year 1954, the delivery of books Act 1954 was passed, accordingly a publisher was supposed to deposit essential one copy of his publication to National Library, Kolkata and 3 to other public libraries of Delhi, Mumbai and Chennai. In order to follow up and execute the act, first attempt to publish INB was made in the year 1955, but it could publish first in 1958, a quarterly issue. Upto 1963, it was continued to publish quarterly but from 1964 it started in monthly publication which continued upto 1967. Some how or the other reasons INB could not be published during the period 1968-70. Again in the year 1971-1977, it continued but discontinued in 1978-84. Now again since 1984 to date is in publishing monthly.

All the books published in 14 major languages of the country are listed in it. These major 14 languages including English are as follows:

1.English 2. Assamese 3. Bengali 4. Gujarati 5. Hindi 6. Kannad 7. Malayalam 8. Marathi 9. Oriya 10. Punjabi 11. Sanskrti 12. Tamil 13. Tamil, Telugu 14. Urdu.

It covers all publications - except musical socires, maps, periodicals and news papers (except the first issue under a new title), keys and guides and ephemeral materials.

The first issue of INB was divided into following two parts:

1. General publications or non-government publications, and
2. Government publications

Later on both parts of the bibliography was merged into one having its internal arrangement of two parts like:

1. Classified part and
2. Alphabetical part

1. Classified Part: Entries in this part are arranged in classified order which contains the bibliographical details:

Author's name, Entry, Joint & Corporate author, Place of publication, Name of publisher, Year of publication, Price, No. of pages, Size, Series, Binding. Dewey Decimal classification scheme is used in arrangement of entries, in addition to this supplemented colon classification and class numbers are mentioned just at right corner of entry and also subject headings by chain indexing system.

2. Alphabetical Part: This part consists author, entry, series, joint or corporate author and arranged all in one alphabetical sequence acting as alphabetical index in use. Besides, English language books published in other language are printed in Roman Script.

Limitations of INB

Though it is very useful bibliography of national importance but it is used by those who wants books on a particular subject published in the country.

As a matter of policy to which it was started to publish, it could not satisfy the objectives in full. It was published very late, the issue of 1976 was completed in press and published in 1978, on the other the publications were included up-to 1975. Thus, it was regarded an irregular and incomplete. Even then it is published regularly after an interval and revised.

Other then English, bibliographies published in other Indian languages are as follows:

–	Assamese	1959
–	Bengali	1958
–	Gujarati	1958-59
–	Hindi	1958
–	Kannad	1959
–	Malayalam	1958
–	Marathi	1958-59
–	Oriya	1958-59
–	Punjabi	1958-59
–	Sanskrit	1958-62, 1963/67
–	Tamil	1958
–	Urdu	1958 etc.

Conclusion : At last we may conclude that bibliographic control at the national level is of utmost importance for control at an international level. As a first step towards this objective we require a current complete national bibliography for each nation, so INB is a good step for the purpose of bibliographic control.

INB is a classified record of current publications published in India so it is useful to the librarians, users and scholars of the country. To over come its limitations, it is suggested that the National Library (Kolkata) should pay the postage for books received by it under the delivery of Books and Newspapers (public libraries) Act, 1954. This might serve as an incentive to publishers and this will enrich its comprehensiveness. Employment of adequate competent staff and also use of computers at Central Reference Library gives us hope for the future. Apart from these limitations it is the only publication which gives information about Indian publications in one source.

2. British National Bibliography (BNB)

British National Bibliography (BNB), London, British Library, Bibliographic Services Division, 1950-weekly - Ed. By A.J. Wells, Annuals in vols. 1987-88, Council of British National Museum.

BNB published by service division of British Library, London, is a listing of new books published in Great Britain. It is a list of those publications which are deposited under copyright to the agents. It was first published in the year 1950 by Council of British National Bibliography.

It is a comprehensive bibliography except the exclusion of cheap novelettes, music, maps, periodicals (except for first issue of a new periodical and first issue under a new title), Government of Ireland's publications, Local Government publication, most of British Government publications and unchanged reprints.

The first issue OF BNB was divided into following two parts.

1. General publications
2. Government publications

After the year 1973, the above two parts were merged into one and again published in another new two parts as follows:

1. Classified part
2. Alphabetical part

1. Classified part : In this part, entries are made with few revisions, class numbers are given according to Dewey Decimal classification and catalogued according to AACR 2. The bibliographical details are given like: author, entry, publisher, edition, yearbook series, maps & tables, pages, price etc. In addition to above a number has been marking i.e., ISBN - International Standard Book Number with a view to standardization.

2. Alphabetical Part : In this part, there is provided an alphabetical index consisting of author and book series. At the end of month, in last week, two alphabetical indexes are added for the books published in that month. Besides, the indexing of author's name, cross reference entries are provided for different forms. Subject index provides class number and subject name both, mentioning subject headings in main and sub headings too in detail.

BNB was started to publish in 1950 & since then it is published regularly. With a view to maintain its updateness it is published weekly, monthly, quarterly, yearly and with a communication of five year volume too, thus it is a regular and up to date. Since 1964, it has been publishing monthly. Besides, year 1958-62 a cumulative index volume was published for all the books published during the period.

Initially chain procedure was used to denote subject headings which was stopped and discontinued after the use of 'PRECIS'.

The cumulated edition published as "Subject list of British Books" (1951-54) 2V, is a land mark in systematic bibliography. It's "chain procedure" subject heading and interest for subject specialists.

Conclustion : BNB is used easily both by the librarians and other users. Though there are some criticism due to its time lag and high subscription rate but the publication is greatly used for the purposes of book selection, bibliographic work and as a guide to cataloguing and classification by other libraries.

Q. : Write short notes on

— Indian Books in Print

— British Books in print

— Guide to Indian Periodical Literature

Ans.

(1) Indian Books in print

A bibliography of English books published in India.

Editor: Sher Singh. New Delhi: India Bibliographies Bureau. 3 Volumes Annual. 1967-. 24th ed.

1. Authority: It was started in 1967 as an annual publication. Its first edition covered period from 1955-67. Since then, it is being regularly published by Shri Sher Singh, Deputy Librarian of Delhi university. The present edition of this bibliography (24th ed) is in 3 Volumes-

(i) Author.

(ii) Title.

(iii) Subject guide.

2. Scope : The current edition of Indian Book in print includes about 1,21,000 titles from 2,700 Indian publishers. It includes all types of books on all subjects except ephemeral audio-visual materials and restricted publications. It also gives a directory of Indian publishers with addresses. There are about 3,21,000 entries in it.

3. Frequency : Its frequency is annual.

4. Arrangement : The three volumed set of Indian book in print is arranged in three sequences.

(i) Authors arranged alphabetically.

(ii) Titles arranged alphabetically.

(iii) Subject - guide arranged according to D.D.C. with modification and features heading rendering is done according to CCC rules.

Volume 1st : In first volume, author entries are arranged alphabetically by their surname. It includes four types of publications:-

(i) Books having persons' name as author.

(ii) Publications of Indian Government.

(iii) Publications of Institutes.

(iv) Publications of Conferences.

Sample entry of Author index entry :

1. BHARATAN (Raju)

Lata Mangeskar: A Bibliography.

New Delhi, UBS publishers, 1995, XI, 38p. 295.00

2. INDIA, HOME AFFAIRS (Ministry of-)

Fertility and Child Mortality Estimates of Haryana.

New Delhi, Demography Division, 1988, 92p.

Honorific words of personal names are excluded from entries. Adequate number of added entries were also provided.

Volume 2nd: In it, titles are arranged in alphabetical order. Articles are excluded from titles. Both title and sub-title are provided.

Sample entry of title Index Entry :

WISBOM: The absolute is adorable by Natraj Guru. New Delhi, D.K. Print world, 1995. VIII, 384p. 190.00.

Volume 3rd: This is subject guide in which entries are arranged according to subject and for provided subject D.D.C. is used. This volume is in two parts:-

Part 1st: In certain subject entries arranged according to DDC.

Sample entry of subject Index Entry:-

923-Persons in Social Sciences.

923-254-Persons in Social Sciences in India.

SESHAN (TN)

Heartful of Burden: New Delhi, UBS publishers.

1995.158p,125.00.

Part 2nd : Directory of Indian Publishers with complete addresses.

5. Treatment : Items of information included in Indian Books in Print are Class no, Author, Co-Author, Editor, Compiler, Full-title, Edition, Place, Publisher, Year, No. of pages and Price.

6. Format : IBIP is in hard bound plastic cover. Volumes are not every bulky and cream wove paper is used. The information is presented in three columns. Total number of pages are about 2500. The type faces are small as generally in bibliographies.

7. Special features: It is a comprehensive index which has been expended to facilitate the location of entry out of the book. All necessary references about any particular state, etc. have been systematically ordered, combined and alphabetized in the index to make it more useful. All entries in the index regardless of number of words are considered single heading and are alphabetized letter by letter.

8. Conclusion: The book is a major contribution to the bibliographical organization of recent Indian material. It is an useful publication for libraries, researchers, auditors, book-traders and publishers. It is a very useful reference sources for providing ready reference service.

(2) British Books in Print

London: Whitaker, 1965 - (Annual).

1. Authority: It is a continuation of the publication entitled *Reference Catalogue of Current Literature* (1874-1964). Since 1965 its tile was changed to *British Books in Print* on the pattern of American Books in Print. In 1988, it again changed the title to Whitaker's Books in Print.

2. Scope : Current edition of Whitaker's Books in Print includes about 6,00,000 titles from 22,000 publishers. It lists all titles published in UK. It is a national inclusive reference index of books in print and on sale in the United Kingdom whether hardbound or paperback. It excludes price below $0.15 and less important government publications.

3. Frequency: It is published annually.

4. Arrangement : It is arranged alphabetically word by word in one sequence of author, title and subject. 5 volumes contain series and their publishers and publisher's addresses.

5. Treatment : In Whitaker's Books in Print, items of information include author, title, subtitle, volume, illustrations, series, ISBN, binding, price and publisher's name in a single sequence.

6. Format : The 5th volume of WBIP are in hard cover cloth binding. Total number of pages are about 11,600. The same information is also available in other formats like monthly microfiche edition, monthly CD-ROM book bank edition and on-line via international data base index.

7. Special format : Volume 5th of WBIP contains completion of main alphabetical sequence, a separate listing of all series and their publishers followed by directory of publishers and their addresses.

8. Conclusion : It is certainly a useful work but we find that very often a publication listed in it may be out of print due to time-lag between receipt of information and the issuing of the above bibliography.

(3) Guide to Indian Periodical literature

Volume 40. No. 4.1964-2003

Indian Documentation Service, Gurgaon

Quarterly (May, August, November, February) Annual Cummulations.

1. Authority: It is an important index of periodical publications of India, which was started as a quarterly publication of Indian documentation service (Gurgaon, Haryana). Since then, it is published regularly. It is an alphabetical subject-author index to articles, research papers, news both national and international, notes, conference proceedings, book views etc in the social sciences and humanities appearing in Indian periodicals. It is an extremely useful service especially because of the regularity of its publication programme.

2. Scope:

1. It includes only Indian publications and gives their bibliographical detail.
2. It only includes publication of social sciences and humanities.
3. In it about 500 Indian periodicals are included.

3. Arrangement : Entries are prepared according to subject heading which are arranged alphabetically word by word. Multiworded headings are inverted. In sub-divisions, entries are divided into two parts :

(i) Set in the bold face type.

(ii) Set in the light face type.

Abbreviated headings are also arranged alphabetically word by word. Every article has two type of entries i.e., author and subject. For articles which do not have author, additional subject entries are prepared.

4. Treatment : Every entry includes article, title and author, title of journal, issue no., volume, page no, and other information viz. illustration, bibliography etc. A plus (+) sign following the page no. indicates that the article has been carried over to some other page. In the same issue in other pages explanation of the article abbreviation used in the guide have been given under "abbreviation and signs".

5. Special Features : Its index includes adequate number of cross references. Specification about signs and symbols are also included.

6. Conclusion : It is an useful index about Indian periodical publication in social sciences and humanities. It also includes dailies like, the Times of India and is cumulated annually.

Q. : What do you mean by subject bibliography ? Describe briefly the important criteria for compiling subject bibliographies.

Ans. : "A subject bibliography is the one which deals with the materials about a given subject, whether the subject be a person, place or thing". Such as, we can have subject bibliographies on Mahatma Gandhi (person), on Kashmir (place), or on Handicrafts (things).

According to Ranganathan "A subject bibliography is a document bibliography confined to a specific subject field, instead of covering the entire universe of subjects". Or in other words, it is limited to a definite topic (which may be quite broad), but not all the topics under the sun.

Thus, a subject bibliography is a systematic listing of documents relating to a specific field of knowledge. The subject could be broad like, Science and Technology, Social Sciences and Humanities, or a minute branch of any subject such as, Social Anthropology, Management by Objectives, etc.

Some important characteristics of subject bibliography are as follows:

(i) Subject bibliographies can occur as parts of books, or as independent.

(ii) Generally a subject bibliography will limit its scope in regard to form of material, time span, sources of origin, language, etc.

(iii) Subject bibliography can either be selective or comprehensive. If it includes only significant items it becomes selective, whereas inclusion of materials of all kinds relating to the subject, makes it comprehensive.

(iv) Depending on time and coverage, a subject bibliography may be current or retrospective.

(v) Indexing and abstracting periodicals relating to specific subject fields are also subject bibliographies.

(vi) Printed catalogues of special subject libraries also serve as subject bibliographies.

(vii) Some subject bibliographies may be annotated.

(viii) Most subject bibliographies become out of date after they are released owing to continuous flow of new literature relating to the field.

Compilation of Subject Bibliography

A bibliography can be regarded basically as a file or recording system. There are a number of books and articles on the compilation and arrangement of subject bibliographies, but they provide no hard and fast rules. This could be attributed to great variations in the size and scope of individual bibliographies. Nevertheless some planning and preliminary decision making is necessary for the success of the bibliographic work undertaken irrespective of the fact whether the bibliography is to be current or retrospective. Before compiling a bibliography, one must consider the following points:

(i) How will one define the subject field and how to limit it?

(ii) Whether the work is to be selective or comprehensive?

(iii) What forms of materials one should include?

(iv) What form of entry is to be used?

(v) Physical form (card, slip etc.) on which entries to be prepared?

(vi) How will one arrange the entries-alphabetically, chronologically, or some classified order?

(vii) What is the final form of subject bibliography in which it will be brought out and presented to users.

(i) How to define the Subject : To have a clear idea about the subject field, it will be advisable to consult subject specialists, research scholars, professional colleagues and other users. Consulting text books and subject encyclopaedias will also be useful. If at any stage of the project, it is discovered that items to be included are many more than first imagined and cannot possible to complete it within some specified period and available funds, it will be desirable to reduce the period and the area covered, or one may omit certain classes of materials. While limiting the scope of the subject one should keep in mind the important factors like requirement of users and availability of resources.

(ii) Selectivity versus Comprehensivenss : This largely depends on the size or extent of the subject. The larger the field, the greater is the need for selection, though it may not always be practical. One of the major problems one will face is to decide where to draw the retrospective line. When a comprehensive survey of subject literature is required, it is necessary to ascertain how much of the published material is of real, practical interest. One should not apply merely physical characteristics such as number of pages, or number of entries. Similarly, exclusion of material based on personal prejudices and biases of the bibliographer is unpardonable.

(iii) Forms of Materials : There are different forms of materials like, books, periodicals, articles from periodicals, pamphlets, reports, manuscripts, gramophone records, tapes, film, microfilms, etc. All these are available in different languages and produced in different countries of the world. Also these materials differ in style depending on for whom they are intended: for scholars, laymen, school students, etc. It is necessary to consider all these aspects and take a decision about the materials one should include in the proposed subject bibliography.

(iv) Form of Entries : It is always good that an entry includes information about authors, collaborators, full title, edition, place of publication, year of publication, publisher's name and number of volumes. One should record the entries according to standard practices e.g. those laid down by AACR, British Standards Institution, or Indian Standards Institution. Abbreviations for periodical titles, should follow international standards. It will be useful to add annotations to the entries.

(v) Physical Format for Recording : The source that are used for preparing a subject bibliography are numerous, like, the catalogue of a general library or special library, periodicals indexes relating to subject field, national bibliographies, bibliographies of bibliographies, bibliographical reviews, etc. Therefore material used for recording bibliographical information from all sources referred to above should be easy to handle and arrange. Flexibility is essential. Catalogue cards of the size 5" × 3" (12.5 × 7.5cm.) are considered most suitable. A separate card need be maintained for each entry. These cards should be arranged in the most beneficial way to the user. One should add necessary guide cards for section headings. This arrangement will be helpful at the time of getting the bibliography mimeographed or printed.

(vi) Methods of Arrangement : The arrangement of entries in a bibliography is of great importance. It makes all the difference between a mere unwieldy list of titles and a useful and systematically arranged bibliography. The arrangement will necessarily depend upon what information one intend that system should provide, and upon the type of user for whom it is designed. The best bibliographies are notable for their consistency of purpose and treatment: the details are given in the same order and form throughout - which facilitates easy reference-and contents and arrangement are based on idea which is a real contribution to knowledge.

There are three methods for arranging subject bibliographies, viz., alphabetical, chronological and logical.

(a) *Alphabetical arrangement* : It is easy to arrange entries under the authors names and arrange alphabetically. Usef finds it easy to follow. But this type of arrangement does not indicate the inter-relationship between different aspects of a subject.

(b) *Chronological arrangement* : This arrangement of subject bibliography depicts listing of items according to date of publication. Most chronological arrangements proceed from the earliest to the latest date. But the reverse is also feasible and is common in science bibliographies. A chronological arrangement can refer to arrangement of material according to period of time with which they deal. Most bibliographies of history and literature group the work of the same period together and arrange the periods, reign, centuries and decades in order beginning with the earliest.

(c) *Logical arrangement* : A logical arrangement involves the use of a general system of classification with specific notation for each class and its subdivisions. Such a system may be a library classification like DDC, UDC, CC, etc. or one especially drawn up for the subject.

There is an another method also, which is :

(d) *Classified cum alphabetical arrangement* : A logical or classified arrangement differs basically from an alphabetical subject arrangement in that classified arrangement starts with broad concepts and proceeds to narrow one, while alphabetical arrangement starts with narrow specific heading. But it is possible to incorporate some of the advantages of classification within an alphabetical subject arrangement by providing of classification within an alphabetical subject arrangement by providing broad headings with subdivisions.

The combination of alphabetical and classified/logical arrangements in order to obtain appropriateness as well as speed in reference is recommended. This will be particularly helpful when topics of equal value or significance are grouped together. The success of classified arrangement combined with alphabetical indexes is demonstrated by INB, BNB, Indian Science Abstracts, Physics Abstracts, etc.

Finally a decision has to be taken about publishing the bibliography. It all depends on the usefulness of the data that is collected for the wider section of people. In that case the bibliography is prepared in book form, printed or mimeographed and sold as a priced publication. But if it is meant for limited use by the scholars of the library or any particular faculty, then it could be kept in the card form and made available to scholars whenever required. In case the bibliography is an outcome of sponsored project by some agency, that agency will take care and publish it. But it is always good to disseminate information about the work to as many people as possible, who are concerned with that subject.

Q. : Bibliographical control is a necessary pre-requisite in the age of information explosion. Justify the statement.

or

What do you understand by the expression 'Bibliographic Control'? How it is related to bibliographic organization? Indicate the different phases of bibliographic control.

or

What is bibliographic control? Discuss the major efforts in this direction.

Ans. : Since printing, paper and electronic techniques of publications developed, there is an explostion of literature in publishing world. Literature is spreading multi-directional and multi-dimensional both. It is published in many languages of the world. This rate of alarming of publishing books and other reading material was felt to make useful and thus bibliographical control needed. The efforts for making reading materials useful is called Bibliographical Control.

Bibliographical control is a term variously defined but converying the idea of a goal which has proved to be tantalizingly elusive. It is an idea which Dorothy Anderson sums up as "Ever since published material appeared in quantity-since the advent of printing in fact-librarians have been concerned with problems of controlling the bibliographic record of that material and in the process have developed an assortment of bibliographical tools with their purpose to supply answers to a variety of questions". In the first two hundred years of the printing era it was independent scholars rather than librarians who were the principal compilers of bibliographies.

Bibliographical control can be defined to mean the mastery over written or published records, which is provided by and for the purpose of bibliography. The purpose of bibliographical control is location of information source or of materials and the speed with which it can be located. Therefore, the librarians should have access to complete records of human civilization and culture and then the ability to organize them effectively for use.

Plan of Bibliographical Control

Bibliographical control consists of four aspects:

(a) Complete recording of all types of printed and other types of library materials;

(b) Systematic acquisition of these materials in libraries and other information organizations;

(c) Location of materials through union catalogue, union lists and like devices; and

(d) Provision of subject bibliography in all areas.

For any distinctive body of printed materials, i.e., of a country, a subject or of a physical or literary form, we can find full and complete information which is required, one can say that the bibliographical control of that set of documents is very good. But in reality the bibliographical control of all types of materials is very difficult, as we are concerned with not only published materials or printed materials but also parts of materials, articles in journals, and any other type of material published or not published.

The bibliographical control actually became efficient or visible only after the World War II due to the efforts of UNESCO which lay emphasis on publication of national bibliographies by all the countries of the world. But the formal event which is considered to be a landmark was in 1974 when IFLA announced 'Universal Bibliographic Control' as one of its core programmes. In the last one decade or so some of the limitations of the bibliographical control have been overcome due to the use of on-line computerized bibliographic records.

The key factors in bibliographic control are subject, form i.e., physical and literary, place, time, scope, i.e., selective or exhaustive and the amount of details given in the individual entries. The number of bibliographies thus is going to be very large if all the subject areas are to be taken into consideration. But in actual practice this has to have some limitations as otherwise their use will be impossible. Therefore, for usage purposes, small bibliographies on a large number of topics are prepared so that the publications are convenient to use.

Bibliography of Bibliographies

These are lists of bibliographies to help users in choosing bibliographies, which help in tracing bibliographies. The bibliographic control of bibliographies presents many difficulties due to many reasons. The main reason being the total number of usable bibliographies being considerable. Besides this, it is difficult to find out whether or not a bibliography exists on a given topic, suitable for a particular user, and also whether it is worthwhile getting hold of it if not in the stock. The last reason is the cost as the major bibliographies are expensive to buy and house.

The bibliographic control bibliographies thus is somewhat patchy. A very famous publication Besterman's *World Bibliography of Bibliographies* is presently out of date. The only choice lift ot the user thus is H.W. Wilson's half-yearly *Bibliographic Index 1937-*. Many of the major bibliographies in current use may be found in Walford's *Guide to Reference Materials* or in Sheehy's *Guide to Reference Books.*

Efforts at International and National Levels

The bibliographic control of documents at the international level has always been a problem. The approaches for universal bibliographic control have been concerned principally with author/title listings and the cumulative patterns of current bibliographies. As far as the subject approach has been present it has been incidental to the main purpose of the works so far described. National library catalogues, general bibliographies and retrospective and current national bibliographies are the basic groundwork upon which a total bibliographic control system is erected. Their modes of arrangement are usually those which will facilitate the widest possible access to as great as possible a range of people. Inevitably this presupposes priority for the author/title approach.

Thus there are no known universal bibliographies as such, but after the second World War, UNESCO took leadership and emphasized that if all nations maintain their current national bibliographies, it might lead to having an effective control on the publicatons universally. Many years have passed but still nothing concrete has come out of this.

The Universal Bibliographic Control (UBC) programme sponsored by IFLA in 1974, appeared to be far more realistic, as it was based on the recognition of the fact that effective bibliographic control must begin within individual countries, and that the exchange of bibliographic information between them is facilitated if there is international agreement on bibliographical description. The UBC programme has since been merged with IFLA's another programme, namely the International MARC and is presently known as UBCIMP.

IFLA and UNESCO have also been in collaboration in this regard and their efforts have resulted in programmes like-International Standard

Bibliographic Description (ISBD), International Serials Data System (ISDS), Cataloguing-in-Publication (CIP) and Union lists of Serials.

Bibliographical Activities at National Level

In India, presently a large number of organizations are engaged in providing bibliographic services at various levels. At the national level organizations like National Library, Calcutta, INSDOC (now NISCAIR) in Science and Technology, National Medical Library in Medical Information and NASSDOC in Social Sciences are carrying out various bibliographic activities which involve international and national information sources.

The *Indian National Bibliography* is being brought out by the National Library since 1957 as our Government recognized the importance of bibliographical control at the national level. Bibliographies of books in Indian regional languages have also been compiled by INB.

The Association of Indian Universities (AIU) has been bringing out a series of bibliographies on Doctoral Dissertations accepted by Indian Universities since 1957 thus providing bibliographic control on dissertations.

NASSDOC has brought out bibliographies on various subjects/ topics in social sciences and is also carrying out indexing and abstracting services in these areas.

INSDOC (now NISCAIR), has been bringing out Union Catalogues of Scientific Serials from various regions of India besides its popular periodical Indian Science Abstracts. The various computerized databases of this, are also efforts to bring about bibliographic control in various kinds of S & T publications.

NISSAT Sectoral Information Centres and Documentation Centres at special libraries in India have compiled various bibliographies for use of their clientele. Bibliographies of books in Indian regional languages have also been complied. One of the example of this nature is in Marathi language. Shankar Ganesh Date, compiled Marathi Gantha Sudhi covering the period 1832 to 1960 published in 2 volumes. After death of S.G. Date, Suchi Mangal, was settled at Pune, who has also compiled a bibliography of articles published in Marathi language in 6 volumes. Attempts are being made to compile bibliographies in other languages also.

Q. : What is a database? Discuss briefly some of the major bibliographic databases.

Ans. A data base can be defined as a collection of records in an accessible sequence, stored on magnetic tapes, etc. There are bibliographic data bases, non- bibliographic data bases and catalogue record data bases.

Bibliographic data bases hold comprehensive bibliographic records in various subjects. They contain complete bibliographies details of each document, i.e. document number, title, author, source reference, abstract, author's/organization's address, language of document, location etc.

Some of the examples of subject bibliographic data bases, are as under:-

(i) MEDLARS (Medical Literature Analysis and Retrieval System)

This data base is maintained by the National Library of Medicine, U.S.A, which is described as an integrated bibliographical service in the field of medicine. The Index Medicus provides a comprehensive bibliography of medical literature. Recurring bibliographies and bibliographies on demand by a particular group are also provided. Mediline is the online version of the index.

(ii) BISOS (Bio-Science Information Service)

This data base covers 9000 periodicals in biology and biomedicine. It publishes a fortnightly 'Biological Abstracts'. This service covers entire literature in Life Sciences. Each issue contains the four indexes (a) BASIC - A key word in context subject index; (b) CROSS - Index bases on subject context; (c) Bio-system index consisting of taxonomic categories and (d) Author index. This data base is also responsible for other abstracting and indexing publications. Bio-research index is one such service which is monthly. It covers research reports which do not appear in Biological Abstracts. This computerized data base is increasingly being used for bibliographical purposes all over the world.

(iii) SA Data Base

This data base covers the World Literature on Sociology since 1963. It is searchable online through DIALOG Information Service, Inc. and Bibliographical Retrieval Services, Inc. (BRS).

It comprehensively covers the world literature in Sociology, in the form of periodical articles, books, proceedings, etc. It offers abstracting service - Sociological Abstracts and International Review of Publications in Sociology (IRPS) which comprises a bibliography of book reviews appearing in the journals abstracted.

(iv) COMPENDEX (Computerized Engineering Index)

This data base is an outcome of Engineering Index Service that was introduced in 1962. It is available online and covers periodical literature, proceedings, books, reports and standards.

(v) ERIC (Educational Resources Information Centre)

This data base is sponsored by the Department of Health Education and Welfare, Govt, of United States. It comprises of data from abstracting and indexing services in education and also fugitive materials. It brings out current bibliographies, Resources in Education (monthly) and Index to Journals in Education (monthly).

Q. : What are Ready Reference Sources? Discuss some of them in details.

Ans. : The ready reference sources are those sources of information that help in locating the right and factual answers to questions. They usually contain brief, pinpointed answers and are serial publications. These are published annually and mostly cover information about the previous year.

The ready reference sources are of different types, namely, yearbooks and annuals, almanacs, directories, handbooks, manuals, guides to statistical sources etc.

1. Year Book and Annuals

The *yearbooks and annuals* are the sources which are issued each year to review developments during the year and to record current information of a descriptive or statistical type. Yearbooks often review and present the events of the preceding year. They can be general yearbooks or supplements to encyclopaedias. The general yearbooks cover annual activities internationally, nationally of an organization, or of a subject. The 'supplements to encyclopaedias' on the other hand are meant to supplement main set of an encyclopaedia. They record major events of the preceding year providing update to the original encyclopaedia. For example, "*Britannica Book of the Year*" supplements

Encyclopaedia Britannica and "*Americana Annual, an Encyclopaedia of Event*" supplements the *Encyclopaedia Americana.*

Types of Yearbooks

A year book may be of four kinds:

(i) International

(ii) National

(iii) Organizational

(iv) Subject based

(i) International Year Books: These yearbooks include the facts and figures pertaining to world. Such yearbooks contain: the organizations of International level; the facts and figures of each country regarding their geographical area, population, constitution, government, political parties, industries, commerce, finance, Defence, social welfare, education, educational institutions, political relation, representatives, flags etc. Such year books are:

(a) Statesmen's Year Book

(b) Europa World Year Book

(ii) National Year Book: A yearbook of national level gives the details of the states of that country and generally includes: area, population, government, constitution, administration, economic condition, commerce, social welfare, communication, national flag, national bird, national animal, national song etc. For example:

India : a Reference Annual

(iii) Organizational Year Book: Such yearbooks are published by an organization which contain the activities, various decisions, plans and proposals, memberships etc. pertaining to that organization. For example:

United Nations: Year Book of United Nations (UN).

A Year Book of Commonwealth (London).

(iv) Subject Based YearBook: These yearbooks contain the information pertaining to a particular subject. For example:

Yearbook of Higher Education (Los Angeles)

Yearbook of Human Rights (New York)

Purpose of the Yearbooks

The yearbook and annuals serve many purposes. Some important purposes of thesc sources are :

(a) Recentness is the backbone of its compilation wherein the user can get recent information on a subject of personality.

(b) Brief facts are provided in the annuals or yearbook serves the useful purposes.

(c) Indicates trends in the development and the regression of civilization.

(d) Information index cited may guide the reader quickly to locate the primary material.

(e) Directory and bibliographical information may provide the address and short biographical sketches.

(f) Browsing is possible through a mass of unrelated and frequently fascinating bits of information.

Some of the important yearbooks are evaluated below:

(i) **Europa Yearbook,** *1959-,* London, Europa, 1959-, 2 vols, annual.

Europa Publications is a leading publisher of yearbooks. Out of these the present one is a general yearbook.

First part of first volume covers international organizations, arranged alphabetically. This part gives detailed information about the UN and other leading international organizations. Besides, it describes functions, membership, address and the date of foundation for less known international organizations. Second part of first volume deals with countries of Europe in the alphabetical order. Third part of first volume deals with countries from Afghanistan to Burundi. The index to volume one lists international organizations. Its second volume describes rest of the countries of the world, listing each alphabetically from Cameroon to Zimbabwe. The index to volume second lists alphabetically all countries of the world.

The work provides a great deal of information about every country including recent history, economic and statistical surveys, details of the constitution, government, diplomatic representatives, political parties, judicial system and religions. For each country, there is also a directory section giving the names, addresses and other useful facts about newspapers and periodicals, publishers, radio and television, banks, insurance, chambers of commerce, industry, trade associations and trade unions, airlines, railway and shipping organization. Statistical data in many cases is given for a number of years, which facilitates comparison of figures.

All in all, this work provides fairly up-to-date information. This is an excellent source for names and addresses of international organizations. This also serves as a good source for brief descriptive and statistical information on different countries of the world.

(ii) Statesman's Year-book, 1865-, London Macmillan Press, 1864-, annual.

First published in 1864 and its 140th edition was published in 2002. Macmillan press, its publisher is a leading publisher with high reputation.

This is statistical and historical annual of the states of the world. Comparative statistical tables have been provided in the beginning. The tables are followed by main portions of the work divided into two parts. Part I International organizations; Part II countries of the World A-Z. Part II is followed by a detailed index.

Part I gives information about the United Nations, agencies related to the UN, World Council of Churches, European Organization like OECD, NATO etc. Other international organizations covered include Colombo Plan, ASEAN, Arab League, Organization of African Unity, etc. Information is usually provided about origin, functions, organization, headquarters, President, Secretary and publications, etc.

For each country and political unit, usually information is given about constitution and government, area and population, religion, education, health, justice, finance, defence, planning, agriculture, forestry, industry, oil, commerce, shipping, railways, roads, aviation, post, banking, weights and measures, diplomatic representatives, books of reference. As this yearbook is not an almanac, therefore there is general absence of astronomical data.

A useful list of books of reference is given at the end of each item. Comparative statistical tables have been provided. Two indexes have been given at the end-place and international organization index and product index.

This is a work of British origin, which lays emphasis on providing information about British Commonwealth. Special attention has been paid to Great Britain and USA.

Briefly, this is a highly useful, most popular and comprehensive general yearbook containing concise, accurate and up-to-date descriptive and statistical information about the government of different countries of the world.

(iii) Times of India Directory and Yearbook including Who's Who 1914-, Bombay, Times of India Press, 1914-, annual.

This publication has a long history. First it was published under the title *Indian yearbook.* Later its title was changed to *Indian and Pakistan Yearbook and Who's who.* The present title was adopted from 1954/55 edition onwards.

This is trade directory, yearbook and a biographical dictionary combined in one. The information is confined to India only. The topics covered include trade directory for buyers, the country, nature and resources, Agro-based industries, education and science, welfare programmes, demography, general compendium, trade and industry, finance, communications, states and union territories, administrative and diplomatic personnel, elections and legislatures, late particulars, who's who, maps of India, states and the world.

A great deal of information, which is not easily available elsewhere, has been provided. It provides list of commercial firms arranged item-wise. Lists of research organizations, names of Government of India and state administrative personnel, names of Indian diplomatic representative's abroad, foreign diplomatic representatives in India have also been given. Who's who in India forms a useful part. Its index is quite detailed.

It is a must for Indian libraries. Eighty-third edition was published in 1988. It has now stopped publication.

(iv) India; a Reference Annual, 1953-, New Delhi, Publications Division, Ministry of Information and Broadcasting, Government of India, 1953-, annual.

It is a national level yearbook, which is an important ready reference source to know various things about India. It is published by the Ministry of Information and Broadcasting of India. Its first issue was published in 1953 and since then it is being published regularly each year with new amendments. It includes information almost on all aspects and field of India. Its 48th edition has appeared in 2004.

This yearbook contains information on major services of the Indian government including the states as well as various important activities taking place in the country. This annual contains information on diverse aspects of Indian national life, covering land and the people, national symbols, government, defence, education, cultural activities, scientific research, health, social welfare, mass communication, basic economic data, finance, planning, agriculture, rural development, civil supplies and cooperation, energy, industry, commerce, transport, communications, labour, housing, justice and law, sports and games, India and the world, states and union territories, diary of events from Jan to Dec., general information. Besides, there are a number of appendices covering personnel of the government, members of parliament, awards given by different organizations and the bibliography.

For each state and union territory, it provides information concerning area, capital, population, principle languages, agriculture, industry, irrigation and power, important tourist centres, government and area, population and headquarters of districts. Similar information is also available for India as a whole. It lists important Indian events in a chronological order. A long bibliography has been provided, which should serve as a useful guide for further reading. A detailed index has been given at the end.

It is of Indian origin and is limited to India only. Being government publication, the information and statistics are official. This is an authoritative work, which is a must for Indian libraries.

(v) Manorama: Yearbook

Manorama Yearbook is an International level yearbook. The latest 37th edition of Manorama has been published in 2001. It is being published every year by Malayala Manorama, Kottyam (Kerala) and is one of the frequently and widely used ready reference tools, equally useful for the researchers, teachers, executives, tourists, particularly for the persons intend to appear in various competitive examinations and all others seeking knowledge. Its Chief Editor is Sh. K.M. Mathew, assisted by other members of editorial board. It is being published in as much as in five languages i.e., Hindi, Tamil, Malayalam, Bengali and English with special focus on the relevant regions.

The information given there in, are reliable and up-to-date. The yearbook has gained much more popularity among the mass of people of all categories. The publishers are well established and known for several years.

The yearbook has been divided into many parts and furnishes valuable information. Each part gives following information:

Part I : Cover Story : It covers various topics such as Indian economy, agriculture, foreign trade, globalization, world trade organization, Indian population, and current affairs: national, a review of India 2001 etc.

Part- II : Information Technology : The information under this heading relates to internet, internet enabling technologies, e-education, e-governance, computers, viruses, worms and logic bombs, enterprise resource planning.

Part -III: Science Panorama : This part of the yearbook deals with some burning issues such as science scan 2001, the universe, space exploration, the earth, solar storms destroy ozone, world of plants and animals, food and nutrition, human body and disease, medicine in 21st century, TB epidemic in India, inventions and discoveries, Numerals etc.

Part - IV: World Panorama : In this part the nations of the world, UN world's peacemaker, international organizations, world population trends, world religions, world languages, Indians abroad, India's turbulent neigh bourhood have been taken up.

Part -V: Education & Career : This section of the yearbook throws light on technology careers in 21st century: surviving change, civil service: A gateway to distinction, model question paper of civil services.

Part -VI: General Knowledge : This part includes what is what, who is who, mythological characters, well known books, abbreviations, national days, important days sobriquets, awards & honours, Nobel prize winners, records, beauty queens, women rulers of world, women chief ministers, quiz-2002, 100 tourist destinations in India etc.

Part - VII: Indian Panorama : This part gives information on different aspects of India such as the country, national insignia, budget, geology, the people, languages, religions, constitutions, plans, livestock, dams, defense, nuclear research, space research, environment, transport, tourism, education, media, states and territories etc.

Part - VIII: Sports Area : It covers the world of sports and provides valuable information regarding all types of sports and games such as athletics, world athletic meet, cricket, snippets, records, Ranji trophy, tennis, football, 2002 world cup in Asia, 2006 world cup, German, Olympic games, Asian games, chess, hockey etc.

Part-IX: People & Events : This part includes Calendar of events 2001: world, Calendar of events 2001: India, Council of Ministers, Heads of important offices, obituary 2001, Stop press etc.

About 204 boxes have been given in the yearbook, which provide very important and new information, which is generally not available in other sources. Such type of data/facts/description enhances the knowledge of the readers. A number of photographs, maps, figures have been given frequently. Colour national flags of all the countries have been separately provided. It is a paperback publication with attractive title page and so designed that it may become more user-friendly. The typeface used and its size, and the layout is considerably pleasing. The text has been composed in double columns. At the end an index has been provided duly arranged alphabetically.

The yearbook, primarily intended to serve the information need of young men and women on the there should of career options, has also become a ready reference companion for executives, researchers, teachers and all others seeking knowledge.

2. Almanacs

There are some sources which are considered as ready reference sources, Almanac is one of them. It is the calendar of the astronomical information about stars, moons and sun. It is the compendium of fact or statistical information of the previous year or the preceding year, which provides both current and retrospective information.

In the beginning (1000 B.C.). almanac was regarded as a book arranged chronologically with some miscellaneous information. The almanacs since than have undergone many changes, and they become much informative in nature.

An *almanac* is a publication usually an annual, containing a variety of useful facts of a miscellaneous nature and statistical information. It was originally a projection of the coming year by days, months and holidays covering miscellaneous matters such as astronomical events, planetary tables, astrological predictions and anecdotes, etc. An almanac is different from an yearbook although both are annual publication. An yearbook is an annual compendium of data and statistics of a given year and records year's activities by country, subject of specialized area whereas an almanac usually covers retrospective information too. The difference therefore, is in coverage in the form of duration.

Types of Almanacs : There are three types of Almanacs:-

(i) *Astronomical Almanacs :* It contains information about astronomy, future etc.

(ii) *Informative Almanacs :* These usually contain general type of information.

Eg : Whitaker's Almanac

(iii) *Topical Almanacs:-* In these information is given on a specific subject or topic.

Eg : The Almanacs of American politics.

Usefulness of Almanacs

— They satisfy current as well as everyday approach.

— They provide information in compact forms such as tables, diagrams etc.

— They provide comprehensive coverage.

— They also helpful in knowing about trends in different fields.

Some of the important almanacs are discussed below:-

(i) Whitaker's Almanac, 1869-, London, Whitaker, 1869-, annual.

Joseph Whitaker was the founder, who established it in 1868. The authority behind *Whitaker's Almanac* is recognized universally, is well known for accuracy of information.

This covers, "an account of the astronomical and other phenomena and a vast amount of information respecting the government, finances, population, commerce, and general statistics of the various nations of the world." However, primarily it is a record of recent events and information has been provided in the form of general compendia.

Although, it is called an almanac yet the calendar material forms only a small part of it. It has an excellent index covering some 20,000 entries. Events of the year are listed chronologically. It provides greater emphasis on British Commonwealth with special reference to Great Britain. It is especially useful about British institutions, British Royal Family, peerage, baronage and knightage. Its shorter edition is also available, which may be useful for small libraries.

There is no doubt that *Whitaker's Almanac* contains vast amount of information in a single volume. The facts provided are accurate and up-to-date. It is highly useful for getting facts about different aspects of British life.

(ii) World Almanac and Book of Facts, 1868-, New York, Newspaper Enterprises Association, 1868-, annual,

It contains brief factual information and statistical data on social, political, industrial, financial, educational, cultural and other subjects. Information has been provided on astronomical and meteorological events, museums, art galleries, historic places, disasters, earthquakes, sports events.

For USA, information and statistics for each state has been given, covering population by state and country. For other countries, population of major cities has been provided. Short biographies of US presidents and their wives are included. Names of cabinet officers of the US government from 1789 have been listed. List of signers of the Declaration of Independence is given.

A very useful index has been given in the beginning listing entries under subject occupation and profession. In case of some famous men, author entries have been provided in the index.

Most of the information is related to the United States but small sections have been devoted to history and present conditions in different countries of the world.

It is the most comprehensive of all almanacs of miscellaneous information published in the United States. It lays greater emphasis on providing more information about America. It contains up-to-date and reliable information.

3. Directories

Today's age is of organizations, associations, societies and academies. Many organizations of social, educational industrial, scientific and technological know how have been established. Societal growth and human involvement with these organizations, necessitates the compilation of, a sort of document, wherein information in a condensed and synthesized manner would be quite helpful to locate the addresses, designations, activities, publications, productions, etc., at the time of need. Such situations have necessitated the production of directories.

A directory is a document containing lists of names of residents, organizations or business houses in a city, a group of cities or a country, in alphabetical order, and/or in order of location in roads, or of firms in trade; classified and arranged in alphabetical order, or of professional people, manufacturers, or business houses in a particular trade or profession.

According to ALA Glossary of library terms. "A directory is a list of persons or organizations systematically arranged, usually in alphabetic or classed order, giving addresses, officers, functions and similar data for organizations."

Types of Directories

Directories can be basically international, national, regional and local. But broadly, they can be grouped into two major categories:-

1. General Directories:- There are further divided into two groups :

(A) Topographical directories of cities, towns etc : These are local or city directories, mostly government publication.

Examples :

— Directory of Cities and Towns in India/by O.P. Sharma Delhi: Kripa, 1989.

— Great Britain Post Office: Post Office Guide; London Statistical Office, 1856-.

(B) Telephone, Telegraphic and Telex directories : They are usually compiled by Posts and Telegraphic department of various national and state government. These list the subscriber in alphabetical order with address and phone number. For example :

— The National Directory of Addresses and Telephone Numbers. New York: Bantam Boos, 1977. Irregular.

— Delhi Telephone Directory : 1999, New Delhi : *Mahanagar Telephone Nigam*, 1999. 3 vols.

2. Sepcial Directories : Special directories can be international, national or local in coverage. They are divided into three main groups.

(A) Institutional : These deal exclusively with information regarding institutions such as-structure, functions, objectives, operational activities, addresses, office bearers, members and other important information about different organizations, institutions, associations etc. For example :

(i) *Commonwealth Universities Yearbook* : Directory to the universities of the commonwealth and the handbook of their associations London: Association of Commonwealth Universities, 1914, Annual.

(ii) *Directory of Indian Public Libraries* : A select list of libraries, Assisted by RRRLF/ed. By B.P. Barva. Kolkata : Naya Prakash, 1986.

(B) Professional Directories: Professional associations publish their membership directories which have proved to be very useful information sources to locate the talented scholars in various disciplines. For example :

(i) World directory of Mathematics International, Mathematical Union, 1979.

(ii) A.L.A. Membership Directory. Chicago: American library Association, 1950. Annual.

(C) Trade and Business Directories : Almost all countries have their directories of trade, business, manufacturers and industrialists. For example :

(i) American Register of Exporters and Importers. New York: American Register of Exporters and Importers Corporation, 1946. Annual.

(ii) Kothar's Industrial Directory of India, 1988-89. 36th ed. Madras: Kothari Enterprises, 1988.

Some of the important directories are evaluated below:

(i) Commonwealth Universities Yearbook : *Directory to the Universities of the Commonwealth and the Handbook of their Associations.* London: Association of Commonwealth Universities. 1914. Annual.

It was published as '*Yearbook of the Universities of the Empire*' from 1941-46 and '*Yearbook of the Universities of the Commonwealth*' from 1948-57. Since than in is being published under the present title.

It gives a fairly detailed information of the universities of the 31 British Commonwealth countries. All these countries have been arranged alphabetically. Under each of them, there is a list of universities of that country alphabetically along-with the page number followed by a map of the country indicating the location of the universities. These after it gives the introduction and directory to the subjects of studies and statistics showing the number of students etc.

Then for each university the necessary information is given about the foundation addresses, Chancellor, Vice-Chancellor, Registrar, Deans, Librarian, teaching staff. Under alphabetical arrangement of department name of the teachers are arranged seniority wise, educational qualification is also provided along with a list of regular research scholars and officers, affiliated colleges with name and the addresses of the principals and total teaching, administrative and other staff.

In the end, general information about the universities like location, jurisdiction, constitution, income and expenditure, faculties and Deans, university campus-library and laboratories, admission to various courses, awards offered, fee, postals and health facilities etc is also given.

Information is also provided for the universities which are not the member of the association of commonwealth universities but are in the commonwealth countries. Its four volumes are-

Volume 1st	-	A-B
Volume 2nd	-	C-H
Volume 3rd	-	I-N
Volume 4th	-	P-Z

There are six appendices-

— The Association of commonwealth universities
— Commonwealth scholarship and fellowship plan.
— National and regional inter university bodies.
— University admission.
— Selected Bibliography of publication on higher education in commonwealth.
— Commonwealth learning.

At the end there are two indexes

— General index and

— Name index.

There is a large names index which contains about 165,000 names of all the teachers and administrators of commonwealth universities.

This reference tool is useful for those who are interested in studies, teaching and research as well as for the persons who are interested in university organizations and the students who are looking for opportunity for study and research in commonwealth countries.

(ii) World of Learning. London: Europa Publications. 1947. Annual.

The world of learning is one of the Europa's series of regularly revised reference books covers every aspect of International affairs, politics and economics. This reference work have earned an outstanding reputation for its accuracy and reliability and are used extensively by public and academic libraries, business, government departments, media, embassies, university and colleges, publishers, academic institutions, professional association, charities, policy institutes around the world. The present work is completely impartial view of world affairs information is gathered directly from the institutions, organizations and individual concerned, as well as government and other official sources.

This remarkable book provide information on over 30,000 organizations or institutions and more than two lakh individual who comprised the "world of learning 2000". The unparalleled amount of information covers the entire spectrum of higher education on worldwide scale. It covers all type of academic institutions like universities, colleges, schools of music art and architecture, learned societies, research institutes, libraries and Archives, museum and art galleries.

A separate section is devoted to over 400 international organizations concerned with higher education such as UNESCO, ICSU (International Council of Scientific Union), IAU (International Association of Universities).

Over 180 countries have been arranged alphabetically; each country have their own section and one can find every type of higher education institutions quickly and easily. The detailed standardized entries for maximum usefulness have been provided and each university and college have all the relevant information necessary for contact for further research.

The entries have given like this Name, Address and web address, Senior Administrative staff, Deans, Librarians, Professors at the most major universities, date of foundation, academic year, size of Libraries, number of teachers and students, publications and affiliated institutes etc.

The advantages of having this volume in the reference library is because of its following features :

- World wide coverage.
- Individual chapters on every country.
- 2050 pages on data.
- Standard chapter structure and three columns layout.
- Full index to Universities.
- Up-to-date information provided by the institutions themselves.
- Published annually for 50 years with reputation for reliability and accuracy.
- Research Academy list world wide.
- Create accurate mailing list.
- Broaden professional network and
- Lists of academic centres for excellence.

Concluding it can be said, this is an effective source of information on higher education world wide. It is a master piece of reference to take pride of place in every library.

(iii) Universities Handbook

Association of Indian Universities New Delhi. 30th ed 2004. Biennial.

1. Authority: This is published by Association of Indian Universities. This handbook works as an directory for locating information about Indian universities and important institution. It provides information about various aspects of Indian universities. It is a biennial publication.

2. Scope: It includes Indian universities and their affiliated colleges approved by Indian universities. It includes information about

Universities and University-like institutions. It is a single volume publication. The informations are given into two parts:-

(A) Introductory information.

(B) Information about universities.

(A) Introductory Information : It is further sub-divided in two parts

(a) Structure of higher education and

(b) Indian Universities, which include following type of details:

1. Types of Universities - Unitary, Affiliating.
2. College
3. Educational Programme
4. Admission
5. Academic Calendar
6. Examination System
7. Medium of instruction
8. Open Universities
9. University Governance - Chancellor and Vice-chancellors, the Senate, Executive Council, Syndicate, Academic Council etc.
10. Finance
11. Bodies of higher education such as-
    1. Association of Indian Universities
    2. University Grant Commission
    3. Central Advisory Board of education
    4. Indian Council of Agriculture Research
    5. Council of Scientific and Industrial Research
    6. Indian Council of Social Science Research
    7. All Indian Council of Technical education
    8. Other Coordinating bodies
12. Student Service

(B) Information about Universities: It is also divided into two parts :

1. Main description and
2. Other description

1. **Main Description:**
   - (a) University name
   - (b) Establishment year
   - (c) Address, Cable, Fax, Telephone and Telex Numbers etc.
   - (d) Name of Chancellor
   - (e) Name of Vice-Chancellor
   - (f) Name of Secretary
   - (g) Deans of Faculty
   - (h) Name of Chief Proctor
   - (i) Name of Vice-Chancellor
   - (j) Directors etc
   - (k) Student advisory
   - (l) Librarians
   - (m) Head of Sports etc.
2. **Other description:** In includes information about:-
   - (a) Brief description about its establishment history
   - (b) Jurisdiction
   - (c) Library and Research facilities
   - (d) Scholarships and fellowships
   - (e) Private studies, continuing education
   - (f) Estimated budget
   - (g) Internal assessment, Coaching classes, NCC training, Health Services, Games and Sports, Hostel fees etc
   - (h) Syllabus
   - (i) Ph.D.
   - (j) Diploma and Certificate Course
   - (k) Lecturer's and Readers
   - (l) Affiliated colleges of university with their description
   - (m) Academic year
   - (n) University departments
3. **Special features :** For easy access of information it includes various indexes such as-

1. State - wise list of universities
2. Index according to faculties.

Concluding, it can be said that the information provided it, are reasonably accurate. The publication is extremely useful for students, educationists and educational institutions.

4. Handbooks and Manuals

A handbook is a compilation of miscellaneous information in a compact and handy form which may contain data, procedures, principles, etc. tables, graphs, diagrams and illustrations. Scientists and technologists use handbooks in their fields rather frequently.

In common practice, a manual is an instruction book, which provides instructions as how to perform a job or how to do something by means of specific and clear directions. Shores opined that "handbooks are here considered to be the primary sources that contains facts for knowing and the manuals are the sources that contains instruction for doing."

It is believed that handbooks and manuals are of recent origin. The oldest title known, dates back to early nineteenth century, viz., A Handbook for Modeling Wax Flowers (1814). Kane's Famous First Facts (1933), More First Facts (135), Traveller's Brief Facts (1936). These books give information on (1) Curiosities, (2) Literature, (3) Statistics, (4) Documentary, (5) Parliamentary Debates, and (6) Specific subjects.

Very often the terms handbook and manual are used without a distinction. For the evaluation of these sources, one should keep in view, authority, scope, method of compilation of data, accuracy, regency and format.

A few examples of handbooks and manuals are described below:-

(i) Engineering Mathematics Handbooks, by J.J.Tuma, New York, McGraw-Hill, 1970.

This handbook contains definitions, theorems, formulae, tables from different fields of mathematics including statistics. This is a work, which is comprehensive and highly useful for an engineer. The information has been provided in a readily accessible form.

(ii) Famous First Facts, by Joseph N.Kane, 3rd ed., New York, Wilson, 1964.

This work tells about famous first facts, recording first happenings, discoveries and inventions in the United States. The information is arranged alphabetically by subject. There is a detailed index, which satisfies the approach to the facts geographically, chronologically and by personal name.

This reference work is of general interest to everybody. However, it is invaluable to researchers, who intend to establish a given fact.

(iii) Handbook of Chemistry, compiled and edited by N.A.Lange, 10th revised edition, New York, McGraw-Hill, 1967.

This is a reference work, which provides chemical and physical data required for laboratory work and manufacturing. It contains great amount of data arranged so that it can be located readily. It is especially valuable for a student of chemistry and a professional chemist.

(iv) Guiness Book of World Records. New York: Sterling. 1955. Annual.

It provides facts and figures on records of human achievement, space, arts, scientific world, animal and plant kingdom, etc. It gives content and detailed index for quick search. The success of the publication has resulted tin publishing a series called 'Guiness Family of Books' having titles such as '*Guiness Sports Record Book*', '*Guiness Book of Surprising Accomplishments*', '*Guiness Book of Extraordinary Exploits*' and so on. The editions of the '*Guiness Book of World Records*' are available in twenty-five languages.

5. Statistical Sources

Statistics play an increasingly important role in modern life, as they are used for political, scientific, commercial and other purposes and with care may be made to tell almost any sort of story in qualitative form. If there is, indeed, one tendency dominant today, it is that in interpretation in quantitative terms. Statistical studies or analyses many a time proved as to how the earlier conclusions were wrong.

As such the provision of statistical reference service is becoming increasingly important. It requires adequate knowledge of a large body of sources of information. One should possess some knowledge of how the statistics are collected and processed. The common suspicion of statistics is based on doubts concerning the method of collection and the validity of conclusions drawn from them. With the later, at any rate, the reference assistant has little concern, and he may present statistical information without hesitation so long as he has reason to believe that the facts given have sufficient authority. This provison, however, applies with equal force to the use of all reference material.

The number of sources of statistics is extremely large. Much statistical information is contained in the almanacs and other yearbooks, but the best authorities are the publications of the various wings of the United Nations and that of various national governments.

Almanacs are annual handbooks containing a variety of useful information but with no other description. They merely provide up-to-date information on any subject likely to be useful to the general public. Their original purpose was to serve as calendars and forecasts of coming events being known often as 'prognostications', on any subject likely to be useful to the general public. *Yearbooks* differ from Almanacs by taking the form of a chronicle of events, in general, in some department of knowledge. *Directories* very often provide population statistics. *Biographical dictionaries* provide vital statistics relating to dates of birth and death, sex, age, address, occupation, etc. *Atlases* are some times specialized and provide economic, geographical and physiographical data. Some of the statistical organizations publish *periodicals* giving statistical data.

A few examples of sources of statistics are described below:-

(i) Demographic Yearbook, 1948-, New York, United Nations Statistical Office, 1949-, Annual.

This yearbook provides vital statistics about nations of the world, including birth-rate, deaths, area, population and population movements.

(ii) Europa Yearbook, 1959-, London, Europa, 1959-2 vols, Annual. The first volume contains organization, functions, and history of leading international organizations and the countries of Europe. The Second volume is devoted to countries of Africa, the Middle East, North and South America, and Asia. It aims to provide general statistics and information on publishers, radio and television, trade and industry, finance, transportation, government, the constitution, religion, insurance, etc.

(iii) Statesman's Yearbook; *Statistical and Historical Annual of the States of the World,* 1864-, London, MacMillan, 1864-, vol.1-, Annual.

This yearbook provides statistics on governments of the world.

A bibliography is given for each country, which lists statistical as well as other reference works.

(iv) Census of India, *2001, Census of India, 2001,* Registrar General & Census Commissioner, India.

This publication contains census data, made up of a number of series. Each series consists of parts and subparts to cover different types of tables and reports.

(v) Statistical Abstract, India, 1947-, Central Statistical Organization, Ministry of Planning, Government of India, 1975, annual.

This issue is 20th in the new series of abstract relating to 1974. It gives national aggregates for 1950-51, 1955-56, 1960-61, 1965-66 and for each subsequent year up to 1973-74. State wise information is presented for the latest year. It gives statistics about population, climate, agriculture, irrigation, animal industry, forest industries etc.

This serves as an important source material for authentic data on different sectors of the Indian economy.

Q. : Enumerate different categories of Reference Sources for current events. Describe briefly the Kessing's Record of World Events'.

Ans. : Seeking information on current happenings or events or affairs has become an essential part of modern living. Every individual wants to have access to the latest and current information on any recent event that has taken place. The chief media for this kind of information are the newspapers, magazines, television and radio. The information loses its currency very fast. Thus, there is need to have sources of information that provide current information all the time to sustain the thirst for information of the modern day users. A good solution to this problem is online access to information which has presently become quite cheap due to information available through to INTERNET. However many users still have to depend on the printed sources of information.

The various sources of current information are:

(1) Indexes to newspapers

(2) News summaries and news digests, and

(3) Summaries of television and radio broadcasts.

1. Indexes to Newspapers : Indexes to newspapers surrogate the news items that appear in dailies. They are the time saving sources, particularly regarding current events. These are of two types, viz.,

(i) **Index to Individual Newspaper :** As the name indicates, it is the index of individual newspapers. For example, New York Times Index, is publishing semi-monthly with quarterly and annual cumnulations since 1851. It includes major news items that appear to national and international events in New York Times:

Two more important newspapers, *Le Monde* (Paris) and *The Guardian* (London) have got their indexes, although in both cases the indexing agency is not associated with the newspaper concerned. In India also, attempts have been made to compile newspaper indexes.

In India, *The Hindu (Madras) Index* is publishing which covers indexing of major - events news appear in Hindu newspaper.

(ii) **Index covering many Newspapers :** This type of indexes, as the name indicate contain index of major newspapers' news. Some of the examples are -

— Canadian News Index, covering over 35 newspapers and magazines of Canada.

— National Newspaper Index beginning with only three American newspapers viz. *The New York Times, The Christian Science Monitor and The Wall Street journal,* it now also covers *Los Angles Times* and the *Washington Post* from 1982.

In India, *Indian Press Index* (Delhi) and *Indian News Index* have attempted to index the newspaper. However, they have ceased publication for want of support.

2. News Summaries and News Digests

These sources are referred to quite frequently by the Reference Librarians to answer questions relating to current events. It could be inferred from the terms used that news summaries/news digests are again newspaper indexes but with a difference that in addition to bibliographical and locational details, brief summaries of the news items are provided by them. Thus, unlike newspaper indexes, in news summaries one can get brief information without referring to newspapers provided he is interested in factual and brief details about current events. Examples:

— Kessing's Record of World Events

— Facts on file etc.

Now-a-days most of the newspapers provide Internet based services. Apart from the National Newspapers like Times of India, Hindu, Indian Express, Deccan Herald etc, a large number of regional newspaper are available in various languages with the facility of downloading of fonts of the required language. The news items are provided in HTML format, which facilitates the user to search for the specific information. India World Samachar is an example of an Indian News digest service on the net which provides news on various aspects viz. daily news headlines, business news, sports, entertainment etc. It also provides links to most of the Indian newspapers on the net.

3. Summaries of Television and Radio Broadcasts

A modern library is expected to have, in addition to conventional media, the non-conventional material in its collection. Audio-visual material like films, television, radio, etc., are important components of the non-conventional sources of information. Particularly for current events, radio and television are effective sources and they occupy important place. The number of people who derive awareness on current affairs from radio and television is increasing day by day. But spoken words, heard from radio and television are difficult to remember and retrieve. Therefore, some bibliographical services are necessary to overcome this problem of retrieval. These services also could be categorized as sources of current events. Some examples are:

— *Summary of World Broadcasts.* Caversham: British Broadcasting Corporation, 1947.

It is published daily except on Sundays, in four parts -USSR, Eastern Europe, the Far East and the Middle East and Africa. Each part has its supplement 'Weekly Economic Report'. It does not have an index. Hence for a reference librarian, it is difficult to use.

— *Foreign Broadcast Information Service.* Washington: D.C.U.S. Department of Commerce.

This service is the US equivalent of Summary of World Broadcasts. Both of them are available in printed and microfiche formats.

— *BBC Six P.M.* Cambridge, Chadwyck-Healery, 1978-.

Chadwyck-Healey has published the BBC Home Service Nine

'O' Clock news from 1939-1945 on microfiche. It has started reproduction of news readers, scripts of radio, six p.m. news bulletins which are collected quarterly with a printed index. It has been produced regularly since 1978.

— *Television News Index and Abstracts: A Guide to the Vanderbilt Television News Archive.* Vanderbilt University.

This is a collection of video-tape cassettes of the evening news broadcasts for each of the three major US television networks.

A few important current reference sources are evaluated below:

(i) Asian Recorder: A Weekly Digest of Asian Events with Index, N. Delhi, K.K.Thomas, 1955-. Weekly.

It is an important source of information of the Asian countries which is published by Mr. C.P.Chacko for Asian Recorder, Delhi. Its first issue was published in Jaunary 1955 and since then it is being published every week. In December 2001, its 2nd volume was completed. The issues are numbered consecutively from the first issue of January 2000. From 2000 the title has been changed as "*Asian News Digest*"

Asian Recorder provides weekly news summary of current events happending in all countries of Asia as well as those about Asia happening outside Asia. It consists of three parts as given below:

(a) Events in all countries of Asia listed under each country arranged alphabetically, with a summary for each if necessary.

(b) Events about Asia happening outside Asia listed under a separate heading- *Asia outside Asia.*

(c) Sport is listed at the end, without consideration for a country. The special features include the citation of the source from which the information has been taken. These may include newspapers, periodicals, radio, embassies or government departments. Every three months, an index is issued. Besides, annual index is also brought out. The index is quite intensive and there are may see also references listed in the index.

Its loose weekly issues are sent to the subscribers with a binder put the issues in the sequence. The are a number of cross references to avoid in necessary duplication and easy access to the information. The page numbering is kept continue. In end of all issues have a heading 'Analysis' is meant to analyse the current references.

This is an extremely useful source of current events, which provides excellent short biographical sketches for leading personalities useful for names of newly appointed ministers etc. at state and national levels. This is highly recommended for Asian libraries, especially useful for Indian libraries because it gives greater attention to Indian events.

(ii) Keesing's Record of World Events, London; Keesing's World Wide, LLC. 1931 - Monthly

It is one of the most important and monthly international level sources of current information. Its first volume was published under the title "Kessing's Contemporary Achives" including the main events occurred during 1931 to 1934. In a year, its eleven issues are published as for the months of July and August one joint issue is published. Its latest 47th volume has been completed in 2001 and it entered into 70th year of publication.

It covers all main events of the world. The world has been divided into six parts:

1. Africa, 2. Americas, 3. Asia Pacific, 4. Europe, 5. Middle East : Arab World, and 6. International.

The events occurred in the countries of the above parts are summarized in this source. There is a time lag of one month only e.g., the events of February will appear in the month of March. The issue is not published in the month of August every year.

The information pertaining to the countries generally relate to various fields, such as:

1. Treaties; 2. Wars; 3. Elections; 4. Disaster; 5. Changes in the Government or Cabinet; 6. Plans; 7. Visit of VIPs. 8. Experiment in the Space; 9. Invention/Discovery; 10. Changes in President/Prime Minister; 11. Meetings of the Countries; 12. Death of Dignitory; 13. Foreign Affairs etc.

Every issue contains an index which is arranged alphabetically. After the issue of December an Annual Reference Supplement is also published in which some other information of the countries falling in the above parts of the world are given such as the area, capital, population, languages, religion, politics, main leaders, ruling party, other political parties, election, major events, economy etc. An index for the names, arragned alphabetically, is also published covering the issues of first five months, then the yearly index is also published.

To enable the subscribers to keep the issues in proper order and safe binder is also provided. The page numbering is kept continued.

The cross-references are also given wherever necessary which enhance its utility. Most of the information is gathered from the newspapers. The summaries are prepared by the experts. It is one of the most valuable sources for the libraries, institutions, organizations, govt. offices for getting current information at one place.

(iii) Facts on File; a Weekly World News Digest, New York, Facts on File, October 30,1940-, weekly.

This work provides precise factual summary of the important facts relating to news events in the form of objective, brief and factual reports. The emphasis is on the news events taking place in the United States and those international events, which have a bearing on American affairs. The information provided is taken primarily from the major newspapers published in the United States and elsewhere.

News items are usually organized under broad subject headings such as world affairs, national affairs, foreign affairs, finance, economics, sports, etc. but the arrangement is not fully statisfactory.

Facts on File is fully indexed every two weeks. The index is cumulated every month, every three months, and every year. The detailed indexes helps a great deal in overcoming the problems of arrangement of items of information in the weekly issues.

On first page of each issue, it lists this week's news headlines under the headings; world affairs, US affairs, other nations and miscellaneous.

Ephemeral events like sports, arts, or movies are covered in detail unlike *Keesing's Contemporary Archives.* One major drawback of *Facts on File* is that it does not indicate the sources of information.

From 1980, machine readable version known as *Facts on File News Digest CD-ROM* is also available.

Of various news summary type publications, *Facts on File* is considered to be most prompt. The information provided is considered reliable as a whole. This is a good survey of the important events of the week, giving synopsis of standard news events and providing a great deal of facts.

Q. : Enumerate major non-documentary sources and tools of reference and information. Discuss the characteristics of mass media.

Ans. : Non-documentary sources constitute the sources other than documentary ones. Like documentary sources, they provide an immediate answer to certain queries. We frequently come across these reference sources in our pursuits to get information or to gain knowledge on certain areas. These sources can be observed to be to two kinds- the formal and informal sources. The formal sources are the one which are available through the properly established organizations, associations or in other words through formal channels. On the other hand the informal sources are through personal contacts, discussion with others or otherwise by any informal means.

The non-documentary sources can be classified into four categories:

(i) Human Resources

(ii) Institutional Resources

(iii) Mess Media, and

(iv) Audio-visual Resources

(i) Human Resources : The human resource refers to any individual serving as a source of information. For example, if somebody is doing historical research, the best way to get information will be to go to particular place and talk to older persons of that area. Here the individuals from their memories can give a lot of information. Similarly if some people had witnessed some phenomenon, then they become the best sources of information on that phenomenon. Past history of an organization can be traced by talking to senior and older employees of the organization. In addition to the above, talking, interaction with fellow scientists, experts, specialists, family members gives a lot of insight into the various problems of a researcher. Similiary, the extension workers are also an important source of information.

(ii) Institutional Resources : In many cases, information not published in regular publications can be sought directly from research organizations in public, private or government setups. This then becomes the case of an institution being a source of information. Many times, institutions maintain their past records, annual reports or old documents not available in other place in their archives. These too are then institutional resources.

In addition to the above, industrial establishments have unique information which is unavailable elsewhere. The specialized information centers, referral centers, clearing houses, trade promotion councils, learned societies and associations, universities, colleges, etc. are examples of institutions as sources of information.

(iii) Mass Media : As we are all aware, the various communication media for the masses; that is, broadcasting and telecasting or a combination of the two are more effective than any printed document. The situation presently is very different and we have to contend with and consider the impact of these emerging new media on our society. Their value and benefits to the individuals cannot be denied and the technology in this area is advancing all the time. Almost every household today has the cable television being operated by many companies. They not only provide non-stop entertainment to people but also give information and instruction in many new and novel ways. For example, the news prepared by the cable companies are more analytical, critical and thorough and of local nature. Besides being private operators they do not have to face the hindrances of the bureaucracy.

The functions of mass communication are to entertain, inform, instruct, persuade influence, shape and sell all types of messages and information to large mass audiences. This audience includes children, students, young persons, adults of either sex, housewives, laypersons, experts, specialists, professionals; in fact every conceivable group in a society. It is never aimed at individuals but always at groups. All programmes of broadcasting and television, public relations products, advertisements are oriented to be relevant to the appropriate group addressed.

The scope of mass communication could comprise almost every subject in which a society is interested. Although radio and television programmes devote most of their listening and viewing time to political events and activities, and entertainments, other programmes include aids to students in their learning process, information to industry and industrialists, general programmes of historical and geographical interests for non-specialists, travel and tourist information, and many others to inform the public on different matters. Recently, separate channels for educating the students have been launched which provide latest information for students.

As public opinion is shaped through mass media and every political party is interested in promoting its own views on the public to capture political power. Business and trade interests are also promoted through mass media to be competitive in the business world, therefore, librarians and information specialists show great concern towards providing access to the plethora of information, communicated through mass media.

Any resourceful and imaginative Reference Librarian or an Information Officer can use his judicious search capability to tap mass media for queries of the readers.

(iv) Audio-Visual Resources : Sometimes information cannot be conveyed by words alone. Librarians have extensively made use of the audio and visual form of the new technology to their advantage. Sound recordings on tape, reel-to-reel or cassette and audio cassettes have been of great help to libraries especially in providing services to the blind. In recent years, visual aids too have come to be used especially in educating the users in use of library services.

The commercial and institutional production of visual and audio aids to education has become so substantial that many libraries are going for them. The British Library has compiled and published a bibliography called the British Catalogue of Audiovisual Materials.

Videotapes were the first to come to market and were later replaced by video discs. Both the tapes and discs have considerable potential value as sources of information. Presently the Compact Discs (CD-ROMs) and DVDs are capturing the market as they have the advantage of high quality of sound and vision. The value of the audio-visual materials in libraries thus cannot be overlooked.

5
Bibliographic Services

Q. : What do you understand by the term 'Indexing'? Describe the indexing techniques KWIC & KWOC with suitable examples.

or

Clarify difference between Pre-Coordinate and Post-Coordinate indexing techniques?

or

Explain "Uniterm Indexing System' and suggest some methods to overcome its short comings.

or

Discuss the need, purpose and functions of indexing and abstracting services. Describe the features of any one international indexing and abstracting service in science and technology.

Ans. The word 'Index' is derived from 'Indicare' which means to indicate i.e., an index is guide to items contained in a collection'. Index is "a systematic guide to the text of any reading matter or to the contents of other collected documentary material, comprising a series of entries, which headings arranged in alphabetical or other chosen order, and with references to show where each item indexed is located". It provides various access points through which a user can identify the document of his interest.

Indexing is a technique or a combination of techniques of preparing an index. It is a method of document representation, the ultimate aim of which is to provide access to the users through the description used. Sometimes it is difficult to represent a document in a single term. In such a case, more than one form have to be used. These index terms are arranged in a more searchable order. This ordering involves a definite syntax, semantics and orthography. Because of these characteristics, indexing is described as a language, more so, an artificial language. The indexing language may be available in a prepared form for adoption in any information retrieval system or the language may have to be specially designed for a system. A scheme of classification is a ready-made language. Similarly, a thesaurus is also a ready-made indexing language.

Need & Purpose of Indexing

Following are the main needs and purposes of indexing:-

1. Publications of Primary Sources - A Flow

In present age, the importance of primary sources has increased much due to rapid growth in printing and its high technology. This flow is continue. The specific knowledge is published in many forms, Lacs of periodical, research reports, research publications, treatise, standards, patents, proceedings of seminars are the example of this flow. Its growth rate has doubled in ten or fifteen years. The figures indicate that this growth of publication and its rate was 2 million in 1970 which increased to 8 million in 1985.

Under the circumstances, it is very difficult for a reader to study all the huge publication for his specific study, thus to avoid this problem, the indexing is needed.

2. Diversity of Publications

The literature of primary sources are now published in the different forms of publications like books, periodicals, technical reports, conference papers, conference proceedings, patents etc. To get the desired information out of these sources or information retrieval, a reader does not have adequate time, so the index is needed.

3. Language Barrier

English is an international language. If the literature and other knowledge is published in English language, it can be used quite easily in the all parts of the world. The problem arise when the literature is published in regional or specific language other than English. Today more than 50% scientific & technological literature is published in other than English language. Mostly the scientists are well known with English language but not familiar with other regional or specific language. Therefore for other than English language literature, translation and index services are required.

4. Scattering of Literature

The reading material available is much enough but the problem is the scattering. The specific need of a subject can not be fulfilled from the particular subject literature. One subject is scattered in different books. Bradford says that 1/3rd information is available readily while the remaining is to find out by consulting various sources. Thus, indexing is essential to solve this problem.

5. Save of the Time

Time and labour are essential part of library administration like in other organization. Dr. Ranganathan's Five laws-and out of them, one law is important i.e., 'Save the time of the reader.' With the help of original documents from various books or periodicals, it becomes difficult for a reader to trace the specific desired information as they don't have much time. But by indexing it completes in a short or less period.

Techniques of Indexing

There are various ways and means of indexing, but in the broader sense the techniques of indexing may be of following two categories:-

1. Pre-Coordinate indexing or Conventional or Traditional Indexing
2. Post-Coordinate indexing or Neo-Convential Indexing

1. Pre-cordinate Indexing

In a pre-coordinate system, the compound or composite subjects are analyzed into its constituent concepts according to a plan and these constituent concepts are then represented in a particular pattern of coordination of terms.

In such a coordinated string of concepts there are many access points. In order to satisfy the various approaches of a user, many of the systems have evolved patterns of rotation, cycling, shunting, etc. of the terms.

Following are the main characteristics of pre-coordinate indexing:

1. It is based on the subject analysis of a document.
2. Subject heading consists of two or many index terms.
3. The index terms are pre-coordinated; in other words they are arranged in pre-decided order.

4. The arrangement of the terms are fixed in one sequence.
5. More than one copy is being prepared and is given to searchers for their assignments.

Some important Pre-coordinating Indexings are

(i) Alphabetical indexing
(ii) Classified indexing
(iii) Chain indexing
(iv) PRECIS (Preserve content indexing systems)

(i) Alphabetical Indexing: In the process of information retrieval alphabetical indexing is quite old technique. Under this system, the subject matter of the documents is arranged in alphabetical form after analysing into simple language. It may be said that the entries are arranged just alphabetically as per dictionary.

There are two types of Alphabetical indexing:

(a) Alphabetico Specific
(b) Alphabetico Classed

(a) ***Alphabetico Specific Indexing*****:** In this system the various headings of specific subjects are arranged subject-wise. The different ideas of documents are arranged and shown under the heading where they represent most appropriates and made entries. The other terms of the subject are shown in next order. For example :

Treatment of infectious disease of heart, can be analyzed into following manner:-

Treatment, Infectious disease, Heart, Medicine.

Here the term 'Treatment' is the specific while the others are its subsidiary. Since there is depth relation between these terms, both can be used as notation alongwith.

Criticism:

1. Due to alphabetical arrangement the terms are separated though these are interrelated.
2. This system is not useful for complex subject.

(b) ***Alphabetico Classed Indexing*****:** In this system the mixed merits of alphabetical and classified terms and its arrangement are available. In Alphabetico classed indexing, the specific subject headings are represented as a sub headings of an higher terms of subjects. The subject titles are arranged alphabetical but the last collection of the entries depends upon any specific classification scheme. For example:

In transportation in Economics, Banking, Finance & Taxation are the main divisions, and subdivision of these main headings are arranged in alphabetical order like:

Transport	Taxation
Land	Income tax
Rail	Sales tax
Water	Wealth tax

The subjects in this system are arranged in two ways. First the main division are classified and arranged and its subsidiaries are arranged in alphabetical order. Secondly main divisions are arranged in alphabetical order and its subsidiaries in classified sequence.

Criticism:

1. Due to lack of control over terminology of general language the subject coverts into pieces of headings. Therefore, there is no continuity and lack of standardisation and uniformity, hence it become difficult to control.
2. It is difficult to decide the intershape of the subjects by adding its guide and directories.
3. Entries are scattered as a result many guide entries are made.

(ii) Classified Indexing: The search of literature can be made very easily and quickly by classified index. The entries are arranged according to classified, with the help of denoting in signs, symbols, numbers. This system brings together the related different subjects as well as finishes the need of guide cards and entries. The problem of synonymous and anonymous is solved. Thus, the system is logically sound.

(iii) Chain Indexing: Chain indexing is a direct and specific indexing which is based on the concluded terminology, of a classification scheme. Under this system the necessary or useful references are taken and unusual or not useful terms and references are deleted.

The colon classification scheme was introduced with a view to provide chain indexing and to derive subject headings from the class numbers. The objective of a classification scheme is not only to classify the subject in helpful sequence, but classification means to a language which can denote a specific subject in detailed form in hierarchical chain from the most specific to most general.

For example - the topic Computer Hardware Manufacturer in India during Twentieth Century is represented by a notation *ABCDE*. This class number will make following entries:-

Twentieth Century	India	Manufacturer	Hardware	Computer
(A)	(B)	(C)	(D)	(E)

India	Manufacturer	Hardware	Computer
(A)	(B)	(C)	(D)

ABCDE

Manufacturer	Hardware	Computer
(A)	(B)	(C)

Hardware	Computer
(A)	(B)

Computer
(A)

While determining the sequence, Dr. Ranganathan arrived at PMEST (Fundamental categories) sequence for putting index term together. This sequence is very useful and got popular "PMEST" which named as follows with connecting symbols:

- Personality (,)
- Matter (;)
- Energy (:)
- Space (.)
- Time (')

Principle : The systems is based on a general principle. If the subjects are classified according to Analytico synthetic classification scheme i.e., Colon classification, the retranslated class number, can be ascertained the subject headings. Thus an indexer can get and decide the headings of the related subjects direct instead of wasting time in analysing or subject deciding. He can go to the class number and get the subject headings for indexing. For example:

If a document is-

'Treatment of Retinal Disease in Children'. The classifier will analyze the subject and represent the following terms:

Medicine (BF), Child (Special), Retina (P), Disease (E), Treatment (2E)

In ordinal language, the cardinal number of classification language, the following class number will be available for use:-

L 9 C, 18517: 4 : 6

The job of indexer starts from this point. If the indexer again retranslate the each number the standard term will appear automatically. While analysing every digit of class number can be shown as below:-

L	=	Medicine
L9C	=	Child
L9C, 18517	=	Retina
L9C, 185 : 4	=	Disease
L9C, 185 : 4 : 6	=	Treatment

If false and unsought links are ignored, then the subject of the document can be derived as follows by the use of sought link:

TREATMENT, DISEASE, RETINA, CHILD, MEDICINE.

Steps in Chain Procedure

Following are the main steps in Chain Procedure:

1. Chain procedure is completely based on classification scheme. Therefore the merits and demerits in a scheme of classification will follows in indexing too.
2. In indexing, the specific subject of document is determined only.
3. In this system only one major heading is ascertained which will be decided by the last term. In order to satisfy the needs of the searcher there are other added entries used like:

   DISEASE, RETINA, CHILD, MEDICINE

   RETINA, CHILD, MEDICINE,

   CHILD, MEDICINE

   MEDICINE

Criticism or Limitations:

Following are the main limitations of Chain Procedure:

1. Chain procedure is entirely dependent upon the colon

classification. Naturally the limitations of the scheme reflects to the indexing too.

2. Only specific entry of a document contains in an index.

To avoid these problems and lacunae, Prof. Bhattacharya and Neelameghan introduced and developed POPSI i.e., Postulate-base-permuted subject indexing.

(iv) 'PRECIS' (Preserve Content Indexing System): Precis is a set of procedures for generating index entries. It uses computerized thesaurus for assigining standard terms. It is an alphabetical index system where subject content of documents are displayed at each entry point. A user can find the index through any of the concept present in the document. For example:

Cotton Industries, Personnel Training

The input term for the above mentioned example would be:

— India

— Cotton industries

— Personnel

— Training

References

1. Asia - See also India.
2. Industries - see also Textile industries.
3. Textile industries - See also cotton industry.
4. Employees see - personnel
5. Labour see - personnel
6. Staff - see - personnel
7. Work - see - personnel
8. Manpower - see also Personnel.

2. Post Coordinate Indexing

In a post - coordinate system, the concepts are kept separately and these can be coordinated by the user at the time of search. It should be noted that the process of coordination is there in both the systems, only they are done at two different stages.

In this system, a separate entry is prepared for every term. Thus, a searcher is not needed to remember its order. The desired information can be ascertained and retrieved at the time of search.

Following are the main characteristics of Post-cordinate Indexing:

1. The determination of the subject is being done at the time of indexing.
2. The clause is made related with subject.
3. Subject clause is analyzed in different terms.
4. Separate cards are prepared for every term.
5. The sequence of the terms it not arranged at the time of indexing.
6. The sequence of the term is determined by the searcher at the time of search.

Process Adopted in Post Coordinate Indexing:

1. A document profile is prepared in the form of card. Separate card is prepared for every document and is given a special serial number which is called Accession number.

> Acc. No. 152
>
> KAKU (Lal Chand) Treatment of Lung Disease through Ayurveda. Journal of Respiratory Disease. 25 1.; Jan. , 1994; 15-24.8 ref.
>
> Abstract describes various types of disease related with Lungs, Discuss various Ayurvedic formulations and their side effects to care the disease.

2. Specific subject of the document is determined, then the specific subject is analyzed in its different terms. These different terms are represented in the form of terms of indexing.
3. A separate card is prepared for every indexing terms. Cards are prepared accessing to number of terms. These cards are called term cards and these are arranged in alphabetical order.
4. The concepts are translated into index terms on the demand of researcher.
5. Each term is written at the top of separate card.
6. The accession numbers of the document are posted in specific columns of all the term cards.

The first Post-coordinate indexing system known as 'peek-a-boo' introduced in 1940's by Batten in England. Batten indexed chemistry documents with this technique in first instant.

7. On the basis of the demand of researcher, his desired subject is analyzed into terms. The related cards of these terms are selected and discarded from the index cover. The uniform number of the document noted in the cards are tallied and identified the related document. To do this job, the following are the different techniques :
   (i) Uniterm Indexing System
   (ii) Keyword in Content or KWIC
   (iii) Keyword out of Content or KWOC
   (iv) Citation Index
   (v) Pee-Ka-boo Indexing system
   (vi) Zatacoding Indexing system.

Out of the above, some of the very important techniques are discussing in detail as follows:

(I) Uniterm Indexing System : The simplest form of Post-Coordinate index is the uniterm index, which was introduced by Mortimer Taube in 1953. The name is made of two-word, i.e. Unit & Term and is intended to emphasize the system's use of single terms as opposed to composite headings. In other words, the uniterm systems involves the indexing of documents under single word (uniterm) extended from the documents itself or chosen from a prescribed list of subjects. A uniterm card has a space at the top for headings. The rest of the card being divided into ten vertical columns. For example:

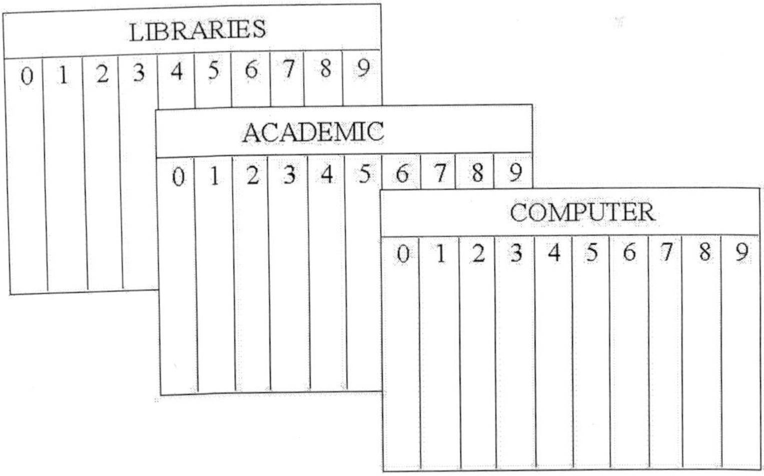

The accession numbers of the documents, to which a particular term is assigned, are written on the cards. Here the final digit determines the filing columns i.e., 692 will be entered in Col. 2 & 695 in Col. 5. This helps in spreading entries over the card. These index cards are filed in alphabetical order. At the time of searching cards representing related index terms (subjects) are picked from the tray and accession numbers are matched manually. Number that are common to all selected cards identify documents deal with the subject of inquiry. In the above mentioned example, documents having accession number 692 deals with computer applications in academic libraries.

Steps in Search Process

1. Analysis of demand
2. Selection of related term cards
3. Recognition of suitable document

1. Analysis of Demand

1. When a demand of a document from the reader for a particular subject is to be answered, then first of all the subject is analyzed into different terms. For example:

   'Treatment of Lung Disease through Ayurveda

   Analysing the above term, we get the following:-

   Treatment, Lung, Disease & Ayurveda

2. Selection of Term Cards:

After analysing of the terms, the related cards which are alphabetically arragned in card index are stretched.

3. Identification of the Related Document :

Having after searching the term card related with the subject, is verified and is known which accession number is common in all cards. This card having Acc. No. will satisfy the need of the reader. For example:

Specific subject 'Treatment of Lung Disease through Ayurveda'. We get the term card form the above mentioned subject-Treatment, Disease, Lung & Ayurveda. It will be tallied into following manner :

TREATMENT									
0	1	2	3	4	5	6	7	8	9
	101	322 142	63 123	44	75 365	26 166	187 217	58	199

DISEASE									
0	1	2	3	4	5	6	7	8	9
10	101	112	123	34	75	26	187	248	199
		142	453	124	455	166			

LUNG									
0	1	2	3	4	5	6	7	8	9
	101	142	453		35	166	237		289
				124	125				

AYURVEDA									
0	1	2	3	4	5	6	7	8	9
10	301	312		124	75	86	347	58	
		142			455	416			

When these all cards are tallied, we get that No. 142 is noted in all cards. Therefore 142 Acc. No. document is referred for all knowledge and references. Thus, the uniterm card is traced in index file.

Merits

1. No need of classification scheme.
2. It becomes easy to prepare index file.
3. Natural language is used.
4. Many documents are included in one term card.
5. The reading material can be traced easily.
6. Documents are arranged in receipt order.

Demerits

1. Taub has limited uniterm in one word while various document cannot be represented in one term.
2. In this index system only the serial number of the documents are provided. Which term is useful cannot be ascertained without going through all term cards.

3. The vocabulary is changeable and difficult to choose correct words.
4. Limitations of the term cards restricts the use and therefore new cards are prepared.
5. Search problem is to be faced when new cards are prepared.
6. A fear of false coordination is possible.

(II) Key Words in Content: KWIC : This is a non-traditional indexing system, which was started in 1856 by Andriya Christadora and known as Keyword in Titles. In the year 1952, the central Agencies of America started the mechanized based vocabulary from title index. In the year 1958, H.P. Luhan started to use this with the help of machine in detail. Thus, the credit of modern KWIC system goes to Mr. Luhan.

In the real sense, KWIC was popularized in 1960. The system was used by American chemical society to index chemical titles.

Basic principles of KWIC

1. This new scheme of indexing was introduced with a view to improve the lacunae of traditional systems.
2. In the traditional system there is always a fear of one man decision taken on his experience and intellectual, 'KWIC' started with a view to improve this limitation.
3. Mr. Luhan introduced the mechanical devices instead of personal decisions.
4. In this system the 'word' and the vocabulary is the base which is named as Keywords instead of the hypothesis.
5. The important word and speeches of the subject are represented through technique.
6. This system is based on natural language.

Structure & Size of 'KWIC'

KWIC has three parts as under :

1. Keyword
2. Content
3. Code

Process

This indexing system has the following base points:

1. To select the main word.
2. To mention all main words in index at the top.
3. To delete unused word as article, conjunction word, auxiliary verbs etc.
4. To arrange these words alphabetically.
5. In which reference the main word represent.
6. Guiding symbol is mentioned at the right of entry card, so that availability of document can be ascertained.

As 'KWIC' indexing is prepared with the help of computer, therefore it is also known as mechanized system. All the entries of documents to be indexed are entered in the computer. Useless and non-essential words are listed already in the computer. Thus, computer tally all the entries with this non essential list and use only those words which are not listed in the computer. Thus, computer arranges the essential words in alphabetical order and print in central processing unit. Base and followed words are printed in capital letters or in bold printing while the words prior to base are printed in ordinary letters.

Example :

'Use of Roles & links in Indexing 56'

The entries of this subject will be as follows:-

INDEXING/ use of Roles and links in ——	56
Links in indexing/use of Roles and ——	56
ROLES and links in indexing/use of ——	56
And links in INDEXING/use of roles	56
Of Roles and LINKS in indexing/use	56
Indexing/use of ROLES and links in	56

Merits

1. It is useful in providing CAS-Current awareness service.
2. Being it is mechanized system, there is least burden on human power.
3. A person having little knowledge of computer can do it easily, as there is no need of depth knowledge.
4. Cumulative figures in tables are prepared with the help of computer.

5. Indexing can be prepared speedily and without mistake.

Demerits

1. This system depends upon entries, but few entries are not very clear, and does not reveal the real sense of the document as a result index can not provide the subject in real sense.
2. In this system the base terms related with one subject scatter as these terms are divided into different alphabet, as a result a reader can not get his desired material.
3. This system is not suitable for the research already done in the past.
4. Reader wants to get his desired material at one place which is not possible in this system.

Suggestions

There are few suggestions to be more useful and practical of the system which are as follows:-

1. The entry of document should be edited so that the subject can be clarified.
2. In order to coordinate the terms each other the related reference should be presented.
3. A thesaurus should be used to understand the meaning of the words used therein.

(III) Keywords Out of Content: KWOC : H.P. Luhan of the IBI was a pioneer in developing a completely mechanized indexing system which was named KWIC. Since then a number of variations of KWIC index e.g. KWOC & KWAC developed.

Under the system 'KWOC' too, the index is prepared on the entry base. The base words are deleted from the entry and these are used as an title heading of the entry. The entries will be as per base terms. The base term is used for entry. The complete entry is repeated just after the title and heading.

Format of Entry

Classification of Books in a Library - 1001

Format I

CLASSIFICATION	Classification of books in a library	1001

BOOKS	Classification of books in a library	1001
LIBRARY	Classification of books in a library	1001

Format II

CLASSIFICATION	Classification of books in a library	1001
BOOKS	Classification of books in a library	1001
LIBRARY	Classification of books in a library	1001

Difference between KWIC and KWOC

The difference between KWIC and KWOC and other variations like KWOC, KWAC, etc is more in the matter of format. There is least difference so far as indexing technique is concerned. As a result there is hardly any difference so far as the retrieval efficiency of these varieties are concerned.

Difference between Pre-Coordinate and Post - Coordinate Systems

The purpose of all kind of indexing is the retrieval of pin-pointed information with minimum efforts. There are basically two types of coordinate indexing systems i.e., pre-coordinating and post - coordinating. The differences between two, are summarized as under :

1. Coordination between the terms is established in Pre-coordinate at the time of preparing indexing while in post coordinate it is done at the time of search.
2. Order of the term - There is a fix order of the terms in pre-coordination when it is uncertain in post coordination.
3. Pre-coordination system is based on analysis where post coordination is on entry base.
4. To search the subject in pre-coordinate system, a subject heading list is used while in post coordination, a thesaurus is used for synonymous.
5. Pre-coordination system is based on any particular classification scheme while there is no use in classification scheme in post coordination.
6. Pre-content system of indexing is a traditional system while post content system is neo-traditional based on computer.
7. Pre-coordinate entry is based on combined term whereas post coordinate system is used unit term.

Q. : Describe the purpose and need of abstracts in the journal. Enumerate the qualities of a good abstractor.

or

Define abstract & abstracting. Discuss various types of abstracts and explain the difference between informative & indicative abstracts.

or

Give the difference between an abstract and summary and suggest the appropriate personnel for preparing an abstracts.

or

Explain the difference between informative & indicative abstracts and describe the principles for abstracting.

Ans. An abstract simply defined, is a condensation that present succinetly, the objective, scope and findings of a document. This information is usually conveyed together with an indexing system, which further helps as a rule, is aimed at a specific group of users what either may not have easy access to the original document.

In brief, it is a summary of essential contents of work or it is a bibliography in which periodical articles are summarized.

Though in general sense, it seems that both abstract and summary are the same. If we study it in depth we will find that there are certain basic differences which are as follows:-

1. While preparing abstract, the essential part is taken and unrequired is left, but in summary it is not necessary.
2. Abstracting is a scientific method while summary not need any technique.
3. While making abstract an abstractor must be a subject expert or professionally trained personnel, but a summary can be prepared by any one or little knower.

Abstracts are useful in the following ways:

(i) The selection of papers to be read by the research scholar or a scientist is facilitated. Due to information explosion it is not practicable for a specialist to keep in touch by reading a few select journals.

(ii) Papers in science and technology are published in more than 50 languages. The user needs to know only the language in which the abstract is published.

(iii) The preparation of articles, bibliographies, reviews, and talks requires organization of the material used. Abstracts can be used to facilitate this organization .

(iv) Informative abstracts can substitute for original literature in many cases.

(v) Retrospective searches can be greatly facilitated by classified and indexed abstracts.

(vi) Accuracy of selection of literature to be read or translated is increased over that of selection from titles plus annotations by the use of abstracts. Moreover, additional information in the abstract increases the accuracy.

Types of Abstract

Various persons have categorized the abstracts into different types in their own way. But broadly, an abstract can be divided into following two categories on the basis of quantity of information-

1. Informative Abstract
2. Indicative Abstract

1. Informative Abstract : An informative abstract (also called comprehensive abstract or abstract synopsis) contains in an abridged form all the significant findings or ideas contained in the original document. It is said that at the time of informative abstract may serve as an adequate substitute of the original for getting some information. The average length of the abstract is about 200-300 words.

2. Indicative Abstract : An indicative abstract (also called descriptive abstract or abstract-summary) indicates very briefly the nature and scope of a document or what the document is about. Because of its very nature, an indicative abstract can not serve as a substitute of the original document. It can provide only clues about the information content of a document.

Apart from the two main types of abstract mentioned above, there are few other varieties.

3. Titular abstract or title-only abstract : The title of a document is used without any elaboration to describe the contents of the document. It is only concerned with the subject and not the findings.

4. Annotation : A sentence or clause is added to amplify the title of the article. Annotations and indicative abstracts differ only in length.

5. Slanted Abstract : Description or information reported in a document is oriented to a specific discipline to which the abstracting service is devoted. In such abstracts emphasis may sometimes be placed on methods, equipment, or findings that were only incidental to author's major purpose, while the latter may even be omitted or minimized.

6. Auto-abstract : It is produced by a computerized analysis of the frequency of use of significant words in a document and of the frequency with which these high-use words appear in the same sentence. The "high-frequency" words are then traced back to the sentence in which they occurred, and their position noted. A score is then assigned to each sentence based on the number and position of the high frequency words it contains. The resultant auto-abstract is a collection of typical sentences from the original document.

7. Telegraphic or Standardized or Encoded Abstract : It is a detailed index to a graphic record which is composed of : (a) significant words selected from the document; (b) code symbols called role indicators which supply a context for the selected words; and (c) punctuation symbols which separate and group the words and role indicators into various units in somewhat the same fashion as conventional punctuation does.

Need and Objectives of Abstracting

Abstracting is an operation which offers two important advantages; first, it reduces considerably the amount of primary information, and second, it lays emphasis on aspects of particular interest to users.

Following are the main need and objectives of abstracting :

1. Language Barrier : Today there is explosion of knowledge which is published in different languages. Generally a reader might be knowing one or two script of language only. If he gets the desired information in his language it becomes easy for him to get it translated. He will get translated those only which is needed. Thus he will get help of abstract and problem of language shall be solved. Abstract will be helpful to choose his own needed subject field.

2. Facility of Selection : In today's world, the number of published journals are in millions. To get, study and read of his choiced magazine for a reader is not only difficult but rather impossible. With the help of 'abstract' he will select only those articles to be read.

3. Save of the Time : According to Dr. Ranganathan, having after studying abstract, a reader saves time to select his needed article and the ratio is 1/1000.

4. Arrangement of Abstracts : The original documents contain more detailed and different subject field and it is difficult for a reader to divide into subject field while the abstracts can be arranged in classified order as a result it becomes easy for him.

5. Retrospective Search : Sometimes readers need back issues of the journals. To do this the classified and arranged abstracts are much useful. The old documents can be traced with the help of abstracts easily.

6. Valid Selection of Readable Literature : The documents used by the readers are more authentic and standardized as it is done with the help of abstract.

7. Usefulness in Indexing Work : Since all the documents related with one subject combine together by making abstract, thus indexing work become more easy.

8. Alternative of Original Document : Abstract is the substance of a document. Sometimes a reader satisfy only with the abstract list as he does not need to go through the original.

The above points clarity that every article or document should be in abstract. Without abstract the use of published article is not possible. Unlimited stored knowledge is presented to the subject experts with the help of abstract. Thus, it saves the time of readers which can be utilized for further research.

Techniques of Abstracting

An ideal abstract contains all the necessary information, like the purpose and nature of the work, new findings, and approach, results and conclusion. The essential aspects of the original document are conveyed in a concise but precise manner. The care has to be taken that no redundant words creep in as well as ensuring that no useful information is omitted. It is the art of conveying maximum information contained in the original document in the minimum number of words.

Abstracts can serve their purpose best if they are carefully written to transmit important information to users quickly and accurately. This implies the knowledge of the readers' needs,, habits and desire; ability to identify the key facts in the document; ability to organize these facts to present them in the order best suited to the reader; and ability to write the abstract clearly and concisely. After determining the type of abstract to be written the work on the abstracting of a document begins. This involves

(i) identification of the key information;

(ii) organizing it; and

(iii) Writing.

The writer of the abstract is confronted by a document whose contents are unknown to him before he scans the same. The following sequence may prove useful in identifying the key information.

(i) The introductory paragraphs of the paper should be read carefully. Generally the introduction contains the objective of the author in writing the paper.

(ii) It the paper contains author abstract it should also be examined. If on checking the document the abstract proves to be a good one, it may be used.

(iii) The summary and conclusion at the end of the paper should be noted as they reveal the authors findings, which should be incorporated in the abstract.

(iv) The text should then be scanned for information on the methodology of work, data, and any other additional information.

(v) The important phrases and passages should be marked and marginal notes jotted down in pencil.

(vi) When contents of the paper are completely grasped the abstract should be drafted, read, and if necessary further modified to give the final shape.

Appropriate Personnel for Preparing an Abstract

Abstracting job is highly intellectual and scientific, hence a question arise in mind who is appropriate person to do the job of abstracting. Learned persons have different views, but Dr. S. R. Ranganathan categorized the following personnel:-

1. Author
2. Library specialist
3. Subject expert

1. Author : No-body is more competent than an author of a document in regard to the subject matter or thought contents of it. But he/she is not a technical hand to write an abstract so he/she is not aware of the techniques of abstracting. Therefore an assistance of author should be taken for abstracting.

2. Library specialist : Library expert is fully aware and knower to the principles of abstracting as he is a professionally trained personnel. He/she knows reference service, cataloguing, classification, which are quite helpful in preparing abstract. He might be expert but may be little knowing of subject.

3. Subject Expert : No doubt subject expert is knowing the subject in depth but lack of principles of abstracting techniques. Moreover there is also a fear of biasedness being a subject expert as a result the authenticity of the abstract is doubtful.

So, no person can do the abstracting in a proper way. Therefore it should be assigned and performed in coordination of the above three personnel. The following qualities should be necessary in an abstractor:

1. Abstractor should be subject expert.
2. Abstractor should be knowing techniques.
3. Abstractor should know the use of the readers.
4. Abstractor should know reference service, depth classification and cataloguing etc.

Format of Abstract

An abstract should contain the following elements:

(i) Purpose: The purpose is to help the users in deciding whether the contents of the paper are such that they need to read it in full. An abstract can properly fulfil this requirement if all the significant findings reported in the paper are clearly brought out. In essence, it should reflect the aims and objectives and answer the question as to why the paper was written.

(ii) Methodology and Techniques: The steps involved in using a particular method or technique should be included in brief.

(iii) Results: A statement of significant findings or outcome of the study should be included.

(iv) Conclusion: Finally a statement on describing the significance of the results and its interpretation should be included as a last step.

(v) Specialized contents : In some subject fields, the abstract should contain specialized information, e.g.:

— **Biology:** Names of organisms, new genera, new classification, and distribution records.

— **Chemical Market Analysis:** Company location, plans, dates, capacity, trade name, nature of the product, patents, unit consumption factor etc.

— **Geology:** Orient (paper) in place and geologic time, locate local stratigraphic manes in the general geologic column, name new minerals, fossils etc.

— **Medicine:** Complete details of diagnosis and treatment, technique and procedures (drug dosages, operative techniques etc.)

— **Pharmacology:** Number of individuals in the experimental series, whether human or animal, and the species; what percentage reacted, etc.; and in the case of a new drug, the composition.

Writing of Abstract

The abstract should comprise a brief but factual summary of the contents and conclusions of the paper. It is presumed that the reader has some knowledge of the subject, but has not read the paper. The abstract should, therefore, be intelligible in itself without reference to the original. The title of an abstract is a part of the abstract, and it is both unnecessary and undesirable to repeat details, which are already in the title.

— **Style:** Generally accepted rules for good writing are also applicable to the writing of an abstracts. Clarity of the content and conciseness of expression are the major criteria of a good abstract. It is valuable to indicate the treatment of various aspects of the subject by such words as 'brief', 'exhaustive', 'theoretical', 'experimental', etc.

— **Length:** The abstract should be brief (100-300 words) and non-repetitive. Normally for informative abstracts 100-300 words can be taken as the limit.

— **General instructions:** The following points should be kept in mind while writing the abstract:

(i) Write in fluent, easy-to-read manner. Strive for simplicity and general understandability.

(ii) Be exact, concise, and unambiguous. Avoid general statements where you can be specific.

(iii) Condense but, as a general rule, do not personally interpret the author's remarks.

(iv) Be consistent in tone and emphasis with the document being abstracted.

(v) Use complete sentences and constructions, except when supplying the last bits of descriptive information e.g., 11 ref.

(vi) Use short sentences, but with some variety in length and structure to avoid monotony.

(vii) Place general statements, where needed, towards the end of the abstract.

(viii) Use active voice instead of passive. For example, 'X exceeds Y' makes better reading than 'Y is exceeded by X'.

(ix) The Noun form of verbs makes dull reading. 'Separating butadine from butenes' reads better in the abstract than 'the separation of butadine from butenes'.

(x) Use the past tense to describe the specific activities that the author is reporting, since they are already in the past. However, the conclusions that he draws from these activities are facts of permanent value (until proved otherwise) and therefore prevail in the present; accordingly, they should be written in the present tense.

(xi) Use short, simple, concrete, and familiar words.

(xii) Try to avoid trade jargons.

(xiii) Use well-known abbreviations and symbols in the subject, e.g. NaCl (in Chemistry), DNA and RNA (in biology), TLCX (in analytical chemistry), RBC (in medicine) etc.

Q. : Write an essay on some of the important Indexing and Abstracting services.

Ans. Indexing and Abstracting (I&A) services are the important links in the chain of communication between the originator of information and the ultimate user. The major factors that have contributed to the launching of secondary periodicals like indexing and abstracting services are

(i) enormous growth in published literature

(ii) diversity of publications

(iii) language barrier

(iv) scatter of published information etc.

Indexing and Abstracting services are excellent records of contemporary published literature, analysis of which would provide very useful indicators for planning research and development. These indicators could throw a flood of light on the development of a subject, its rate of growth, unploughed areas for further research and a number of other quantitative and qualitative data.

Indexing and abstracting services bring together all or significant current publications, that lie scattered in number of source documents. I & A services may be pertaining to a subject or discipline, irrespective of the country from which a document originates, language or form (journal article, technical reports or thesis). There are also national I & A services, confining themselves to all documents that emanate from a country. Some of examples of major Indexing & Abstracting given below.

1. Chemical Abstracts: (Chemical Abstracts Service, Columbus, USA). 1907-.

This weekly abstracting and indexing journal is covering new findings in chemistry and chemical engineering reported in the worlds scientific and technical literature. It treats periodical (14,000) Literature published in 50 languages in 150 countries, patents (70,000) issued in 28 different patent offices and reports (14,000) dissertations (6,000) proceedings (1,700) and other types of materials. Divided into 80 topical sections within 5 broad chemical subject groupings: sections 1-34 are published one week and sections 35-80 the following week. Available as printed publication, in microform and on line. The five subject groupings may also be subscribed to individually.

Abstracts in the main section are arranged by entry number under 80 sub-topics within 5 broad subject categories. Each issue also includes key word index, patent index and author index. Cumulated every six months and are issued as part of the twice yearly. CA volumes indexes comprise of general subject index, chemical substance index, formula index, ring index, author index, patent index. Volume indexes are cumulated every 5 years as CA collective indexes. Photocopies or loans of original documents cited in chemical abstracts are available on fee basis from CAS document delivery service. Chemical Abstracts information is accessible through various on-line services world wide.

2. Engineering Index: (Engineering Information Incorporation, New York) 1962.

This is an abstracting and indexing journal providing access to the worlds technological literature significant to all engineering disciplines. It covers materials published in 50 countries in over 15 languages. Available as a printed publication and as an on-line data-base.

About 2,000 periodical titles, proceedings (1000 per year), books (100 per year), reports (100 per year) and standards are covered. List of periodicals covered is published annually.

Entries in the main section are arranged by entry number under specific alphabetical subject headings (Subject Headings for Engineering; SHE) with sub-topics. Each issue also includes the author index, list of conference publications covered, list of acronyms and abbreviations of organization names.

A typical entry includes entry number, article, article title, English title translation (where applicable), abstract, number of references, original language if other than English, author, author affiliation, journal title abbreviation, volume and issue numbers, data, page numbers. It is cumulated annually. Copies of most articles abstract may be obtained from Engineering Societies Library. The information from EI annual is included in the COMPENDEX database, which dates from 1969 to the present and is widely available on line.

3. Sociological Abstracts (Sociological Abstracts Inc. San Diago CA) 1953-.

It is an abstracting and indexing journal providing abstracts and indexes of the world literature in sociology and related disciplines. It includes a supplement, the International Review of Publications in Sociology (IRPS) which comprises a bibliography of book reviews appearing in the journals abstracted.

It covers about 1,500 periodical titles, books (200 per year), proceedings (10 per year). List of periodical sources covered is published in the annual cumulative volume.

Entries in the main section are arranged alphabetically by author under sub-topics within 31 subject categories. Each issue includes subject index; source index; International Review of Publications in Sociology.

Typical entry includes entry number, author, author affiliation and addresses, article title in original language and English, journal title, year of publication, volume and issue numbers, issue date, page numbers, language code if other than English, abstract, number of illustrations, abstractor credit.

It is issued five times per year. Indexes are cumulated annually and issued in a separate volume. Photocopies of most articles abstracted in SA are available through the SA Reproduction Service.

SA database, covers the world literature on Sociology since 1963. It is searchable on-line through DIALOG information services, Inc. and Bibliographical Retrieval Services, Inc. (BRS).

4. Humanities Index (H.W. Wilson Co., New York) 1974.

It is quarterly subject and author index to current English language periodical literature covering various topics in the field of humanities. Periodicals indexed are selected by subscribers vote from a master list of suggested titles.

The coverage includes archaeology and classical studies, area studies, folklore, history, language and literature, literary and political criticisms, performing arts, philosophy, religion and theology and related subjects.

Entries in the main section are arranged alphabetically by article title under author names and subject headings appearing in a single alphabetic sequence. Each issue also includes a book review index, in which citations are arranged alphabetically by book author, and a source list.

Each entry includes article title, indications of bibliography and illustrations, journal title abbreviation, volume number, page number, date, and entries in the book review section include author and title of the book being reviewed and review citations.

5. Index Medicus (US National Library of Medicine) 1879.

It is a monthly subject and author index to current articles published in the world's biomedical journals covers literature in all languages from all countries also includes bibliography of medical reviews which lists articles considered to be well documented surveys of recent biomedical literature. Available as a printed publication and as an on-line database. An abridged version, Abridged Index Medicus and an annual cumulation, Cumulated Index Medicus are issued separately.

Medicine, life sciences, and other health related topics are the subjects covered. Subject Indexing use US National Library of Medicines Medical Subject Heading (MeSH).

Entries in the main subject section are arranged alphabetically by journal title under specific alphabetical subject heading sub-divisions; English language journal titles appear first within a heading.

Entries in the subject section include article title in English, author, journal title abbreviation, date, volume and issue number, page numbers, language code of other than English. 2000 Entries per issue are cumulated annually.

The index is produced from the computerized MEDILARS system. MEDLINE, the on-line version of the index is searchable through the National Library of Medicine, DIALOG Information Service Inc. and Bibliographic Retrieval Services Inc.

6. Current Technology Index (CTI) (Library Association Publishing Limited, London) 1962.

It is a monthly Index providing subject and author access to English language periodical literature dealing with general technology, Engineering and related topics. Covers 350 periodical title published in U.K. Available as printed publication of microfilm and on magnetic tape.

Entries in the main section are classified by subject. Each issue also includes an author index a source list.

Typical entry includes article title, subtitle, journal title, volume and issue numbers, data page numbers etc.

7. INIS Atom Index (International Nuclear Information System Vienna, Austria) 1970.

It is a semi-monthly journal providing abstracts and indexes of scientific and technical periodical and other literature dealing with nuclear science and its peaceful applications. It covers-world wide literature without restriction on language as processed by an international, decentralized information system. It is available as printed publication and on-line database.

It covers nuclear science-physical sciences, chemistry, material science, earth science, life sciences, isotopes and isotope radiation applications, engineering and technology other aspects of nuclear energy.

Abstracts in the main section are arranged by entry number under sub-category and sub topics within six broad subject categories. Each issue also includes the following author index, corporate entry index, subject index, conference index by date, by place, report standard and patent index.

Entries for periodical articles include entry number, English title translation (where necessary), author name and affiliation, language of article if other than English, original title abbreviation, ISSN, date, volume and issue numbers, page numbers, abstract, date flag, subject headings. Its fortnightly, semi-annual and annual cumulative indexes are available, as well as 5-year cumulation report, standard and patent number index. Atom index information is searchable on-line as the INIS database available through ESA-QUEST and BELINDIS.

8. Library and Information Science Abstracts (LISA) (Library Association Publishing Limited, London) 1950.

It is monthly abstracting and indexing journal covering 600 periodicals, books and other literature dealing with library and information science. It treats international literature without restrictions on language of country. It is available as printed publication, on microfilm, magnetic tape and on-line.

Abstracts in the main sections are classified by subject. Each issue also includes detailed subject index, author and proper name index, subject classification scheme outline.

Entries for periodical article include subject classification code, subject descriptor string, entry number, article title in original language and in English, author, journal title, volume and issue numbers, data, page number, indication of illustrations, numbers of references, abstract, abstractors initials.

LISA is searchable on-line through DIALOG Information Services Inc. Systems Development Corporation (SDC).

9. Indian Science Abstracts: (Indian National Scientific Documentation Centre, Delhi; now NISCAIR) 1965.

It is a semi-monthly abstracting periodical reporting original scientific research work published in Indian journals including short communications, research work by Indian scientists published in foreign journals, review and informative articles appearing in Indian scientific and technical journals. Proceedings of conferences, seminars, symposia held in India, monograph and ad-hoc scientific reports from Indian scientific research institutions, Indian Patents and Standards are also noticed in this publication.

Abstracts are broadly classified according to UDC and arranged under appropriate headings alphabetically by the authors name. Entries are serially numbered. Each entry includes author, title followed by language symbol if the article is in other than English language and locus followed by abstract and initials of the abstractors. Each issue gives author and key word indexes. It lists about 1200 entries in each issue.

10. Indian Dissertation Abstracts: (ICSSR, Delhi), 1973;

It is a quarterly journal, sponsored by the Indian Council of Social Science Research and Association of Indian Universities was started in 1973. It is devoted exclusively for publication of synopsis of doctoral dissertation in Education, Economics, Management, Political Science, Psychology Public Administration and Sociology and Social Science aspects of Anthropology, Demography, Geography, History, Law and Linguistic, approved by the Indian Universities.

Entries are arranged subjective. Each entry includes name of the scholar, title of the theses, name of the university, year and name of the guide followed by synopsis. Author index is provided.

11. AGRINDEX: (Food and Agricultural Organization, AGRIS Co-ordinations Centre, Rome) 1975.

Agrindex is a monthly bibliography of the world's current agricultural literature. It covers periodical and other literature monitored by participants in the International Information System for Agricultural Science and Technology in more than 100 countries.

Entries in the main section are arranged alphabetically by author under sub-topics and commodity codes within 17 subject categories. Each issue also includes personal author index, corporate entry index report and patent number index, geographical index and list of participating AGRIS centres.

Entries include entry number, author, author affiliation and address, article title in English, original title and language, journal title, country of publication, data, volume and issue numbers, page numbers, number of reference and illustrations, indication of summary and language summary. Agrindex is searchable on-line as AGRIS database.

12. Indian Library Science Abstracts, (Calcutta, Indian Association of Special Libraries and Information Centres), 1967-, Quarterly.

This abstracting journal reports work published in India. It abstracts original articles including short communication published in library science periodicals issued in India, and proceedings of conferences and symposia held in India. Indian language periodicals have been omitted.

In each issue, entries are arranged in classified order according to *Colon classification* followed by subject and author indexes. The latter are also cumulated annually.

This is a useful service for Indian library literature especially because the *Information Science Abstracts* and *Library and Information Science Abstracts* do not cover Indian literature comprehensively.

13. Biological Abstracts (Biological sciences Information Service) 1926.

It is one of the most important abstracting journal in the field of Biological Sciences, which is a semi-monthly publication. The journal abstracts and indexes current published research from biological and biomedical periodical literature published world-wide. It is available as a printed publication, or magnetic tape and on line as part of the BIOSIS preview data base. It covers 9000 periodicals in biology and biomedicine.

Abstracts in the main section are arranged by entry number under 84 alphabetical subject headings. Each issue also includes: author index, biosystematic index, generic index, concept index and subject index.

Typical entry includes: entry number, author, institution affiliation and address, article title, journal title abbreviation, volume and issue numbers, page numbers, year of publication, original language if other than English and informative abstract. Available on microfiche and microfilm also by subscription.

14. International Political Science Abstracts, Vol. 1-, 1951, London, Blackwell, 1952-, Quarterly (publisher varies).

This service is prepared by the International Political Science Association in cooperation with the International committee for Social Sciences Documentation, and with the support of UNESCO. It abstracts articles from a large number of the world's leading political science journals published in various countries. The abstracts are in English or French. It is classified by large groupings and its cumulative, annual author and subject indexes are available.

This is an excellent service in the filed of political science.

15. Psychological Abstracts. 1972-, Washington, American Psychological Association, 1927-, Monthly.

This abstracts psychological literature published all over the world in all forms including books, chapters of books and articles, doctoral dissertations and occasional reports. In addition to psychological publications, it also covers material in related disciplines like sociology, phychiatry and physiology, of special interest to psychologists. Over 800 journals, technical reports, monographs and other scientific documents are covered.

Psychological abstracts follows classified subject arrangement along with alphabetical author and subject indexes. Its monthly issues contain abstracts listed under seventeen major classification categories, with some categories having subsections.

Abstracts are non-evaluative in nature (annotations are provided for books) and are signed.

Indexes are cumulated semi-annualy. Cumulated author and subject indexes have been published by G.K. Hall and Company.

P A since 1967, is also available on machine readable tapes, which forms the basis for an automatic search and retrieval service known as Psychological Abstracts Information Service (PAIS). *PA* is an indispensible abstracting journal in the field of psychology and is published with a reasonable time-lag between the appearance of the documents and the appearance of abstracts.

16. Economic Abstracts, The Hague, Martinus Nijhoff, 1953, Semi-monthly.

This is a semi-monthly abstracting service, covering economics, finance, trade, industry, foreign aid, management, marketing and labour, compiled by the Library of the Economic Information Service (Ministry of Economic Affairs) of Netherlands.

This contains abstracts of highly selective items, especially articles in important periodicals with a more permanent value.

The main entries containing abstracts are arranged according to UDC (*Universal Decimal Classification*). Each main entry also contains descriptors in the English language. The alphabetical subject index is provided in the beginning of each issue. Author and subject indexes are cumulated on annual basis. A list of periodicals with annual indexes is provided, and short, quite excellent abstracts are given. It is a highly useful selective abstracting service in Economics.

17. Historical Abstracts, Oxford, Clio Press, 1955-, Quarterly.

HA covers all branches of world history excluding the United States and Canada, from 1450 to the present. Its scope is mainly confined to political, diplomatic, military, economic, social, cultural, religious, intellectual, scientific, technological, and medical history. However, social sciences and humanities articles are included "provided they contain a minimum 40% historical content." Area and interdisciplinary studies, economics, psychology, sociology, art, literature, philosophy, education and popular culture are also covered. It contains abstracts and shorter annotations from over 1900 journals published in 84 countries and in 45 languages. It covers books and dissertations. Approximately 23,000 entries are added per year.

HA is published in two parts (Part A: Modern history abstracts, 1450-1914, Part B: Twentieth century abstracts, 1914 to the present). Each part consists of four issues. Five-year indexes are available from V1 to V 30. North American history (United States and Canada) is covered in the sister publication, *America: History and Life*. HA is the world's largest historical abstracting service.

Current status: Most of the Indexing and Abstracting services are making use of information technology by way of computerising their services. There are around 2000 Indexing and Abstracting services at present. These services have expanded their scope, coverage and range of documents covered. A few major services are mentioned below:

Chemical titles, Polymer Science and Technology, Chemical abstracts, Chemical Biological Activities. CA concordances, Chemical Registry system, CA Patent Concordances, CA Subject Index alert, CA Source Index

Mention is also hereby made for emerging on-line databases by DIALOG and other vendors in USA. Consequently, the concept of information industry has emerged out of the recent developments by the use of information technology. In India some efforts have been made by information consultants, publishers, computer processing organizations etc. These developments have led to systematic and organized system for marketing of information.

Q. : Write brief note on Citation Indexing.

or

Briefly discuss-

— Science Citation Index

— Social Science Citation Index

— Arts and Humanities Citation Index

Ans. Citation data provide a unique view of primary research and also primary research journals which act as a vehicle of scientific research communication. A citation is the formal acknowledgement of *intellectual debt* to previously published research, publicly recorded in the references listed by the authors. Hence, citations act as an important indicator to how frequently current researchers are using the journal literature.

When one document (B) refers to another document (A) the latter has been cited by (B) as a source of information. It is said that the document 'A' has been cited in a reference of document 'B'. In this sense, citation and reference are frequently used interchangeably.

Citation Indexing is mainly the contribution of Eugene Garfield of the Institute for Scientific Information, Philadelphia to the field of indexing. The failure of the schemes of classification to meet the challenge of proliferating knowledge is the basis of the new method. The principle of citation indexing has been derived from *Shepard's citations,* a legal tool that has been used in the United States since 1873. By looking up the case number for any given decision in *Shepard's citations,* a lawyer can locate references to all subsequent citing cases. The *science citation index* (1963), *Art and Humanities Citation Index* and *Social sciences citation index* (1973), published by the Institute for Scientific Information are the best examples of the kind.

Citation Indexing is based on the assumption that (1). an author's references (citations) to previously published material indicate *subject relationship* between his current article and the older publications, and (2) articles that cite the same publications usually have subject relationships with each other. Cited items can be books, articles, letters, theses, editorials and other forms of published material.

A citation index is nothing but an-ordered list of cited articles, each accompanied by a list of citing articles. The citing article is identified as a source and the cited articles as a reference. Citations in journals explicitly stated a connection between two documents one which cites, and the other which is cited; whereas citation of secondary journals does not usually imply any connection between documents.

Besides, retrieval, citation indexes can be used for historical research. In addition to identifying individuals whose work had impact on a branch of science, citation networks can also bring into focus many other characteristics of science e.g., disprove or prove certain prevailing scientific myths, anomalies in history of scientific development etc. With the easy access to large computer memories and online databases, it is now possible to specify some starting point - a person, a word, a citation, a place and display not only a list of pertinent papers but also a graphical approximation of a history of development of a subject.

Citation indexes help in :

— retrieving information on new rather than previously published works.

— tracking citations of specific works/authors, etc.

— conducting in-depth searches even if one knows only the name of one active author or bibliographic details of one relevent article.

— identifying currently active of research.

The major defect lies in its inability to be selective. Quality is in danger of being sacrificed at the altar of quantity because of the inherent inability of any mechanical system to be discriminating. Its failure and success also depends on the use of proper terms in the title. The problem is more serious in respect of the humanities and social sciences, due to their imprecise terminology. All said and done citation indexing is a great advance on existing systems and is a welcome response to the Niagra of proliferating literature.

The Institute for Scientific Information (ISI), Philadelphia, PA, publishes three citatin indexes viz. Science Citation Index (SCI), Social

Sciences Citation Index (SSCI) and Arts and Humanities Citation Index (A & HCI). The Science Citation Index (SCI) is one of the most important citation indexes. The advent of Science Citation Index (SCI) in 1963 was a great event not only in the domain of Library and Information Science, but also in the fields of Science and Bibliometrics. Ever since its origin, it has been the most powerful tool in the hands of the bibliometricians and allied professionals.

Science Citation Index, Philadelphia, Institute for Scientific Information, 1963-, bimonthly, cumulated annually and quinquennially.

SCI analyzes 3000 journals, proceedings, symposia, reports, patents, editorials, monographs and multi-authored books (thematic collection of papers). Monographic series are indexed, each chapter being indexed as an article. It covers the most important and significant scientific and technical journals. It is an inter disciplinary index to literature of science, medicine, agriculture, technology and the behavioural sciences.

SCI consists of three separate indexes, though these are related. They include citation index, source index and the permuterm subject index. All of them are published quarterly for the first three quarters of the year. Indexes belonging to the fourth quarter are incorporated in the annual cumulation for each index.

The *Citation index* provides the following entry points to the literature:

— Corporate Index Section: under the name of each organization, citation for all items attributed to the organization and published during the period indexed is to be found.

— Citation Index: arranged alphabetically by cited author and within this the arrangement is by chronology by cited year.

— Source Index: a complete author index for citing authors

— Permuterm Subject Index: an alphabetic list of significant words extracted from the titles of all source items processed for the *Citation Index.*

In a nutshell, the fundamental question answered quickly through the *Citation index* is where and by whom has a paper been cited in the literature? Citation indices provide a new approach to bibliographic reference based not on the principle of subject affinity but on the assumption that the writings of an author have an underlying unity and can form the basis for an initial literature survey.

Source index is arranged alphabetically by source-author. Source-author is the author full title of the citing (source) items. Title of periodical, volume, issue, page, year, type of item and number of references in the bibliography of the source item.

Permuterm subject index is produced by a computer which permutes all significant words within each title and subtitle of every item included in the source index. It uses the searching technique of following up references cited in relevant papers.

SCI tells us for a given specific work, "What has happened since." Thus, it provides (a) for each cited reference, subsequent current works, which cite it, (b) what more recent works cite specific, older works, and (c) subject approach by means of various words or descriptors representative of the main subject matter of an article. The database from which volumes are compiled is maintained on magnetic tapes and is updated on a weekly basis. These tapes are manipulated by computer to produce various kinds of lists.

It is claimed that this form of indexing is able to identify a specific work unambigyously and, thereby, the subject concepts discussed in it are also identified. Thus, *SCI* enables a user to trace a new application, improvements of theories, instruments, chemicals, etc.

Social Sciences Citation Index, Philadelphia, Institute for Scientific Information, 1973-, published in June and October with annual cumulation, within four months of the end of each year.

SSCI indexes every article and every significant editorial item from every issue of over one thousand of the most important social science periodicals. It also covers another 2200 periodicals on a selective basis, indexing only those articles with are relevant to the social sciences. Besides, it also covers many important monographs. Like SCI, it also contains three separate indexes, namely, *source index, citation index*, and the *permuterm subject index*. Its arrangement follows SCI and comments given for SCI are equally applicable for SSCI.

It is certainly an invaluable tool for social scientists but its cost is too high for Indian libraries.

Arts and Humanities Citation Index, Philadelphia Institute for Scientific Information, 1977-

It covers over 1000 journals in literature, history, languages, religion, philosophy, drama/theatre, art, music and other related fields. In addition, over 125 new, multi-authored books are indexed per annum on a chapter-level. Over 80,000 new items are indexed every year. It indexes articles, book reviews, fiction, poetry and correspondence and provides author, title and subject approach. Allows to start a "search with an earlier work central to your topic and find newer items that have cited or referenced it and are thus likely to be on the same subject. When a work of art (a painting, musical composition, film, etc.) is the basic subject of an article, it too appears as an indexing term in *A & HCI's* Index." This is the only large-scale multidisciplinary index to the literature of the arts and humanities.

Q. : What is Current Awareness Service (CAS)? How does it differ from Selective Dissemination of Information (SDI)?

or

What is Selective Dissemination of Information (SDI)? Explain the steps involved in providing SDI in special library. How does SDI differ from CAS.

or

Describe the different methods of dissemination of current information and explain the role of CAS and SDI in this process.

or

What is Current Awareness Service (CAS)? Explain briefly any two CAS Services provided in a special library.

or

Describe the importance and preparation of 'Users Profile' in the SDI service in a information center. Also draw the flow chart of SDI system.

or

What are the components of a SDI system? Explain the role of a user profile in SDI.

Ans. : There has been an exponential growth of information contained in publications originating from various sources, in different languages and forms. The conventional indexes and other dissemination techniques are not adequate to keep pace with the accelerated output of scientific & technical literature. Proliferation of these publications create further problems for those who want to keep abreast of recent developments. The perishable nature of new information and pressing demand for speedier communication in science are the identified problems. It becomes evident that new techniques are required for quickly announcing and disseminating current information and making information system users aware of the most recent developments in their selected fields. It becomes necessary for libraries & information centres to devise ways and means to fulfil this need i.e., by designing and developing new and innovative information services. Two such services are Current Awareness Services (CAS) and Selective Dissemination of Information (SDI).

1. Current Awareness Service

At present time, the libraries and information centres has been providing new documentation services which is helpful in research & development. Industrial productivity, management marketing and explosion of publication in the world is increasing day by day. These publications are in different languages. But for any active researcher it is absolutely essential that he keeps himself up-to-date in the field of his work. In addition, he is also required to know the developments in other broader and peripheral areas which impinge on his field. This type of approach to information is known as current approach to information. Any service intended to meet this current approach is generally known as current awareness service or CAS.

The most important characteristics of CAS, are as under :

— The service is usually in the form of a publication, and attempts to being information that is current or new or of recent origin to the attention of its users.

— The service does not seek to answer any specific questions that the user may have.

— The service is usually confined to a well defined subject area or topic. However topics from related areas are also covered in the service.

— The service may sometimes confine itself to a given type of literature, e.g. patents, or may cover different types of literatures.

— The service could be bibliographical in nature, e.g., a list of references with or without abstracts. This service could also be discursive, e.g. a newsletter. In this type of current awareness service usually there are short contributions from professionals with the objective of highlighting recent developments or exchanging information and ideas.

— The service endeavors to alert its users to recent development or news as quickly as possible.

— The service attempts to make browsing convenient and easy for the user.

Although published current awareness service is the predominant form, more recently the service has also been using electronic means. This usually talks the form of an electronic bulletin board which is computer based, and accessible to users through their terminals. The user browses through items in the electronic board just as he would do in a publication.

Type of CAS

There are four methods which are also considered as types of CAS, are described with their characteristic features. These types of service are: Contents-by-Journal, Current Awareness Lists, Research-in-Progress Bulletin and Newspaper Clipping Services.

(i) Contents-by-Journal Service : In this service, the documentation section of library, publishes the tables lists of commercial publications and serves current aware services. This is the easiest method as compared to others that requires only the reproduction of the content pages of selected periodicals. It is also a cheapest and quickest way of providing current awareness service. This is because very little intellectual effort is involved in providing this service. However, this service also suffers from disadvantages. Some of these are:

— A lot of effort is called for on the part of the user to discover information that is useful to him.

— Since this type of service provides only titles of papers, it is difficult to determine the usefulness of papers without actually examining the full papers.

(ii) Current Awareness Lists : In this service, the library or documentation centre scans primary journals and other sources of current information received in the library to identify potentially useful articles of interest to their users. The bibliographical details of such articles are collected, and classified or grouped into broad or narrow subject groups. At periodic intervals, such as fortnightly, monthly, etc., the collected bibliographic entries are listed under the different subject headings, class numbers, or groups. The list is then duplicated and circulated to users.

Examples: Chemical titles of the chemical abstract service and current chemical papers of the chemical society, Britain.

(iii) Research-in-Progress Bulletins : This is another type of CAS, and as its name suggests, it alerts users to new research projects and progress made in on-going research projects. This type of current-awareness service usually required joint effort of more than one organizations working in similar or closely related research areas.

A research-in-progress bulletin usually contains information about the laboratory at which the project is being done, name of researchers, sources of funds, duration of the project, and special equipment in use, if any. In addition, it includes a short description of the research project and/or progress made till date.

At present the trend is for the creation and maintenance of research-in-progress databases in computer readable form similar to the USDA's CRIS system. Such a database can then be used both for retrospective search before a new project is formulated as well as for current awareness services. This type of database can also be used for other purposes, e.g., to produce an inventory of specialized equipment, centres of specialization, etc.

(iv) Newspaper Clippings : Newspapers are a current awareness media, since they publish news of current happenings on the political, social and economic front of a nation or region. Newspapers cary useful information for everyone form housewives to top management's of companies and cabinet ministers. Again, newspapers are of different kinds. Some of them are local or regional in their orientation and coverage, others are national or international. Further, some newspapers specialize in economic or financial news and contain in depth analysis of industry, trade, banking commerce, sprits, etc.

In the Newspaper Clippings Service, a library subscribes to one or more daily or weekly newspapers, carefully chosen for their coverage of areas of interest to the organization of which the library is a part. Each of these newspapers is scanned and any items of news that are considered to be of interest to the user group are clipped and paisted on a sheet of thicker paper of card. The clipping is then assigned one or more subject heading or group/class codes. At periodic intervals, e.g., daily or weekly, the clippings are arranged by subject headings or group code and disseminated to users.

It is customary for any special library to provide some kind of CAS to its users. There are at least four ways of providing in-house CAS:

(i) display of currently received documents;

(ii) notifying the receipts of new arrivals;

(iii) routing of journals; and

(iv) publication of in-house current awareness bulletins.

The display method is practiced by all libraries. Current issues of journals are displayed of specially designed racks to facilitate browsing by users. Most researchers adopt this method of keeping in touch with the current journal literature. The display of newly acquired books in the library also falls into this category. Besides, there are a number of commercially available current awareness publications. Current Contents, published by the Institute for Scientific Information, reproduces tables of contents of highly cited journals.

2. Selective Dissemination of Information (SDI)

The objective of SDI is to keep users of the system informed of new developments in their respective areas of interest without overburdening them with non-relevant and unwanted documents. It provides notifications of new primary documents.

Luhn of IBM introduced the concept of Selective Dissemination of Information (SDI) in 1961. According to him SDI is "that service within an organization that concerns itself *machine-assisted* channeling of *new* items of information from *whatever source* to those points within the organizations were the *probability of usefulness,* in connection with *current work or interest is high".*

Thus, SDI is a changed form of CAS, based on the mechanized system emphasizing it to personal or every researcher to his need pin-pointedly. User is provided the information actually he needs.

The main characteristics of SDI are:

(i) It uses computers which made their appearance in the 1950s and were beginning to be used in handling information.

(ii) It is concerned with new information or information of recent origin, or that information which is current. Hence, SDI is a form of current awareness service.

(iii) The sources of new or current information may be both within the organization and outside it. The fact that there are too many sources of information necessitated such a service in the first instance.

(iv) SDI ensures that new information which is highly useful should be channelled (i.e., directed or disseminated) to those points (i.e., users, scientists, managers, etc.) within the organization.

(v) The channelling or directing of information to a given user is determined by the nature of his current work or interests.

Work Flow in SDI Service

SDI can be regarded as a by-product CAS, which not only serves current information but is also totally user-oriented. Conceptually, the work flow including the main jobs and activities in SDI are explained in the following diagram.

The different steps for providing SDI service, are discussed below:

(i) User profile: First of all the selection of the group of users who require such a service should be made. The interest of each user or groups of users are ascertained and represented in the form of the pattern of terms, keywords, code numbers, etc. Such a record of interest pattern is called a profile. These individual profiles are then organized into users profile file.

(ii) Documents Profile: The incoming documents are analyzed and the subject content of each of them is represented in the same indexing language that has been used in the preparation of user profiles. The document descriptions are then organized into a document profile file.

(iii) Matching: The users profile file and the documents profile file are compared at fixed intervals. When a close match is observed, as per instructions, between any user profile and a document record, the details of both the records are noted.

(iv) Notification: Each individual user receives notification from the system if any close match was observed between his interest profile and any document record. The notification may include bare citations of the documents, or citations with abstracts or keywords. The notification could be accompanied by the document itself or a copy of it.

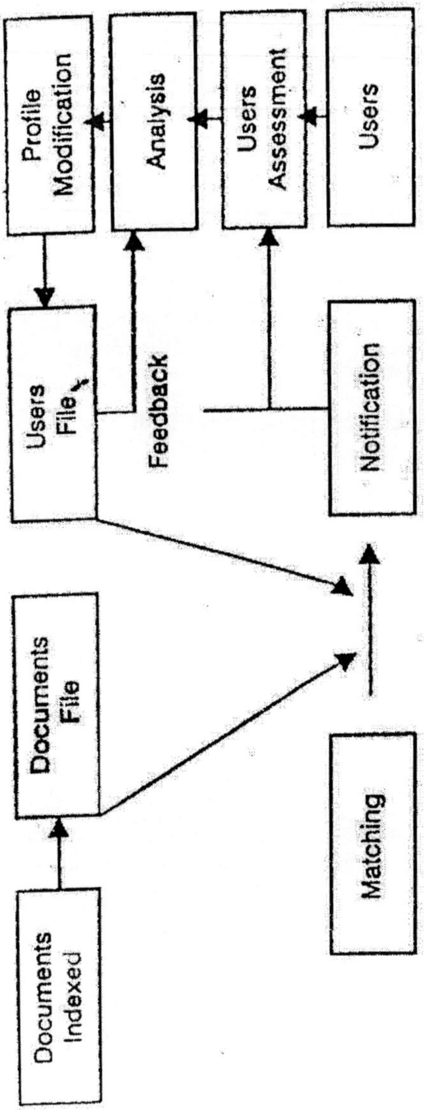

Conceptual Workflow Diagram for SDI Service

(v) **Response or Feedback:** An important feature of SDI system is its mechanism of feedback. It is a mechanism through which the response of each subscriber to each notification can be obtained or observed by the system. For example, the user may be asked to check in a printed card, sent along with each notification, how far the notified references were of relevance to him. Similarly the response of a subscriber could be known by noting whether bare citation was enough for him or he requested an abstract or was he so interested that a copy of the document was requested. Another type of response is the referral response wherein the recipient instructs the system that a particular document, notified to him, would be of interest to another subscriber of SDI.

(vi) **Modification:** In the process of going through the notifications, a user may indicate the usefulness of the documents disseminated to him/her or point out that output was not useful. At this stage, the SDI system is to modify the particular profile. This implies that the modification of the users profile is guided largely by the feedback provided by the user. The SDI system operations analyze the reasons for the dissemination of the items that were not found useful. This could result in the revision or modification of the users profile or search expression for the user. The modified profiles' performance is again monitored to ensure that it is better than the earlier profile.

Another possibility of modification arises when the user tells about a change in his interests. For example, if a user takes up a new research project, then his/her interests may change and to this extent he may inform the SDI system operators to modify the profile suitably.

It is in the provision of a mechanism for the collection of feedback and modification of user profiles that the SDI is fundamentally different from other models of current awareness provision. Personalization and selectivity of service to the user, and the possibility of continuous interaction with them provides an opportunity for effective use of the documentary resources. SDI Services have been known to generate more demand for documents than other modes of dissemination service. The possibility of good interaction between users and information specialists as a result of SDI brings about a better acquisition of documents, indexing and abstracting services.

Recent Developments & Trends in SDI

The concept of SDI from the earlier times when Peter Luhn introduced it has undergone a significant change particularly due to computerized processing facilities. It was the service that required each orgainzation to develop its own computer readable document database or document profile against which the user profiles were to be matched. This was the option during the time that Luhn first thought out of SDI. It is no longer necessary today for each organization to build its own database, since databases are now available in computer-readable form in almost all areas of science, technology and social sciences. These databases can be used locally by an organization for use at their own computer. In other words, the organization subscribes to one or more databases, creates profiles for its users, and periodically matches the profiles against the various issues of the computer-readable database to produce SDI outputs. This method of providing SDI service, however, is costlier since the subscription to the computer-readable database can be expensive. However, the same may be suited to an organization which has a very large number of users who require SDI, and can therefore justify the cost of subscription to the database.

The availability of databases for on-line searching enables also the storage of User Profile on the vendor's computer. The profile is matched periodically against one or more databases to produce SDI outputs that are then sent to the user. The user pays a fee for using the database, the SDI output, and for the computer time used. He also pays the amount for using the telecommunication lines. The charges for access are considerable cheaper than it was when the user had to use the service of a Centralized Information Dissemination Service. Further, the user can modify his profile whenever so desired. Another important advantage of this method is the fact that the User Profile can be built with several elements, such as key words, names of authors, names of languages, etc. It can also contain data of those elements which should be eliminated so that the SDI output becomes a truly customized product.

Thus, it can be seen that the SDI service which began on a local level service to their users by several organizations, has now become a service that is provided centrally by on-line vendor at considerably less cost, and providing far greater access to the worlds' output of information than was possible in the past.

Difference between C.A.S. and S.D.I.

Main differences between C.A.S. and S.D.I are

1. The objective of CAS is not to answer of a specific question but to provide update information of new developments and newly published documents.

   Whereas, SDI provides answer of a specific query to a particular user. It is truely personal base service.

2. CAS consumes time and labour both. Since a long lists are published in this CAS so researcher gets his desired information.

   SDI prepares bibliographies of a specific subject and provide to those user who needs them only. Thus, it is time and labour saving.

3. CAS provides information of detailed and multi-subjects while SDI provides only one subject and its related uses. CAS provides the information to a user other than his need too while SDI assists to the specific need only.

4. CAS can be provided more speedily, while SDI takes time to prepare bibliography.

In short, the 'CAS' helped lot in information collection and retrieval but to avoid its limitations, SDI services started, for which the credit goes to Mr. Luhan. Now-a-days both services are being provided through computer.

Q. : What is translation service? How far are translations are representation of the original text? Elucidate.

or

Discuss translation service. Describe the problem faced by a library in providing translation service.

or

Write the difference between translation and translation service. Describe the translation services in India.

or

Define the translation service. Describe the need for translation service.

Ans. Mostly researchers and scientists are anxious to study basic and primary documents for their research projects. Sometimes the basic documents are in such a language script from which the researcher is not familiar with the language. To make use of such documents translation services are needed. Generally translation services are provided by specialized institutions.

In an ordinary way, a translation is turning, writing or rendering from one language to another. Translator is one who translates from one language into another or from and older form of language into the modern form without changing the meaning of the content of original.

Kinds of translation

Translation may be divided into following two kinds:-

1. **Adhoc Translation :** This type of translation is the selective translation of the articles published in current literature.
2. **Cover to Cover Translation :** In this method every word of the material is being translated into the target language. This method takes extract time, money and labour in comparison to adhoc translation.

Need and Importance of Translation

It is fact, only about 50% of the technical literature produced every year is published in English. An analysis of the balance of non-English literature reveals that Russian occupies the foremost position with a share of nearly 20% followed by German (nearly 8%), French and Japanese (5% each). Italian and Spanish, Portugese, Hungarian, Czech and Chinese are other important languages of world scientific literature. Obviously no one is expected to have proficiency in more than one or two languages, and unless some effective mechanism is created after getting over language barrier, no researcher can have totality of information in his field of specialization.

Therefore, the researcher needs translation to utilize these literature. The research work needs to give its high result to the project assigned, and it is possible only when translation is available. Language barrier is not so effective if translation is good instead of abstracting.

Problems Faced by a Library in Providing Translation

There are so many problems in providing translation by the documentation centres and libraries. These problems are as follows:-

1. **Supply of Translators:** Though there are much possibilities of demand of good translators in libraries but no trained staff are

available. In India there are 16 languages. Documents are quite available in English and Hindi but Sanskrit language needs good translators. Unfortunately in our country the youth is not getting the art of translation training. The need of translation is increasing day by day at one side while good translators are not available on the other side. This problem almost exist in all country but in India it is too much.

2. **Quality of Translators:** It is very difficult to translate the document from one language to another. Merely to know different languages is not adequate. It needs skill and depth knowledge of grammar which is not available in our country.

3. **Knowledge of Language:**It is common feature that translators having little knowledge of foreign languages cannot do translation of high quality. Though these personnel has passed certificates, degrees etc. but to be a successful translator this is sufficient. By passing examination only does not guarantee of a good and successful translator. Therefore, language problem exist in translator.

4. **Delay:** The another problem of translation is of delaying. Sometimes it takes much time that there are many changes, addition and alterations in the document and this makes delay in translation.

5. **Specialization and Vocabulary:** In our country whatever the dictionaries, thesaurus and vocabulary are available, has no uniformity and has difference of words and its meaning. Therefore to avoid and solve this problem, efforts should be made for.

Translation Services

Translation work by its very nature is extremely expensive and time consuming. A good subject knowledge, coupled with fluency in both source and target languages is a rare combination. This has prompted all those who are interested in translation work to seek mutual help and cooperation, both at national and international level. This cooperation has resulted in what are called translation pools or translation banks. Over the years, a number of agencies have come up to help the users with their translation problem.

At international centres following are working.

(a) **National translation centre (NTC) :** In humanities, NTC is located at the John Crerar Library, Chicago. It is a cooperative non-profit enterprise and its services are designed to eliminate costly duplication of translation effort and to provide free funds for translating new material.

The NTC was formally organized in 1953 after having existed for several years as a voluntary project of the Science Technology Division of the Special Libraries Association (SLA). Translations available from the NTC are also available from the BLLD of Great Britain on loan (U.K. only) or in photocopy.

(b) **International Translation Centre (ITC) :** The centre came into existence in 1960 under its former name the "European Translation Centre." The present name was adopted in 1975. Its general aim is to act as an instrument for the exchange of information by means of translations and prevention of duplication of translation work. It is situated in Delft, Netherlands.

(c) **Federation International des Traducturs (FIT)** located at Belgium issues "Babel" quarterly. "Bable" is an international journal devoted to information, development and research in the field of translation and interpreting.

(d) **International Association of Conference Interpretes, Geneva at Switzerland.**

(e) **International Association of Conference Translators, at Vaud, Switzerland.**

Though in India, no satisfactory efforts are being made in comparison to other countries of the world. Some institutions are doing lot but even then the result is not upto the mark. These institutions require to continue research work and translation services.

In India, INSDOC - Indian National Scientific Documentation Centre, New Delhi (now NISCAIR) and DRTC - Documentation Research & Training Centre, Bangalore have been providing translation services. Here about 16000 scientific literature in different foreign languages are stored and every year 700 are translated.

Besides, IASLIC, DESIDOC, BARC, National Agriculture Library, Institution of Technology etc., are doing translation work in their own subject field.

There are many more institutions which are busy in translating work like Lab Institutions, Information Centres, Documentation Centres but there is no coordination between these institution as a result there is no check to duplication.

Q. : Write briefly about literature searching; also differentiate it from reference service.

or

Write short note on literature searching.

Ans. : The ultimate objective of any documentation or information activity is to provide an user with the information he requires, to the extent he requires, within a reasonable time and cost frame. There are occasions when users want to know "everything that has been published" on a subject. The most important reason is that they want to know the state-of-the-art before undertaking a new research project. Such information need can be satisfied by undertaking a comprehensive search in bibliographies - the indexing and abstracting publications. This is known as literature searching. The structure and arrangement of these secondary publications facilitate undertaking comprehensive literature search. *Search* in hard copy documents is known as manual searching, but literature searching can also be done using a computer.

Steps in Literature Searching

Literature searching can be undertaken by the researcher himself or he may delegate the task to a library staff. Many libraries now provide literature search service.

Before intimating a search, it is essential that the searcher understands what the user wants. Understanding what he wants is critical in literature searching, because of the amount of time needed for the purpose. This is more important when an online databases are used. Some of the following information must be sought from the requester before proceeding on literature search:

(i) A clear statement of the subject,

(ii) How far back in-line the search should go,

(iii) Whether the search is to be comprehensive,

(iv) Whether the focus should be on specific regions, and

(v) Whether specific types of document (e.g., patents, reports literature) should be included/excluded. Successful literature search needs a thorough familiarity with the hard copy indexing and abstracting documents as well as their computerized versions, if online databases are used.

The various steps of literature search may be understood as under.

(i) Selection of Sources: One very good approach to literature search is looking up on appropriate selection of articles in a bibliography, an encyclopaedia or a review publication. This will provide a background of technical knowledge and also some useful references. After this preliminary search is over, searches should be carried out with secondary publications like abstracting and indexing services. Depending upon the topic, any one of the following situations may arise:

(a) Secondary periodicals are available on the subject.

(b) Secondary periodicals are available on the subject as well as on broader subjects.

(c) No secondary periodical is available on the subject, but available on a broader subject.

(d) No secondary periodical is available on the subject, not even on a broader subject.

(ii) Search in Secondary Sources: When secondary periodicals are available on the subject as well as on broader subjects, search must first begin with the secondary periodicals on the subject proper, supplemented by references collected from the periodicals covering broader subject. Usually, the secondary periodicals covering broader subjects will cover journals peripheral and some times quite alien to the main subject of search. But it is a well known fact that there is a considerable scatter of information on a given topic over a whole range of periodicals covering core, peripheral and alien fields. Although a few core journals, cover considerable part (50-60%) of the published literature on a given topic, yet sizeable portion (30-40%) can be covered by scanning a very large number of peripheral journals in the alien field, for example, an article of medical interest, say malaria eradication, may be published in a sociology journal.

Skills are to be developed for the consultation of secondary periodicals, since wide variation is observed in the pattern of the arrangement of the entries as well as in the methods of indexing, and also the types of indexes provided. Usually the indexing method used is explained in the introduction to the index. Pertinent subject headings vary from one secondary periodical to the other. The searcher should acquaint himself not only with scientific nomenclature and terminology, but also with popular and trade names.

(iii) Search in Other Sources: No search will be complete without a look at other sources of information, specially for topics for which there are no secondary periodicals available like conference proceedings, research reports, theses, patens, standards and specifications, trade literature and in some cases monographs and treatises. There may be cases where information will be available from non-documentary sources, like institutions and experts.

Any of the above type of information, sources may be needed to consult at sometime or the other. So a knowledge of the main characteristics of all types and familiarity with these sources are needed. Much of the expertise of searching for information lies in choosing the appropriate sources to consult in each case and the best order in which to consult them.

(iv) Recording of References or Information: Every literature searcher develops his own style of taking notes of references. While every effort should be made to optimize the time and efficiency of search; it is well to remember that a few extra seconds spent to make proper preliminary records may save many frustrating hours later. The first principle in saving search time, is to use a single operation to serve multiple purposes. For example, reference recorded on sheets of paper can serve only one purpose- providing a list of reference without any order. Records on cards or slips, with one reference per card or slip, can serve several purposes. Abstracts can be added under each reference, if required, and the cards can be arranged by subject, or author or chronologically, as required.

(v) Presentation of Results : To be most effective, presentation of search results, require as much skill and care as correctly defining the subject and parameters of search. Reading lists need only be selective and may require brief annotations. But a search on behalf of a researcher will need exhaustive treatment, and may need slanted abstracts confirming to the users need. Choice of arrangements also depends on what the user needs-alphabetical (by author's surname), chronological source-wise (monographic, periodical), non-conventional (microfilms, audio visuals etc.), subject classified, or some hybrid arrangement. The best one is the one from which the user gets the most help with the least effort. An indication should be given as to how authoritative and how complete the bibliography is? The sources should be stated giving the exact references.

Online Searching

The real difference between manual searching and online searching lies, according to William A. Katz, in the mechanics and the jargon of the latter. However, after doing a number of searches, one becomes proficient in searching databases online. In short, it is practice that makes one perfect in the art. Besides, each international information service has brought out its user guide which helps attain mastery over, what Katz calls 'mechanics'.

Online searching is particularly helpful and resorted to when (i) depth search is involved, and (ii) exhaustive search is called for. Yet another merit of the online searching is the facility it offers of using Boolean logic which allows limiting or expanding the search as required. Because of the three logical operations symbolized by OR, AND and NOT, it is possible in co-ordinate the relevant forms by modifying the search strategy. The online search, unlike the manual search, ensures at once enhanced, quick and refined access.

Some Examples of Online Databases

The adoption of modern technology has resulted in the proliferation of machine readable databases. The National Library of Medicine (USA) designed its MEDLARS which became operational in 1964. Later appeared its online version as MEDLINIE. Engineering Index of the Engineers' Joint Council (USA) and Biological Abstracts soon had their corresponding online versions, viz., COMPENDEX and BIOSIS. Yet another very large online database is that of information services for Physics and Engineering Communities, called INSPEC (UK) representing the three printed versions of Physics Abstracts,

Electrical and Electronic Abstracts and Computers and Control Abstracts. CA search and AGRICOLA, the online counterparts respectively of Chemical Abstracts and Bibliography of Agriculture (NAIUSA) are worth mentioning. These are all also devoted to sciences.

Of the social scinces, there exist a number of large online databases particularly in economics, psychology, political science and management. For example, PsychINFO is the online version of Psychological Abstracts.

MARC database of the Library of Congress is a good source to search for resources in humanities. It is also worth while to know about two full text online databases one is LEXIS in law and the other is NEXIS that offers several newspapers and business publications. But whatever the type of search may be, expertise in literature search can be gained only by experience. Some attitudes or traits conducive to a good literature search are: imagination, mental flexibility, thoroughness and orderliness, persistency, judgment in resolving contradictory information and accuracy in recording. A basic knowledge in the field of search is considered helpful though not absolutely essential.

Reference Service versus Literature Search

Reference service, according to the A.L.A Glossary of Library Terms, is "that phase of library work which is directly concerned with assistance to reader in securing information and in using the resources of the library in study and research". Usually a reference service responds to a specific piece of information-about a person, about a place or event, a method, procedure, formula etc. The nature of information sought in such a situation is very specific and quite often the answer could be found from the conventional reference tools, like dictionaries, encyclopaedias, manuals, handbooks, gazetteers, directories, yearbooks, etc.

Literature search, on the other hand, can be equated to "long range reference service", where the search has to be more exhaustive-both in depth and extent. The range and complexity of reference sources to be consulted are wider and generally more than one source has to be consulted to adequately carry out a literature search. Besides bibliographies, secondary sources like abstracting and indexing services, reviewing periodicals are the main sources of information. The demand for this service has been growing with the growth of scientific and technical literature which has assumed frightening proportion in the post-Second World War era.

Q. : Write an essay on Document Delivery Services with special reference to India.

or

Write short note on document delivery service.

Ans. : The foremost objective of libraries is to provide documents demanded by scholars. It is not an easy task to cope with in the present conditions, when on the one hand there is a phenomenal increase in published and unpublished material, and on the other increasing publication costs have rendered libraries less and less self-sufficient. Non-availability of a document however does not always mean that it is not physically available in a particular library or libraries but that it is not located on demand. Therefore it is necessary to devise ways and means to increase access to records and materials to two groups of people librarians and users. Document delivery service is the solution for this problem, which provides a copy of the desired documents against the request of users. It can be made available to the users as photocopies, microforms or through electronic transfer through online networks. While the photocopies and microforms are sent by post, electronic transfer can be made by fax, electronic mail, or Internet or any other available network. Normally, the copies are not supplied by fax or electronic mail, etc., due to various reasons.

Document delivery service is a restrictive service and it usually constrained by the provisions of copyright and intellectual property rights.

The efficiency of DDS is based on three basic criteria:-

1. Satisfaction level,
2. Speed of supply, and
3. Cost.

1. Satisfaction Level: It is the proportion of request satisfied out of the total number of requests received. A satisfaction rate of 90% will be very good level to aim at.

2. Speed of supply: The speed of supply depends on:-

(a) the speed with which a user wants literature so that there is no genuine dislocation in his work schedule.

(b) the speed of supply he expects and below which he feels frustrated.

The success is determined by:-

(a) the ability to locate a copy.

(b) the probability that the item is actually available e.g. not misplaced, not in use or at binding etc.

(c) the willingness of the holding library to lend it-reasons for not lending include fragility, rarity, reference, value or regency of acquisition or a blanket policy of not to lend.

3. Cost : In devising a cost effective system, all types of costs should be taken into account-direct, indirect and capital cost as well.

Need of Document Delivery Service

(i) The literature output has been phenomenal.

(ii) No library, not even the largest one, can afford to subscribe to such a large amount of literature.

(iii) The hike in the cost of publications imposes a definite strat on the number of titles a library can subscribe to and leaves. Thus, user has to look elsewhere for their requirements.

(iv) Institutions invariably grow over the syears, as represented in the broadening of their purview as well as in the number of scientific and technical personnel. But if this increase in the personnel is contrasted with the feable increase in the library budgets, we find a definite fall in the ratio of new acquisitions to the library users, so the need to seek publications/copies from other institutions and centres is becoming an unavoidable reality day by day.

(v) Demand for document copies has been stimulated by improvements in bibliographic access; users are thus presented with larger and wider access of references than here-to-before and a lightening speed that heightens the expectation of quick access to the actual document copies.

Type (Models) of Document Delivery System

UNESCO has identified four basic supply models for Documentary Delivery Service.

1. Centralized model.

2. Completely decentralized unplanned model.
3. Planned decentralized model.
4. Partially centralized model.

1. Centralized Model: In this model a highly comprehensive collection is especially developed in a single institution. The main advantages of this model are:-

(i) Being a single channel of request and supply saves time and money as well.

(ii) The speed of supply is maximum.

(iii) Direct costs of handling requests are low.

(iv) The demand can be monitored and analyzed for effective collection building and as well as monitor performance as a routine job.

(v) It can be geared specifically for document supply, i.e., for fast retrieval and supply of specific terms.

But there are some disadvantages too :

(i) The costs of setting up and maintaining a central collection-stock, buildings staff equipment etc. are high.

(ii) Unit costs are high unless demand is heavy.

(iii) Any future failure to finance in adequality could undermine the whole system.

2. Completely Decentralized Unplanned Model : Most existing systems are basically of this nature, i.e. without any special attempt at subject or other specialization, the resources of libraries are made known to other libraries by means of union catalogues.

Its advantages are :

(i) Libraries need not require additional resources.

(ii) Libraries are not under any obligation to participate in this cooperative activity.

(iii) The libraries are free to build their collection based on the local demands.

The disadvantages of this model are :

(i) The services is slow, inefficient and costly.

(ii) To achieve the active and continuing co-operation of a large number of libraries is very difficult.

(iii) There is no coordination in building the collection. This results in unnecessary duplication.

(iv) This system places the burden mainly on large libraries.

(v) Substantial resources are necessary to contract and maintain the union catalogue on which success of the whole system depends.

3. Planned Decentralized Model : In this system a number of libraries build a collection in a planned manner, depending upon their area of specialization. In addition to a core collection, they acquire additional sources as are identified by the system to participate in this cooperative venture.

The advantages of this model are :

(i) Most of the requests can be sent direct.

(ii) Extensive resources can be developed serving both local subject specialists as well as national needs.

(iii) The cost of additions to resources are not high.

(iv) The system does not place a heavy interlending burden on any one particular library.

(v) The planned collection building results in optional utilization of the collection budget.

But there are some disadvantages also,

(i) The total national cost may be high because of the extensive duplication among the special subject libraries and other research libraries.

(ii) Conflict may arise between lending and other normal functions.

(iii) Procedures of the library have to be adjusted to give an efficient lending service.

(iv) It requires libraries to subscribe those materials that they do not need for their own clients.

(v) Requests have to be directed to a large number of libraries.

4. Partially Centralized Model : The partially centralized model attempts a reasonable resource building of heavy demand materials and depends on a limited number of libraries in the country for the supply of document copies not available with it.

Both the advantages and disadvantages to be effective, strong central planning and coordination is done by one centre viz. a National document delivery centre. A partially centralized model is more advisable as total centralization in the strict sense is unattainable.

Methods of Requests and Supply

Requests for documents are received by mail, telephone, telex, fascimile system, e-mail or on-line computerized database systems. Any of the above methods can be used for the delivery of the documents.

Some examples of Document Delivery Supply Centre: *International scene*

1. **British Library Document Supply Centre:** BLDSC is an example of partially centralized model with some back-up libraries. The centre was formed in 1973 (earlier known as British library, lending division) by amalgamation of National Central Library (NCL) in London and National lending library for science and technology in Boston.
2. National Periodicals Centre in USA.
3. Document Delivery Service of Australian National Science and Technical Library (ANSTEL).
4. USSR, Lenin State Library provides document supply service at National level.

Indian Scene

1. Document supply service of INSDOC : It is a national level decentralized collection of resources held in various science libraries in the country.

2. Contents, Abstracts and Photocopies Service (CAPS) of INSDOC : This service is started by INSDOC in April 1992. Under this service, the individual or institutional subscriber can get monthly dispatches of contents of 40 journals selected from about 50000 core Indian and foreign journals.

3. SSDC Inter-Library Resource Centre (ILRC) in collaboration with Jawaharlal Nehru University.

Electronic Document Delivery System

The systems using optical disc based technology or on-line computerized databases or any other electronic media for receipt and supply of requests of documents are known as "Electronic document delivery system". The main advantage of these systems is its speed. Among other advantages are, sharing of resources by different centres, offering scanning facility to the requester to assess the utility of a document before placing an order etc. However, these systems are expensive to set up and cost of delivery of items is also very high as compared to the conventional systems.

Example of Electronic Delivery System

1. **ADONIS (Article Delivery Over Network Information System) :** It supplies full text articles of selected biomedical journals on CD-ROM. It is an co-operative venture of 10 major international publishers of biomedical journals such as Elsevier, Springer Verlag, Pergamon, Blackwell, etc. and 12 test libraries in Europe, USA, Mexico, Australia and Japan.
2. **OCLC and ILL system:-** OCLC is a non-profit computerized library network linking more than 11,000 libraries in 41 countries and territories, founded in 1967. Original purpose of OCLC was to establish an automated cooperative cataloguing venture. Over the years, it expanded its services to include interlibrary loan system (1979), serial control (1989) and acquisition (1981).

OCLC with "Faxon" research services has recently started journal article table of contents and document delivery service.

In our country, document supply is greatly confined to interlibrary loan and supply of a photocopy of the desired document. The activity is taken up on an individual library level. There has been so far no organization set up at national or regional level to take up document supply as its primary activity.

In the years to come, the document supply system (DSS) has an increasingly prominent role in the over all national information system. The present time demands a national outlook or still better a universal outlook from the library professionals, and the needs of the users should be accorded top priority. The potential of information technology for document delivery service is enormous. Today, the electronic telecommunication media is pushing fast knowledge through variety of its media. It has become a space and time binder. Thus, utilization of knowledge through its instant transmission has added value and variety to our life.

Q. : Write an essay on Reprographic Services.

Ans. Due to the invention of printing the concept of libraries changed a lot, after the invention of printing technique and as its result the heap of literature being started publishing everyday. As the result, the large volume of literature received in the library in the form of books, periodicals, pamphlets, reports, patents etc, makes it possible for any one to persue, let alone read all the literature relevant to a particular field of study. This problem as faced by the user lead libraries to launch a new concept known as Documentation. This concept is introduced to save the time of users and specially researchers and as a part of documentation, "reprography service" was started because sometime user does not have much time to read the material in the library or if he feels some problem in coming to the library he simple, ask for a duplicate copy of it. This gave rise the concept of Reprography Services in libraries.

Reprography is the art of producing single or multiple copies of documents, whether by photographic or other means. The term 'reprography' includes - photocopying, microcopy, duplicating and in-plant printing. It is a term used to refer to photocopying as well as duplicating documents whereby one or more copies of the same size or in reduced or enlarged form are produced.

Methods of Reprography

Copying processes and techniques are employed for making a very limited number of copies of a document quickly for personal or official use. Three methods of reprography are in vogue at present. They are:

1. Copying process and techniques
2. Duplicating process and techniques
3. Micrographic process and techniques

1. Copying Process and Techniques

Copying process enables librarians to have photocopies of any size enlarged, reduced or full size. In it copies of an original document can be made quickly and economically. Sometimes the world "photocopies" can be used for this purpose. There are a number of processes available for making copies; of which important are:

(i) Electrostatic Process

(ii) Diazographic Proces

(iii) Thermographic Process

(iv) Silver Halide Process

(i) Electrostatic Process : Static electric charge plays a dominant role in the creation of photocopies by this process so this process is commonly known as electrostatic process and the photocopy made by the process, an electrostatic copy.

There are two methods of making electrostatic photocopy :

(a) Indirect or transfer method

(b) Direct method

Indirect method is popularly known as xerography and the copies obtained by this method are known xerox copies. This method use photo conductive plates, camera, developing unit, transferring the developed image on plate and fixing the transferred image.

Direct method is commonly known as "Electrofax" and copies prepared by this method are called "Electrofax copies". In it, two methods are used :

(a) Dry method

(b) Wet method

(ii) Diazographic Process : In this method, a photosensitive substance known as Diazonium compound is used for making photocopies and copies prepared by this method is known as "diazocopies."

By it photocopies of one-sided documents are prepared. For making copy document with its right side up is placed over a sheet of paper coated with diazonium compound. Diazo copies are prepared by three process :

(a) Vapour process,

(b) Moist process, and

(c) Thermal process.

(iii) Thermographic Process: In this process, image is created by the use of heat sensitive substance. It is a dry method of copying, but it does not require separate development and drying of fixing operations. Both one side or two sides copies are made by this process. It is also known as the "Thermofax process."

(iv) Silver Halide Process: It is the oldest method, in which light sensitive material is used for making copies. There are two methods by which copies can be made by this process. They are:

(a) Transmission

(b) Reflex

In transmission method negative print are used for making copies from a single sided document. While reflex method is used for making copies of double sided documents.

2. Duplicating Process and Techniques

By this process a large number of copies of a document are produced quickly and economically. The various techniques of duplicating process are as follows:-

(i) Offset Duplication : In it, all kinds of documents (written/typed/printed) can be reproduced by offset duplication which is a modified form of offset printing. In it, a convenient copying technique is employed, for transferring the text of document on an offset master of paper or metal.

(ii) Stencil Duplication : It is known by many other names: mimeography and cyclostyling. It is most economical method of duplication. Stencil duplication process has following two steps:-

Advantages and disadvantages of different copying processes.

Advantages	***Disadvantages***
	Reflex Copying
High-contrast copies from line and half-tone (excluding verifax) originals of any colour (except yellow)	Copies require drying and tend to darken or fade out with time. Their cost is rather high.
	Diazo Copying
Lasting and most cheap copies From originals of any colour (except blue and violet)	Requires translucent original with image on one side and involves the use of highly odorous chemicals.
	Thermography
The fastest and easiest method of copying of letterpress of typescript images and line drawings. Dry Process in lighted room.	Does not copy inscriptions in writing ink and other organic dyes. Copies darken and become brittle in time.

Xerography	
Lasting copies of excellent quality from textual and line originals of any colour on standard stationery and many other materials. Dry processes in lighted room.	Poor copies from half-tone illustrations and originals with large solid areas expensive equipment requiring skilled personnel to service.
Electrofax	
The basic merits of xerography, plus quality copies from illustrations and originals with large solid areas.	Requires special stationery, from which the image may be easily scratched with metal objects. Some apparatus involves wet processes.

(a) To begin with stencil/matrix of the original document is made. Stencil can be prepared by hand; with the help of a type writer or by using an electronic stencil maker.

(b) Then the prepared stencil is run on a machine to make the duplicate copies.

(iii) Spirit Duplication : This process is also named as "Hectography". In this process a carbon paper and receiver sheet is used. In place of normal carbon, an alcohol (spirit) soluble dye is used. The receiver sheet consists of a stiff glazed sheet of paper.

3. Micrographic Process and Techniques

Micrography may be described as miniaturization of document. In it, documents are highly reduced in size and recorded on microfilm for saving storage space and handling convenience. All kinds of documents can be microfilmed. Any kind of microform is used for this process such as:

(i) Microfilm : It is the most popular of the microforms. Though microfilm reels are available in 8mm, 16mm, 35mm, 70mm and 105mm; 16mm and 35mm are the most commonly used sizes in libraries. A 35mm reel of 30mts can accommodate as many as 2100 pages which occupies only one inch of shelf-space.

(ii) Microfiche : Its sizes range from 3" x 5" to 6" x 8". It is piece of flat and transparent film that can record 98 pages or more depending on the reduction ratio adopted. They are easily duplicated for mailing, security or reference purpose.

(iii) Ultrafiche : It contains images reduced more than 90x, thus, permitting thousands of pages/images per fiche. Ultrafiche offers the advantage of storing more information in less space than a standard microfiche.

(iv) Microcards : These are similar to microfiche in configuration but images are on opaque stock. Therefore images can be stored on both sides. For blow-back opaques use reflected light.

(v) Apeture Cards : These are available in many sizes. 80.5mm × 187.2mm or 3 ½" × 7 ½" is the most commonly used size. They combine keypunched data and access information with microfilm. Aperture card may cotain a single image, or upto eight page-size images on one 35mm frame.

(vi) Microfilm Cartridges : It functions as convenience packaging for rolls of microfilm. Unlike microfilm on reels, which require threading, cartridges can be self-threading. Microfilm in cartridges is well protected and not subject to fingerprints and other sources of damage.

(vii) Microfilm in Cassettes : This gives added convenience to the handling of continuous rools of microfilm. Each cassette contains two film cores - the feed and the take-up. There is no need to rewind a cassette when it is removed from the reader. Any frame may be held in a viewing position for further reference at a later time.

(viii) Jacket : It is a plastic carrier with single or multiple sleeves or channels designed to accept strips of 16mm or 35mm film. Images may be copied or read directly from the jacket without removing film. Jacket can be visibly titled for easy reference.

(ix) Computer Output Microfilming (COM) : It is a process by which computer data are translated into human readable form and recorded in microfilm.

There are three types of COM devices described by Synder: *Business* - an alphanumeric printer which prints lists of data for business; *Graphic Arts* - a special quality alphanumeric printer and plotter, useful for preparing business reports and graphs; and *Scientific* - the digital output of computers is reduced to usable plots and curves that are annotated with alphanumeric information.

Importance of Reprography Service

These can be enumerated as under :

1. It helps in the dissemination of information.
2. It facilitate the work of Inter-library loan.
3. The documents reproduced in microforms helps in solving the space problem.
4. It act as a duplicate of the original copy.
5. It helps in saving the original document.
6. It saves the time of the users.

Concluding it can be said, the objective of the reprographic services is "to produce copies of documents in the form, format and quanity desired by the management or the user at minimum steps in operation and in minimum time but having due regard to optimum quality of the copies consistent with their end use."

So reproduction of documents is an integral part of the functions of the documentation and information services.

Q. : Briefly describe the reprographic services in India.

or

Write note on "reprography services in India"

Ans. India has been affected by the phenomenal progress in abroad with respect to the reprographic technology. Development work in certain directions have been fruitful at the National Physical Laboratory, New Delhi; Indian Institute of Technology, New Delhi; INSDOC, New Delhi; and Central Electrochemical Research Institute, Karaikudi.

The various organizations which are providing reprographic services in India, may be discussed as under :

1. Indian National Scientific Documentation Centre (INSDOC) (now NISCAIR), Delhi

It has adequate facilities for microfilming, photocopying and slide making. The centre also undertakes microfilming of old documents to help institutions in storage and archival keeping. It provides a full range of documentation services in all fields of science and technology inclusive medicine and agriculture. All the services are provided on specific requests and are charged.

2. National Social Science Documentation Centre (NASSDOC), Delhi

It provides single or multiple copies of articles/text from documents, subject to the provisions of the Copyright Act, and the possibility of making a photocopy without damaging the library's originals, to officers, staffs, staff members of ICSSR and other scholars/ institutions, to be used for research purposes only. These services are available on week days only. In addition to this, services in cyclostating/ rotating/ stencil cutting etc. are also provided on payment.

3. Defence Scientific Infromation and Documentation Centre (DESIDOC), Delhi

DESIDOC provides reprographic services, including photography, Xeroxing, colour slide preparation, slide projection and microfilming facilities to DRDO, H.Q. and local Laboratories and Establishments.

4. Bhabha Atomic Research Centre (BARC), Mumbai

Reprographic and printing unit in BARC, was started working in 1953 under the technical information section of library. This has a number of equipments to cater the needs of scientists in BARC Complex by providing reprographic services in the form of microfilm, xerox copies, offset printing. It also has several micro-documents, reader-cum-printers and duplicate machines etc.

5. Indian Agriculture Research Institute (IARI), Delhi

IARI has a reprographic unit to cater the needs of thousands of scientists, students and research workers by supplying them microfilm strips, photocopies, diazo copies and slides etc.

6. National Archives of India (NA), Delhi

The National Archives of India is considered the richest depository of the nation's records relating to the British period. It possesses million archives and microfilm copies of records obtained from the India Office Library and other public and private sources in Great Britain. Besides, it has an excellent collection on modern India including a large collection of government publications.

It has also the oldest organized reprographic unit set up with the support of the Government of India. No other organization has reached the volume of microfilming work as done by National Archives of India.

It has continuous programme of micro-recording. This unit is equipped with a battery of recorder cameras and ancillary equipment. But it has yet to put on microfilm, our state records of this century, particularly the bulk of documents created after independence.

7. Nehru Memorial Museum Library (NMML), Delhi

NMML has an independent reprographic unit which caters to the need of the research scholars working at different institutions.

8. National Information System for Science and Technology (NISSAT), New Delhi

The sector and regional centres under National Information System for Science and Technology, as one of its objectives serve its users with efficient and rapid reprographic services. For example, the Reprographic Division at CLRI, Madras is equipped with sophisticated reprographic equipment and offers various beginning with photocopy, processing facilities for a full range of copying and duplication systems like Xerox, Electronic stenciling, micrographics, thermofax process, camera operation, diazo duplicating system, visual making etc.

9. Small Enterprises National Documentation Centers (SENDOC), Hyderabad

SENDOC established in 1976 at SIET (Small Industries Extension Training Institute, has set up a Reprographic Unit, as one of its six sections. This unit is well equipped. It has microfilming and photographic units, electrostating copy units, diazo copying unit, electronic scanner and a full-fledged offset unit with a battery of electronic typewriters and vari-typers for cold composition. This reprographic service, the centre has listed under its Responsible Documentation Services.

10. Indian Association of Special Libraries and Information Centres (IASLIC), Kolkata

IASLIC established in 1955 has one of its functional division of Decoumentary Reproduction and Translation. The services were started in 1958, providing microfilms and photocopies of documents available in the major libraries in Kolkata to any individual research institutions, learned bodies etc.

11. Universities

There are many universities providing reprographic facilities to their faculty members, research scholars and students. It is considered that Tagore Library of the Lucknow University introduced the first photocopying services in India. Now a days, almost all universities and advanced study institution's library has such facility.

Besides all these government institutions, research centers and universities, there are quite a large and well established industrial units which offer reprographic services. Some of them are HMT, Bangalore; BHEL, Hyyderabad; HEL, Bhopal; Bokaro Steel Plant; Tata Iron and Steel Company, Jamshedpur etc.

Q. : Write short notes on the followings:

(a) Digest Services

(b) Information Analysis Centres

(c) Referral Centres and Services

Ans.

(a) Digest Services

It is of course primarily for current information that yearbooks are consulted, but their historical value should not be overlooked. While much of their text is repeated with appropriate updating from year to year-unlike, for example, the pure *Annual Register-type* yearbooks whose content each year is unique-they can be invaluable for ascertaining the exact status at a particular point in time of a international organization or a country. A run of the *Statesman's Yearbook* from 1864, for instance, provides an unrivalled quick-reference source for historical states that are now defunct as such, e.g., Brunswick, Crete, Montenegro, Palestine, Sarawak.

But it does occasionally happen that the information required is too recent even for a current yearbook. The obvious current affairs source supplementing the yearbook it the newspaper, but such searches are usually very time-consuming and often frustrating. A *Digest* is a methodically arranged compendium or summary of literary, historical, legal, scientific or other written material. Generally, in *Digest Services,* the summary of the last events or the news is provided for the quick-review of the readers. Just as frequently perhaps librarians turn to such *indexed* sources of current information as *Facts* on *File.* Its appearance weekly ensures that it is more up-to-date than a newspaper index would be, and of course the text that is indexed appears within the same covers, obviating the second step that consultation of a newspaper index requires. Its coverage is international, though its United States emphasis reflects its American origin. An older British Service, *Keesing's Contemporary Archives,* with its international coverage slanted towards the United Kingdom, the Commonwealth and Europe, used to provide a valuable counterpart to *Facts* on *File,* but now appears to have fallen on hard times. Far less prompt for many years than its American rival, from 1983 it became a monthly after appearing weekly for over 50 years. Though indexing is vital for such a digest service, its very brief and almost perfunctory outline index now cumulates three times a year only. The much superior *Facts on File Index* appears every two weeks, cumulating throughout the year. Retrospectively of course the indexed sets serve, like yearbooks, as summaries of a year's events, back to 1940 and 1931 respectively. And *Kessing's* in its prime, used to make a particular point of including texts of documents (such as the first international treaty covering space exploration, approved by the United Nations in December 1966) where appropriate among its 5,000 condensed reports per year from the world's press.

One advantage not to be disregarded is that these news digest services do strive in reporting controversial events to achieve a balance that is not always found in newspaper accounts.

At least one news digest service saw some years ago that the most effective way to keep as up-to-date as possible was to call on the aid of the computer. *Infobank,* now available on NEXIS, is an online service providing abstracts of articles selected from the *New York Times* and some 60 other English-language newspapers and periodicals. Updated daily, the two million-item database goes back as far as 1969 and is growing at the rate of 100,000 items a year. More recently both *Kessing's* and *Facts on File* have also become available online.

(b) Information Analysis Centres

An Information Analysis Centre (IAC) has been defined as an organization which indexes, abstracts, translates, reviews, synthesizes, and evaluates information and/or data in clearly defined specialized fields. The key activities of IAC are analysis, interpretation, synthesis, evaluation and repackaging of information or numerical data. The IAC is the most efficient system for transferring authoritative and evaluating information to a user in a convenient form.

(c) Referral Centes and Services

A referral centre is some sort of an "information desk" for the scientific and technical community which does into provide enquirers directly with the information they need, but suggests sources i.e., organizations or individuals, likely to satisfy the clients. The Science and Technology Division of the Library of Congress maintains one of the most active referral centres-the National Referral Centre. An efficient referral centre maintains an exhaustive inventory of significant information sources and also publishes directories of such sources.

A referral centre is differ from a conventional library in the following manner:

Referral Centre	***Library***
(i) It provides source of information.	It provides not only sources of information but also documents as well as the needed information.
(ii) It stocks only access tools, such as directories, guides, and lists.	It stocks primary, secondary and tertiary literature.
(iii) It provides only enquiry service.	A library provides enquiry, reference, bibliographical and other range of services.

Referral services are the services which do not provide the user with the documents or information actually needed for his query but refer him to the sources such as secondary publications, information units, professional organizations, research institutes and individual specialists, etc. and tell him where to find them. They utilize directories and files on sources. If is very difficult to measure he effectiveness of such services unless they keep themselves in close touch with their sources and users. Such a task is easier only when referral services offered for the clientele is in a small geographical area.

6
Documentation and Information Centres and their Activities

Q. : Write short notes on the following :

1. NASSDOC **2. FID**

3. UNESCO **4. INSDOC or NISCAIR**

5. VINITI

or

Give an account on information activities in India with special reference to NISCAIR.

or

Give an account of information activities in India in the field of social sciences.

or

Describe the contribution of UNESCO in the field of dissemination of information and documentation.

or

Describe the organisation and functions of NASSDOC (India).

Ans. The documentation and information centres can be defined as the organisation that (i) selects, acquires, stores, organizes and retrieves specific documents to meet users' requirements, (ii) announces, abstracts, extracts and indexes documents, and (iii) disseminates documents in response to requests from users.

Traditionally, libraries have been collecting various kinds of publications and holding them in readiness for use by scholars, who generally know what they want. After the World War II, there has been a knowledge explosion and consequently, exponential growth of literature and information, besides, complexities in information generation, handling and use. The users have been increasingly feeling helpless duc to lack of time and skill to go through the vast amount of literature or to find the information directly. Traditional library services had to be supplemented with more active service provisions. As a result, documentation and information centres began emerging to take care of the changing needs of information users for specialised services. The emphasis first shifted to documentation where periodical articles, etc. were required to be handled and served and then to information, where the information contained in the documents became the product of service.

Now-a-days, libraries, particularly special libraries, and documentation and information centres have been known to scan current literature sources, select items of interest to the users, prepare bibliographical entries and maintain a file to offer current and retrospective literature search services. These files are known as databases. In these files bibliographic data are recorded. A documentation and information centre may create databases in its areas of interest from internal and external sources and also provide on-line access to external databases for providing current and retrospective literature search services.

Some of the important documentation and information centres and their activities are briefly discussed below :

I. United Nations Educational, Scientific and Cultural Organisations (UNESCO)

'United Nations Organisation' (UNO) established a separate organisation with a view to develop, education, science & culture in the world and also to establish peace, brotherhood-sentiments of the people on 4th November 1946. It was named UNESCO of UNO.

Organisation

To run successfully and smooth functioning it has following three parts:

(A) General Conference : It is the main body of the UNESCO, which makes policies. There are its two meetings in a year.

(B) Executive Board: This board is responsible to execute its policies and programmes. Its members are elected in general meeting by the members of member nations of UNESCO.

(C) Secretariat : Director General is the head of secretariat, which is elected in general meeting, by the nominated members of executive board.

Membership

Any nation member of UNO can get the membership of UNESCO. Other than UNO member nation, others could get membership by getting 2/3 majority of its general meeting.

Objectives of UNESCO

These are following :

(1) To motivate and inspire the educational development so as to develop peace and brotherhood feelings between different nations of the world.

(2) Unesco was established with a view to help those nation members who were developing and got freedom in their educational, scientific & cultural life.

(3) To help the member nations of the world in their national plans of education research & training and to solve its related problem.

(4) To promote the inter exchange of intellectuals between nation members to achieve the objectives of scientific and cultural need.

(5) To work as a nodel agency for documentation services.

Activities of UNESCO

The various activities of UNESCO can be described in the following manner:

(1) Bibliographic Services : An international seminar was organised by UNESCO in Paris in the year 1950. National bibliographical services were considered in the conference and a cooperation policy between nation member and library of congress was framed as a cooperation. An international agency-was established as "International committee on social science documentation". The following four bibliographies were published by this institution:

(i) International Bibliography of Social science (1951-59)

(ii) International Bibliography of Political science (1952-59)

(iii) International Bibliography of Economics (1952-59)

(iv) International Bibliographic of Social & Cultural of Human Science (1955-59)

In the year 1960, a new advisory board was organised having after merged of two advisory board, and named an "Bibliography, documentation & technical terminology of international advisory board." In continuation of the above, with the help of IFLA, a seminar of international level was organised in the year 1977. Universal bibliographical control - a project was also started with the assistance of IFLA.

(2) Documentation & Information Service : Its various services include :

(i) Computerised documentation services: The year 1971 was a landmark in starting of computerised library services & information retrieval & also documentation services. In the year 1972, Data Retrieval System (DARE) for the social and human science was experimented. The project was also assigned by UNESCO to the centres of documentation established at Europe, Latin America, Africa and Asia. An economic assistance was provided in 1972 to establish a project of National industrial institution of textile in Argentina.

(ii) ISORID : International Information System on Research in Documentation was established in the year 1972 with the help of FID. It is an information system, which maintains:

1. Central information files on research projects and research reports; and
2. Research report depository.

The Central Information files are maintained in information data sheets provided by the National Information Transfer Centres of ISORID. It renders the following central services:

— Provision of information on research projects;

— Provision of information on research reports;

— Provision of copies of research reports.

The information services include a Current Awareness Service, Cumulative Indexes and information retrieval on specific requests.

(iii) UNISIST : United Nations Information System in Science & Technology, was introduced in 1972, in the 17th Conference of general meeting of Unesco with the help of ICSU- International Council of Scientific Unions. The UNISIST emphasized the application of information, particularly scientific and technological information, in the service of development, the importance of developing user-oriented information systems, the need for national information policies & planning and importance of education and training. Initially UNISIST started to provide its services in science & technology only but it was extended in the field of social sciences since 1974.

(iv) NATIS : National information system (NATIS) established in the year 1974 by UNESCO, aims at the integrated development of national information infrastructures - particularly libraries, archives and documentation Centres - with a view to establishing national information systems capable of meeting all the economic and social development needs of member states.

(v) PGI: (General Information Programme) - The general information programme was formally established by decision of General Conference of UNESCO at its 19th session in 1976. It was directed towards the development and promotion of information systems and services at the national, regional and international levels to formulate of information policies and plans, as well as the education and training of information specialists and users. The duties were given in 5 themes as below:

— Information policies & plans.

— Standards of information handling & retrieval.

— Contribution to the development of information infrastructure.

— Specialized information systems in the field of education & culture, communication.

— Promotion of the training & education of specialists in and users information.

(3) Professional Training : UNESCO established research centres at special libraries. It has made efforts to provide efficient and skilled professional and arranged for their training schools at regional, national & international centres. It also provides subject experts to the nation members in exchange policy.

(4) Publications : The main publications include :

— Index translationeum.

— UNESCO journal of information science, librarianship & archive administration.

- Copyright bulletin.
- Directory of educational, documentation & information services.
- World guide to library school & training courses in documentation.
- UNISIST- Reference manual for machine readable description of research projects & institutions.
- UNISIST Newsletters.
- Informatics.

II. Indian National Scientific Documentation Centre: INSDOC (or NISCAIR)

After independence, the educationists and intellectual of the nation had an ambition to make the nation self dependent in scientific and technical field and to start a centre of learning which can be responsible in developing and guiding for research. In the year 1947, International standard organisation motivated to Indian standard institution by a letter to establish such a centre in the country, but the effort was in vain. Again in the year 1956, a well known scientist Shantiswarup Bhatnagar and Maurice Gwayer, Vice-chancellor, Delhi university, Delhi, insisted Dr. S.R. Ranganathan, to make a plan, and constituted a committee to implement. In the year 1952, INSDOC was formally inaugurated and started.

The main objectives of the INSDOC are:

- To receive and retain all scientific periodicals which may be of use to the country.
- To inform scientists and engineers of articles which may be of value to them by issuing a monthly bulletin of abstracts.
- To answer specific enquiries from information available in the center.
- To supply photocopier and translations of articles required by individual workers.
- To be a national depository for reports of the scientific work of the nation, both published and unpublished; and
- To be a channel through which the scientific work of the nation is made known and available to the rest of the World.

Organisation

To run INSDOC and its functioning smooth, research association and administrative associations are organised having a Director. Apart from this following departments are established :

— Information service department
— Information extension services
— Information source department.
— Computerised information department
— Training and orientation department
— Research and development department
— Information use and marketing department
— Planning and coordination department
— Administration and office.

Regional centres of INSDOC are situated at Kolkata, Bangalore, and Chennai, where printing, information service, bibliographical and reprography services are provided.

Functions and Activities of INSDOC

'INSDOC' is responsible for development of educational research and development and provides assistance to research institutions, universities, industrial institutions, administrative and government departments in regards to documentation. It's working sector and coverage are as follows :

1. Documentation Services : The centre has been providing documentation services since its inception. Scientists and researchers have direct link with this department. Any needed researcher and scientist can demand photocopy or microfilm of the documents available at the centre. If the document is not available even then it can be provided under inter library loan/ photocopying from other centres of national or international in the form of microfilm. These services are provided at very cheap cost. Thus, the centre performs the following jobs:

(a) Centre verifies the documents received from the scientist.
(b) Information needed is assessed and then- is known availability of the information.
(c) Microfilm/photocopy of the needed article is provided.
(d) On demand of the scientist/research scholar bibliography is prepared and delivered.

(e) Answers the query of a scientist/researcher.

Besides, now-a-days, CD-ROM database service and on-line services are also provided.

2. Translation Service : Scientific and technical literature is almost published in 50 languages of the world. The centre provides translation service in about 20 languages. The translation work is being done by the experts of fully trained and well aware of translation job who are permanent employee. Sometimes to finish the extra job or backlog of the work, some part-time personnel are appointed. Every year 10.000 papers are translated at the centre. A computerised list is published containing translated at this centre and including of different centres too. The demand of researchers is supplied for the papers published/translated earlier too.

3. Bibliographical Service : The centre provides bibliographical services and prepares 250 bibliographies in a year. Bibliographies are needed by small entrepreneurs, researchers studying in foreign. Therefore, on demand centre provides them, bibliography of their needed subject. It includes books, articles in periodicals published, patents, government reports.

4. Reprographic Service : This section of INSDOC provides microfilm and photocopy of the documents and articles. This service is highly demanded by researchers, scientists, engineers, departments, institutions. If the needed article is not easily available at the centre, the same is traced with the help of union cataloguing or by Internet and then provided to the reader. Here 1,00,000 pages and 20,000 microfilms are prepared every year. To solve the problem of space, centre also make microfilms of old records of the libraries.

5. Printing : This centre of INSDOC, does the printing of published material. The centre is provided the facility of modern techniques of printing photo, offset, Xerox machine, electronic typewriter, Copier and Laser printer. In addition to its own publication, it publishes the material of other scientific institutions too. This facility is available at Bangalore centre too.

6. Advisory Service : On demand, the centre provides advises to other institutions in regard to information system, information services, productions, manufacturing. Training and orientation of information science printing & photography etc.

7. Audio-Visual Service : The centre makes slides too. In this way it is helpful to serve scientist by making programmes of audiovisual aids.

8. Publications : Important publications are :

— Union Catalogue of Scientific Serials in India (Now available in CD form);

— National Index of Translations;

— Indian Science Abstracts;

— Annals of Library Science and Information Studies.

INSDOC has further to its credit the following publications:

— *Directory of Indian Scientific Periodicals (1964).*

— *Directory of Scientific Research Institutions (1869).*

— *Directory of Current Research Projects in CSIR Laboratories* (1972). Its revised edition contains materials up to 1984.

— *Directory of Scientific Research in Indian Universities* (1974).

— *Work done in India on Viral and Rickettsial Infection of Vertebrates - a bibliography,* 1900-1965 (1967).

— *Directory of Ongoing Research Projects in India.*

— *Directory of Testing Facilities in India.*

— *Contents List of Soviet Scientific Periodicals, Russian Scientific and Technical Publications.*

It also maintains close relation with DESIDOC NASSDOC, and National Medical Library, New Delhi.

9. Training Programme : In the year 1964, a course– "Documentation & Bibliography" was introduced. Today it is run as 'Associationship in Information Science' for two years. This course is regarded equivalent as postgraduate degree of library science.

Apart from this, documentation and reprography orientation is to be given to the scholars. Training and orientation service is provided to in-service library personnel. Seminars and conferences with the assistance of national and international agencies are also conducted from time to time.

10. International Cooperation : The centre maintains its relations with the international institutions in order to extend its cooperation. F.I.D. UNESCO, UNISIST are such institutions, which are very useful and helpful.

11. Research & Development : The centre and its activities are fully devoted to the development of library science and information systems and research too. The centre also prepares bibliometrics, thesaurus etc.

In the year 2000, INSDOC has been merged with NISCOM (National Institute of Science and Communication) and both are working under its new name NISCAIR (National Institute of Science Communication and Information Resources).

III. International Federation for Information and Documentation (F.I.D.)

It was the year of 1895, Bibliographer Paul Outlet & Henry La Fountaine of Belgium, whose efforts gave a result into establishing an institution. International de Bibliography.' The objective to establish this institution was to publish an universal bibliography. The idea was hypothetical only due to Ist world war and the financial position became poor to poorer.

In the year 1920, Mr Frits Donker Duyuis financed to this institution and devised to decentralise its work programmes. On his recommendations, memberships was started to given to the nation members from the year 1924. In the year 1931, its name was changed as 'International Institute of Documentation. Again in the year 1938 its name changed as 'International Federation for Documentation".

On 12 Sept, 1986, in its general assembly the word 'Information' added thus, finally it is known as 'International Federation for Information & Documentation.'

Objectives of F.I.D.

Initially the following were its objectives:

— To publish a journal with a view to inter exchange of bibliographical information.

— To act as distributor of bibliographical information.

— To revise Dewey Decimal Classification.

— To prepare an international union cataloguing.

— To organise international seminars.

Gradually, the scope of F.I.D. increased and as a result of which its objective too changed. At present, its objective can be summarised as below:

— To coordinate the activities of various organisations and personnel in regard to documentation.

— To avoid and reduce the language barriers in documentation.

— To develop mechanised and computerised techniques for storing as well as retrieval of information.

— To coordinate the activities in regards to revision and enlarging U.D.C. scheme.

— To cooperate in establishing documentation centres and information centres in various nations.

— To decide about the standardisation of terminology of classification.

— To coordinate with other international organisations involved in documentation and scientific developments.

— To train those personnel who are engaged in documentation information sciences.

Functions of F.I.D.

To achieve its objectives, F.I.D. has been serving many important works. Some of its functions and activities are as follows :

1. Development of Classification Scheme : Most important activity of FID was to extension and revision of UDC scheme. To get this job done, a committee was constituted for the purpose in the year of 1960 and 1965. This Committee had 30 special developments sub-committees. The committees prepared new and revised editions of UDC scheme. The main objectives of this committee were :

(a) Standardisation of classification terminology.

(b) To publish a critical treatise on classification literature.

(c) To assist in preparing thesaurus for bibliographic centres.

(d) To provide assistance in indexing and research work.

2. Research in Information and Documentation Terminology: A committee was constituted to make research on the nature and scope of documentation problems, information systems. The main objective was to make available the reading material in different languages of the world.

3. Education and Training : This institution provides the advanced training programme on documentation to those countries where such facility is not available or exist. For this purpose a committee was constituted in the year 1953 and again in the year 1959, it was reorganised. The committee prepared a list of those learning professors and teachers of library and documentation officers who could teach documentation in other foreign countries as well as can write text books.

4. Information for Industries : FID constituted a committee in the year 1959 to provide useful information to the industry. The committee published a series list of National bibliographies and also the directory.

5. Informatics : A job of the use of information science in mathematics and its evaluation was delivered to a committee. An international platform was made available to do the job by this committee.

6. Linguistics in Documentation : For this job a committee for languages studying for documentation was constituted. This committee works for research work linguistics in documentation. A journal named Linguistics in Documentation-current Abstract is being published.

7. Patent Information and Documentation : The information relating to patents and its use is encouraged by arranging various programmes.

8. Research on Theoretical Basis for Information Science : For this project a committee was made by FID in the year 1965. The main functions of the committee were to :

(a) decide the standards for evaluation of information retrieval.

(b) study the systems and techniques of abstracting used by various information centres.

9. Development of Machinery System in Documentation : The institution establish the research centre to develop the mechanised systems of documentation.

10. International Cooperation : The institution also organizes the seminars, conferences, symposiums, from time to time at international level. It cooperates with UNESCO & its organisations like; FAO, IAEA, NIDO, ITU, ICSSD, ICA, ISO.

11. Publications : FID has brought various publications, the important ones are as follows :

— A guide to world training facilities in documentation.
— Manual of documentation reproduction and selection.
— Manual of modern documentation practices.
— A list of 2000 abstracting services in science, technology and medicine.
— World list of library and documentation journals.
— FID news bulletin (Monthly).
— FID-Directory (Bi-annual).
— Extension and corrections to UDC (Annual).
— FID projects in documentation and librarianship (Bi-monthly).
— International form of informations and documentations (Qtly).

Contribution of India : India has been actively participating in the activities of F.I.D. since 1948. Dr. Ranganathan convened the activities of FID/CA & FID/CR. INSDOC is the active member since its inception. In the year 1957, Dr. Ranganathan was honoured by FID. India hosted in IIIrd international research conference (1975) and second regional conference on classification (1985).

IV. NASSDOC (National Social Science Documentation Centre)

The National Social Science Documentation Centre (NASSDOC) was set up in 1970 by the Indian Council of Social Science Research (ICSSR).

Objectives

Its objectives are following:

1. To provide progress report to research scholars in the field of social science.
2. To motivate the high quality of research projects in the national interest.
3. To make coordination with the international social science documentation service and also to provide information to researchers.
4. To cooperate and motivate to the eligible, meritorious researchers at various levels.
5. To coordinate between international technology and business centres.

6. To prepare bibliography of books related with research.

Functions of NASSDOC

It's a great landmark achievement to establish ICSSR and its documentation centre This documentation centre has the following main functions:-

1. To collect research projects published approved by Indian universities as well as foreign scholars.
2. To make available the reports of research projects completed with the help of ICSSR.
3. To make available the reports and speeches of conferences and seminars organised by ICSSR and submission of them onwards to the researchers and learned subject experts.
4. To collect research periodicals-related with social sciences.
5. To provide documentation information to the institutions of international repute.
6. To publish bibliographies.
7. To provide bibliographies, translation, base material, Photostat, textbooks, etc. on the demand of researchers at a very cheap cost.
8. To assist in establishing of documentation centre.
9. To provide facility of participating in seminars etc. to the employees.
10. To avail facility of providing documents to the researchers residing outside Delhi.
11. To edit the syllabi of continuing education for business teaching.
12. To exchange the national and international publications. At present 2500 journals are being used in exchange from 1000 institutions.

Activities of NASSDOC

Activities of NASSDOC can be described in the following manner:

1. Library : NASSDOC has its own library, which remains open for the whole year. In this library, reference material, periodicals, ICSSR publications, unpublished Ph.D. thesis, research reports, microfilm & microfiche, plan reports, are collected.

2. Inter Library Centre : The centre collected and organised back issues of periodical publications of social science available at centre, Delhi.

3. Exchange Programme : NASSDOC is exchanging with the institutions of national and international in lieu of the publications of ICSSR. At present 2500 periodicals are exchanged with 1000 institutions.

4. Establishment of Information Bank : Information bank was established to provide information of incidents and developments occurred in the field of social science. Assistance is also given to various institutions.

5. Documentation Programme : These programmes are being performed by NASSDOC itself and it also helps other institutions in organizing such programmes. Economic assistance is provided by the ICSSR.

6. Publications : NASSDOC has brought out the following publications in the series of research information.

— Union list of social science periodicals.

— Union Catalogue of social science serials.

— Union catalogue of newspapers in Delhi libraries.

— Directory of social science research institutes and Directory of professional organisations in India.

— Mahatma Gandhi bibliography.

— Retrospective cumulative index of Indian social science periodicals.

— Area studies bibliographies.

— Language bibliographies.

No doubt NASSDOC has provided much information of documentation to the scientists of social sciences. Improving its services qualitatively NASSDOC won the award of DR. Kalia trophy. The centre is being prepared to equip with computerised services. The centre is trying to networking of information system all over the country.

Thus, NASSDOC has contributed in the field of social science and assisted in developing research work.

V. NISSAT (National Information System for Science and Technology)

Realising the urgency for a strong national information system, India made an appeal to UNESCO for a short-term mission of a consultant to advise the INSDOC in these matters. Accordingly, UNESCO deputed Dr Peter Lazar during March-April 1972, who, after a thorough study, recommended the establishment of a National Information System for Science and Technology (NISSAT) for India. The Panel Group on the Information Sector of the National Committee on Science and Technology (NCST) of the Government of India in its report, prepared in 1973, also recommended the establishment of NISSAT under the Department of Science and Technology (DST). A sum of Rs. 150 million was proposed for this scheme during the plan period. As a result, the planning of NISSAT was started in 1975 and was completed and approved by the Planning Commission and the Ministry of Finance for implementation since July 1977.

Objectives

The NISSAT aims at fulfilling the following objectives:

— Provision of national information service relevant to present needs and capable of development to meet the future needs of the generators, processors, disseminators and users of information.

— Optimum utilization of existing information services, and systems and the development of new ones.

— Promotion of national and international cooperation and liaison for exchange of information.

— Support and active encouragement for the development of facilities for education and training in information science and technology and in, communication to provide qualified manpower for the implementation of the national science information policy.

— Support and active participation in research, development and innovation in information sciences and communication to enhance both the efficiency of information services and the quality of the information provided by these services.

— Support and promotion of research, development and innovation in information technology.

Structure

(i) *National Focal Point:* The DST has been designated as the National Focal Point (NFP) of NISSAT. This advised and guided by:

(a) Advisory Committee

(b) Executive Committee

(c) Ad hoc Working Groups and Expert Groups. It is serviced by a small Secretariat.

(ii) *Network*: The NISSAT Network comprises:

(a) *Sectorial System* with

(i) Sectorial Information Centres and

(ii) Local Information Units.

(b) *Regional System* with

Regional Centres

(c) *Specialised Services.*

Sectoral System : Presently, ten information centres are designated as NISSAT's Sectoral Centres; which are working in their own specialization at CLRI, Chennai, CFTRI, Mysore, CMTI, Bangalore, CDRI, Lucknow, ATIRA, Ahemdabad, NCL, Pune, CGCRI, Kolkata, University of Madras, Chennai, INSDOC (Now NISCAIR), Delhi and NAL, Bangalore.

NISSAT's Sectoral Centres

S.No.	*Sectoral Centre*	*Institution*	*Information System*
1	*2*	*3*	*4*
1.	Leather Technology	Central Leather Research Institute (CLRI), Chennai	National Information Centre for Leather and Allied Industries (NICLAI)
2.	Food Technology	Central Food Technological Research Institute (CFTRI), Mysore	National Information Centre for Food Science and Technology (FOSTIS)
3.	Machine Tool	Central Machine Tools Institute (CMTI), Bangalore	National Information Centre for Machine Tools and Allied Products (NICMAP)

4.	Drugs and Pharmaceuticals	Central Drugs Research Institute (CDRI), Lucknow	National Information Centre for Drugs and Pharmaceutical (NICDAP)
5.	Textiles	Ahmedabad Textile Industry Research Association (ATIRA), Ahmedabad	National Information Centre for Textiles and Allied Subjects (NICTAS)
6.	Chemicals	National Chemical Laboratory (NCL), Pune	National Information Centre for Chemicals (NICHEM)
7.	Glass and Ceramics	Central Glass and Ceramics Res. Instt. (CGCRI), Kolkata	National Information Centre for Advanced Ceramics (NICAS)
8.	Crystallography	Deptt. of Crystallography and Biophysics, Univ. of Madras, Chennai.	National Information Centre for Crystallography (NICRYS)
9.	Bibliometrics	INSDOC (NISCAIR), Delhi	National Centre for Bibliometrics (NCB)
10.	CD-ROM	National Aerospace Laboratory, Bangalore	National Information Centre for CD-ROM (NICDROM)

VI. DESIDOC (Defence Scientific Information and Documentation Centre)

Realizing the importance of information, the Defence Research & Development Organization (DRDO) created a Scientific Information Bureau {SIB} in 1958, soon after the formation of the organization. The job of SIB was to collect and process scientific and technical information of defence interest and communicate it to the concerned R & D Scientists and other agencies of the Ministry of Defence. On May 4, 1967, SIB was reorganized and renamed as Defence Scientific Information and Documentation Centre (DESIDOC) with wider scope and responsibilities. It became a self accounting unit in July 1970 to function as one of the DRDO establishments headed by a Director. Today, DESIDOC has become one of India's premier national information centres. Its working can be broadly grouped as under:

(i) Defence Science Library (DSL) : The Defence Science Library acquires books, journals, reports, patents, etc. for the use of scientists and research scholars of DRDO. In addition the library has built-up a comprehensive collection of microforms, CDs, etc. in the recent past.

(ii) Dissemination of Information : The library and information scientist of DESIDOC provide information in 'anticipation' as well as against specific requests from the users. As anticipatory information services, DESIDOC brings out abstracts/indexes bulletins, state of the art reports, technical digests etc. Literature searches are regularly conducted for providing information to the Scientific Adviser to the Union Defence Minister, Chief Controller of R & D, and other users in DRDO headquarter and its laboratories. Modern information technologies have been inducted into the system for quick and effective communication of the processed information.

Desidoc's information service includes online searching of information from various international databases.

(iii) Networking : Desidoc has established an information network of DRDO laboratories spread all over India.

Objectives

Its objectives are :

(a) to functions as a central resource for providing scientific information/documentation/library/reprographic/translation service to the Defence Research and Development Organization Headquarters, laboratories, establishments and to coordinate DRDO scientific information programmes.

(b) to develop a data bank on scientific information system for Defence Science and Technology and to cooperate with other national and international agencies in the field of scientific information.

(c) to provide training and user's education programmes for Defence Research and Development Organization and carry out research and development work in the field of scientific information.

(d) to provide consultancy and referral services to Technical Information Centres.

(e) to publish scientific and technical journals including books and monographs of the defence research and development organization.

Functions and Activities

Its main functions are :

(i) maintaining an up-to-date research and reference library capable of catering the needs of the scientists engaged in defence research and development work.

(ii) sifting through current literature indexing and subject classification of scientific and technical information of interest to defence research and development.

(iii) providing bibliographical service to scientists in all defence establishments/laboratories on demand as well as in anticipation of demand.

(iv) abstracting Information under specific topics of interest to defence research and development.

(v) translating into English language scientific and technical documents appearing in other languages.

(vi) disseminating information to the scientists in defence research and development establishment and laboratories through:

   (a) List of latest arrival in the library;

   (b) Abstracts of selected papers from current scientific periodicals and technical reports;

   (c) Microfilms/photocopies of articles/documents when required by the defence research and development scientists.

(vii) maintaining liaison with universities, research institutions in India and abroad, and

(viii) editing and publishing science journals, and other defence research and development publications.

As far as its activities are concerned, DESIDOC provides translation service and also maintaining a 'translation bank'. It has a potential unit for software development, designing of networks; management: training and also organised several seminars and conferences on key areas and issues of information management.

To perform its functions, DESIDOC has the following primary functional divisions:

(1) Library;

(2) Documentation;

(3) Polygraphy;

(4) Publications;

(5) Reprography;

(6) Translation;

(7) Technical Coordination; and

(8) Administration.

Publications

1. Bibliographies/Literature Searches on Demand,
2. SDI Bulletins : DESIDOC issues from time to time SDI Bulletins on various subjects like military warfare, documents, missiles and rockets, nuclear weapons, etc.
3. Current Abstracts on Electronics
4. Patents Information Alert.
5. Defence Report Abstracts.
6. DESIDOC List.
7. State-of-the-Art Reports.

The following are also worthy of mentioning:

(1) Thermal Imaging System. (2) Defence R & D in Coming Decades. (3) Remotely Piloted Vehicles. (4) Reconnaissance Sensor System. (5) Chinese Space Programme. (6] Falkland Wars : A Literature Survey Report.

Some Others are :

(i) *Popular Science & Technology;*

(ii) *Defence Science Journal;*

(iii) *Defence Reports Abstracts;*

(iv) *DESIDOC Bulletin of Information Technology;*

(v) *DESIDOC List of Current Scientific Literature;*

(vi) *Patent Information Alert;*

(vii) *R & D Bulletin;*

(viii) *R&D Digest.*

VII. INIS (International Nuclear Information System)

International Nuclear Information System (INIS) was set up by the International Atomic Energy Agency in order to facilitate the exchange of scientific and technical information on the peaceful use of atomic energy. This system came into operation on a limited scale in 1970 and reached the present stage in 1976. It processes the world literature on all aspects of the peaceful use of atomic energy; say, physics, chemistry, materials, earth science, biology, agriculture, medicine, health, safety and environment; the industrial application of radio isotopes and radiation, engineering and reactor technology, legal and economic aspects, etc.

Procedure

INIS has a 'decentralised input and centralised output". Fortynine national centres and thirteen International organisations send input to the international centre in a prescribed format. INIS brought out seventeen reference documents to assist the national centres for preparing the data. These documents which are called as INIS Reference Series, give standardized formats, carriers, rules for description and descriptors. The data gathered are recorded on an input sheet, on an OCR worksheet or magnetic tape and sent to IAEA International Processing Centre in Vienna, which checks that the records confirm with the established standards and merges them into a single database. Copies of the database are made available on magnetic tape or as a printed bulletin, the IMS *Atom index* issued twice a month. Apart from bibliographic references and abstracts, this bulletin contains indexes by author, corporate author, subject, conference report number and patent number or standard number. Its cumulative indexes are produced twice a year.

It is estimated that INIS covers 95 per cent of world literature on the subject including about 30 per cent of non-conventional documents, which are not available in the commercial circuits. The participating centres also send the full text of the document to the international centre which Is stored in a clearing-house for consultation of users.

The cost of the international centre in Rome by the IAEA and that of the national centres is met by the participating countries. The INIS system also offers training to the participating countries in the installation and use of various services.

VIII. AGRIS (Agricultural Information System)

Food and Agricultural Organisation (FAO) of the United Nations (UN) is continuously involved in collection, collation and dissemination of scientific and technological information in the field of agriculture, forestry, fisheries, nutrition, rural development, etc. among the member nations. FAO's Library and Documentation Systems Division in Rome (Italy) is involved in the information systems like AGRIS, CARIS, AGINET etc.

AGRIS is a cooperation worldwide information system on current agricultural literature.

AGRIS aims at improving the flow of information and services to users through cooperative action involving all countries and their specialised documentation centres, in order to achieve a better coverage of the newly produced agricultural literature, avoiding gaps as well as duplication of efforts and increasing the variety and efficiency of services.

AGRIS is in operation since 1975. It pools bibliographic information from national and regional participating centres through duly filled-in data-sheets. The data includes monographic material; meetings and project reports, theses, surveys etc. relevant to agricultural research and development

Services

(i) AGRIS publishes monthly AGRINDEX both in hardcopy; as well as, magnetic tape form. The tapes are generally used for providing SDI service, current as well as retrospective searches.

(ii) The AGRIS Coordinating Centre at FAO headquarters is responsible for the development, processing, training of staff from participating countries, etc.

(iii) *CARIS (Current Agricultural Research Information System)* is a cooperative information system on current research in developing countries. It aims at improving the collection and dissemination of information on agricultural research currently being carried out in developing countries, through cooperative action involving all these countries and the setting-up of a worldwide information bank and a network of services to users.

From 1978 onwards data processing and data base updating were decentralised to regional and national CARIS centres.

(iv) *AGLINET (Agricultural Libraries Network)* is also a cooperative system for the exchange of services and information among the main agricultural libraries. The primary aims of AGLINET are to promote mutual and national exploitation of agricultural library resources for world's agricultural development through systematic collaboration among agricultural libraries for the efficient provision of inter-library loan services, photo-reproduction and exchange of bibliographic information and data on the participating libraries' holdings. The network consists of a chair of major agricultural libraries in each region or country of the world supported by the international centre.

IX. MEDLARS (Medical Literature Analysis and Retrieval System)

United States National Library of Medicine (NLM) began publication of *Index Medicus* a bibliographic bulletin of world literature in the field of medicine in 1889. In the year 1964, a computerised system known, as MEDLARS (Medical Literature Analysis and Retrieval System) was set up for producing *Index Medicus.*

In Index Medicus, more than 2,200 periodicals are scanned and indexed by means of a controlled vocabulary called MeSH (Medical Subject Headings) with an average of thirteen keywords assigned to each document. Since 1963, a data base of medical literature is maintained at NLM Medline

An online retrieval system MEDLINE came into operation in late 1971 with access via the TYMNET (a computerised telecommunication network managed as a commercial undertaking by a company of the same name).

Medical Library Network (MLN) : MLN serves as a national resource for all US health science libraries. It consists of 400 Basic Unit Libraries, mostly at hospitals, 125 Resource Libraries at Medical schools, 7 Regional Medical Libraries. About 2 million inter-library loan requests are attended *to* every year.

Office of Computer and Communications Systems (OCCS) : It provides information processing capability to meet MLN needs for disseminating biomedical information, operating library programmes and providing Management Information System to MLN including office automation. It has the following 4 branches:

(i) Development Branch

(ii) Applications Services Branch

(iii) Systems Support Branch

(iv) Computer Service Branch.

Its *Special Information Services* were started in 1967 with Toxicology Information Programme (TIP). The SIS includes :

— TOXLINE (Toxicology Information Online);

— CHEMLINE (Chemical Dictionary Online);

— RTECS (Registry of Toxic Effects of Chemical Substances);

— DIRLINE (Directory of Information Resources Online);

— HSDB (Hazardous Substances Data Bank); and

— CCRIS (Chemical Carcinogenesis Research Information System).

X. VINITI (All Union Institute for Scientific & Technical Information)

The Institute of Scientific Information of the Academy of Sciences, USSR was established in 1952, which was later on renamed as All Union Institute for Scientific and Technical Information. In Russian, it is known as Vsesoiuznyi Institute Nauchnoii Technicheskol Informatosvi for which the acronym is VINITI, and it started functioning in 1953. VINITI is subordinate to the USSR State Committee for the Coordination of Scientific Research, Moscow and to the USSR Academy of Sciences, Moscow.

Organisation

To run successfully and smooth functioning VINITI is working by decentralisation of jobs assigned to its various departments, which are :

— Acquisition department

— Technical department

— Bibliography department

— Abstracting department

— Translation department

— Publication department

— Instruction department

— Reference service department.

Objectives of VINITI

It has the following objectives:

1. Coordination to Collect Information : It manages the networking of institutions to provide scientific and technical information by means of collecting and retrieval of information. Registration and representation of collect material for use by analytico synthetic classification scheme and also to make available magnetic tapes, etc.

2. To motivate for Growth of Scientific Research : It helps in scientific research & development, editing of scientific research as well as to remove the difficulties in the field of informatics and scientific information.

3. Training and Orientation : It provides training and orientation to increase in knowledge of the personnel at different times on need.

Functions of VINITI

'VINITI' includes the entire literature of the world in the subject field of science and technology. Every year it receives about 40000 entries; 1,00,000 other publications from 133 Nations which is in 66 scripts. Approximately 2,50,000 patents too and its related information is collected for further use.

VINITI provides full information of published documents to the scientists and subject experts. To do this, VINITI works as follows:-

(i) First of all the material received is presented by analytico synthetic classification scheme.

(ii) After presentation the documents are provided on the reader's demand.

(iii) Provides magnetic taps of suitable information by establishing information centres at other cities and places.

Gradually, it was felt that VINITI, collects the entire literature from almost parts of the world but its services are comparitively immaterial. To avoid this misconception, in the year 1969 few plans of modernization were presented for implementation. It was also felt after its self evaluation that it should be reconstructed in providing services.

The whole system was to be mechanised and indexing, translation services started.

To achieve these all targets VINITI established an integrated informal system VIIS. It was called as ASSISTANT, which stands for Automated Reference Information System for Science & Technology.

'ASSISTANT' planned to provide the following services :

— SDI- Selective dissemination of information.

— Retrospective search.

— Online and fact retrieval

— Providing fail copy of periodicals article.

Computerised Information Service

VINITI has developed computerised mechanic system. The following services are provided:-

1. Information removal of facts and figures related with science technology.
2. Computerised information of collected material at centre.
3. To provide extension service through SDI.
4. To provide retrospective search.
5. To provide information in Machine readable format.

Publications

VINITI has the following publications of its own:

— Referativnzi Zhurnal

— Express Information

— Itogi Nauki (1962)

— Pilot Information

— Scientific & Technical Information.

Besides, VINITI is coordinated and related with main international agencies like UNESCO, F.I.D., I.C.S.U. etc. It exchanges the textbooks with other nations. VINITI has direct and active relations with UNISIST. It has also established coordination between different international organizations and established a information system.

7
Users and User Education

Q. : What do you mean by users? Giving different categories of library users, briefly discuss methods or techniques of user studies.

or

What are different categories of information users ? What is the role of reference librarian to these users ?

or

Discuss the purpose of identifying the users need for information. Describe the various methods used in ascertaining the users need.

Ans. : In library and information field, a number of terms are used to represent users, such as clients, customers, borrowers, members, etc. Some of these terms are used in particular contexts (e.g., borrowers) or borrowed from other areas of human endeavour (e.g., customers). But the most frequently used term in libraries is user. It specifies the context clearly and has a wide acceptability in the profession. It represents a person who uses the library for his information needs. But to define the terms library user is still not easy, as some persons may be frequent visitors of library, while some others may use the library once in many years. Some may use many of the services provided by the library, and others may use only one service. Some may visit the library while others may use the library services through messenger or telephone or other facilities. Still another category of persons may visit the library but not for using its collection or services, instead for paying personal visit to a staff member. Out of these many conditions, when we can call a person, a library user is sometimes difficult. According to Kenneth Whittaker, "a user may be defined as a person who uses one or more of a library's services at least once a year". It is not necessary for the user to visit the library's premises personally; he may use telephone or other communication facility for this purpose.

Types of Users

Categories of users may include a specialist, a student, a housewife, an average layman, a businessman, or a teacher, etc. Moreover, the categories of users will vary from library to library. According to Whittaker, for a general analysis, the users may be divided according to the kind of use they make or are likely to make of the library's services. Five groups of users can be distinguished on this, basis general readers, subject readers, special readers and non-reading users; and one more as non-users.

(i) General Readers : This group of users makes use of fiction and non-fiction collection of the library. The non-fiction collection may include documents from a variety of subject fields. This group may be further broken down into adult or mature general readers and the children. The adult general readers use libraries for a variety of purposes, but mainly for leisure needs, and they are mostly associated with public libraries. The children may also use public libraries in addition to their school libraries. Children have both educational and leisure needs, which must be, provide for, and, being children, their needs must be addressed at level, which are appropriate for them.

(ii) Subject Readers : These types of users concentrate their use of library materials on a subject field, which they are working in or are studying. This category can be further subdivided into students and subject specialists. Students are the main user category of academic library. The educational needs of this subgroup are considerable, but fairly easy to workout, being linked to the courses they are taking. The services required by the subject specialists are available from many types of libraries, but special libraries are in a position best suited to cater to their requirements. There are several reasons for this, but basically it is because the typical special library is particularly geared to satisfying only the needs of the users this category.

(iii) Special Readers : This group of readers has some special needs, which are the result of disabilities of one kind or another. In this context, physical and intellectual disabilities may be distinguished. The physically handicapped subgroup such as wheel chair users, have the ability intellectually to access library materials, but have difficulty physically in accessing them, unless special help and services are offered by the libraries. The intellectually disadvantaged include the educational subnormal and those who are illiterate or semi-literate for other reasons.

This subgroup too needs special services or materials to have its needs satisfied.

(iv) Non-reading Users : This category of users can not be called as readers, as they make no use of the reading materials offered by the library. In this category one subgroup makes the use of the library materials but not reading materials. A good example is of the users, who come into the library just to borrow videos. The other subgroup consists of those users who only make use of the library services, which are not connected with its stock e.g., they may enter the library to listen to a library lecture or in order to view a book exhibition.

(v) Non-Users : Non-users in the context of a library, are the persons entitled to use library services, but are not able to use them at present. They may be socially, culturally, economically, educationally, or even physically disadvantaged persons of the society or they may have a different life-style or inclination that does not match the functioning of the library. Libraries make effort to eliminate the hurdles and make these non-users their regular users.

Information Needs of Users

Libraries endeavour to provide what the users require. These requirements are expressed in terms of needs for specific piece of information or document. Libraries serve a large community of users and make efforts to organize all their resources so that maximum

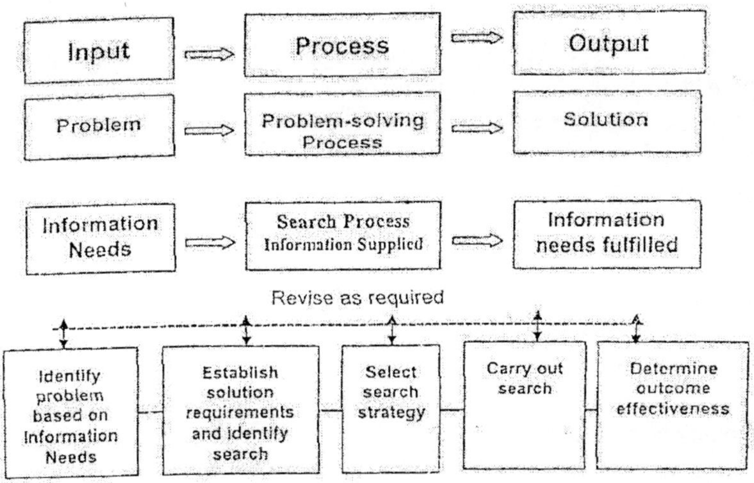

Input-Output Model-Process

information needs of maximum number of users are satisfied. But information needs depend upon a number of factors and differ depending upon individual's own functions and tasks, the level of their knowledge and experience, their particular interest as well as on the breadth and depth of their interest profiles. The information needs also depend upon the hierarchical position of the individuals. The explanation of the identification of information needs can be best expressed as an Input-Process- Output model.

The basic components of the system are (1) Problem, (2) problem solving process, and (3) solution. The problem is analyzed to determine information needs. It is indicative of the state of uncertainty in knowledge. Solution results in resolving of the situation by filling the gap in knowledge.

Kinds of Information Needs

The information needs of the users vary in particular cases for a particular point of time. In general, there are four kinds of information needs:

1. Current Information Need : In order to keep the users up-to-date in their respective fields of development, the necessity of current information is intended to make available right information in the right format of the seeker at the earliest possible. This need becomes more and more essential in the fields of R & D institutions, where development is take place in many areas such new activity, new services rendered, new products and processes, new methods and techniques etc. with the help of modern information technologies. Therefore, demand for current or instant information is much required for the users.

2. Exhaustive Information Need : This is required when a particular information user needs particular information exhaustively. Detailed information on a particular field helps the users to draw a suitable conclusion for the purpose. Unless exhaustive coverage of information sources is done so as to study a total picture of that particular area or activity, the users become helpless to arrive at a suitable conclusion.

3. Everyday Information Need : As day-to-day activity vary from person to person, different kinds of users need different kind of information at different points of time. There are some users who need information on a particular activity every day. This goes on changing from one day to another. Therefore, everyday information is expected to be fast, reliable and up-to-date. This is one of the important information needs of the users.

4. Catching-up Information Need : This type of needs is also known, as brushing-up needs. Brief and precise information are the characteristics of this kind of need of the users. The information should be as simple and to the point so that the users can easily catch it. This is an easy approach or access to information by the users in a particular field of activity, which gives the complete picture of that area in a precise form.

Medhods or Techniques of User Studies

User studies are useful in bridging the gap between the kind of information services needed and the kind in existence. The usefulness of conducting surveys for understanding users' needs is still not beyond doubt, as each user has distinct information needs that call for a personal attention. So a general survey of the entire community of users may not lead to the understanding of the individual's needs. This doubt has made the selection of an appropriate technique all the more important as some of the techniques are very effective in specific cases.

There are a variety of method which can be used for determining the users' needs for information with strong as well as weak points. However, taken together, these can give us a better idea about the needs of the users.

The following methods may be used for ascertaining the information regarding users' needs:

(i) General or Conventional Methods
- Questionnaire
- Interview method
- Diary method
- Observation by self
- Operations research study

(ii) Indirect Methods
- Analysis of library records
- Citation analysis

(iii) Special and Unconventional Methods
- Computer feedback

— Unconventional methods

(i) General or Conventional Methods

These are the methods used for social surveys, but one can also use them for conducting user studies.

(a) Questionnaire Technique : A questionnaire is essentially a skillful translation of objectives of a particular study into a set of questions intended to be answered in writing. The questions may request the user for some fact, or his opinion. They may be framed in any one of the three ways: those answered in yes or no; those answered by selecting one of the given answers; and open-ended questions, that may be answered in one or more sentences.

Sample Questionnaire for Users' Survey

You are kindly requested to assist in collecting information so as to enable Librarians to provide you more effective library services.

Please answer the questions and make any additional suggestion(s) on the back of these pages or on a separate sheet of paper.

Your cooperation is appreciated and the information provided will be kept confidential.

1. *Bio-data*

   Name........................... Qualifications.......................

   Status ....

   Area of specialization ....

   Specific field of research ....

   Languages known (to be able to read literature)......................

2. *Collection*

21. Do you find reference collection strong enough to meet your demands?.......

22. Give suggestions as to how the reference collection can be improved?....................

3. *Reference service*

31. Do you ask for assistance from the Reference Librarian or other members of the reference staff....................

    to locate books ....

    to search books ....

to seek information ....

to understand the use of various tools ....

to locate reference books................................

to find bibliographical publications ....

to use library catalogue......... ....

32. Do you seek advice about your research project from reference staff at the stages:

(i) selection of research projects....... .

(ii) preparation of a bibliography... ......

(iii) initiating work on it... ... ...

33. Do you ask for documents not available in this library (x) yes/ no

34. How many times in the past 12 months did the library succeed in getting material from other sources?... ... ...

35. How much time did it take to get the material on inter-library loan?... ... ...

36. What kind of services do you expect from the reference section?... ... ...

37. Give your impression and make suggestions for improvement in the services provided by reference section... ... ...

Signature

(b) Interview Method : Interviews are of two types: Structured and unstructured. In structured interview, a previously prepared set of questions is asked in the same order, while in unstructured interview there is no prepared set of questions, only the topic is decided in advance. Answer to one question may be used as the basis for the next question. It has a great degree of flexibility and may look like a discussion.

A set of questions is given below, which can be used as a basis for discussion:

(i) What are your needs for information in terms of amount, kinds and levels, variations in information needs at different times such as at the beginning, during and at the end of a research project?

(ii) How do you get the information you need?

(iii) Which types of publications do you use? (e.g., books i.e., monographs, handbooks, literature guides, journals, abstracts, indexes, reviews, research reports, advances in-, progress in-, etc.) For what purpose do you use each of the type of publication?

(iv) Are you able to keep up with literature in your field? What the reference section can do in this regard?

(v) What services not now provided by the reference section would you like to be made available? (examples may be listed)

(vi) Give your impressions about reference service provided by the reference section.

The problem of misinterpretation of questions generally attributed to questionnaires can easily be solved in interview as it takes place by asking the questions in person and required clarification can be given at the same time. There is also no problem of poor response in interview. But this technique is more time consuming and costly, and some special communication skills are also required for a successful interview. Besides these, sometimes, interviewee's behaviour may become slightly unnatural, usually known as 'spotlight effect'.

(c) Diary Method : In this method, the users are asked to record their particular information activities performed during a given period of time. This recording may include the time spent on searching for information, actual reading, and discussion with colleagues, etc. They may be provided with predetermine data diary forms for this purpose.

The diary is a useful tool for recording the behaviour but it requires a great degree of cooperation from the users, which is not always possible for various reasons. When applied on specialist users engaged in research, it may be possible that some of them forget to note these activities and later on fill-up the columns in approximate way. Such instances may distort the actual findings.

Now, recording of information activities can also be done on audio or videotapes instead of diary forms.

(d) Observation by Self : It is a modification of the diary method. A selected sample of participants is asked to record the information activity at different points of time. It is generally conducted within one building or floor with a facility to inform each participant, when he has to record his activity.

In this method, demand on the participants' time is reduced to a great extent. Moreover, they have to record only the activity they are performing at that point of time. A number of such observations are recorded and later analyzed to reach on some definite conclusions on information behaviour of the participants.

(e) Operations Research Study : This technique or method is also called observation by other. A selected group of participants is observed at random times during working hours and time spent by them on various information activities is recorded. Later these observations are analyzed and time spent by them on information activities, like perusing literature, looking up for references, actual reading, talking or listening to a colleague and so on, is calculated.

A number of such studies have revealed that scientists generally spend almost half of their working hours in some form of communication and out of this only half the time is spent in actual reading, while rest half is exhausted in searching for information. Now, the problem of the information system is to design such services that reduce the searching time and provide more time for reading.

(ii) Indirect Methods

The above mentioned five techniques were general and used in conducting all types of social surveys. Besides them, there are some indirect methods used mainly for information need surveys.

(a) Analysis of Library Records : Every library maintains a number of records regarding its functioning. Records of reference and circulation sections are very important. Number of queries on different subject fields received and answered, time taken in answering the queries, sources used for this purpose, number of books issued on different subjects, are valuable records that help in understanding the reading habits and ascertaining information needs of the users.

(b) Citation Analysis : Citation analysis is another indirect method of identifying literature use pattern of users. It is based on the premise that people refer relevant earlier studies they consulted while writing a particular paper. The bibliographical references appended to every scientific communication can reveal a number of facts about the information use pattern of authors of the documents. An analysis of these citations reveal the relative use of different categories of documents, age of documents used, most frequently used periodicals, literature preference with regard to country, language, etc., Although findings of citation studies are objective in nature but they do not reveal the whole picture. Citation studies do not reveal use secondary services like indexing/abstracting services, and use of different channels of communication. Moreover, citation practice varies with individual authors. Some cite very selectively while others are too liberal in this respect, still others prefer self-citations. All these practices limit the usefulness of citation analysis.

(iii) Special and Unconventional Methods

These methods either have special areas of application or are used rarely.

(a) Computer Feedback : This technique is used in computerized information services. The producers of computerized databases analyze the search statements of users and if a particular pattern is visible, they make use of this information for enhancing the usefulness of their database. With the expansion of Internet based services this technique is increasingly being used.

(b) Unconventional methods : In addition to the above direct and indirect methods of conducting user surveys there are some unconventional methods that can also be used for this purpose. One such technique may include asking the authors of contributions in a conference about use of various channels and sources in writing their contributions. In a different situation, reading of biography of a renowned scientist or social scientist may give vital clues regarding their information-seeking behavior.

Thus, the information needs of various users are ascertained.

Q. : What is User Education ? Identify various levels and methods of user education.

Ans. The libraries and information centres spend large amounts of money in acquisition, processing and the maintenance of a variety of information sources, but many of these sources either remain unused or are underutilized. This is to some extent, due to a large number of users being unaware of these sources. Libraries as public institution are founded by public money. All their resources need to be used to the fullest extent possible. This can be achieved only when users are aware of what they may get and how to use the items they have got. The field of user education addresses these problems.

Mews defines user education as "instruction given to readers to help them to make best use of the library". A more elaborate definition is given by Tocatlion, to which "user education is to include any effort or programme which will guide and instruct existing and potential users in the recognition and formulation of their information needs, in the effective and efficient use of information services and in their assessment". Thus, user education is a continuous programme aimed to making the users of information aware of the value of information and to motivate them for use of information sources.

Need of User Education

The library collection is an important resource. But its utility is when the requisite information is available to the readers or say the document should be reached to the right person at a right time. If an attempt of assistance is made to ascertain requirements from the users, then they would get a feeling that at least the library is willing to look into their problems. This feed back is essential for establishing a rapport between the library and its users.

There are certain questions ?

Why to give personal assistance to the comer readers ?

Why they don't use the library themselves ?

Should library staff serve to them etc ?

It's very easy to get new invention in a laboratory but difficult to find out the required information from the library. So, user education is provided to a user to get full use of library resources.

Purpose of User Education

The specific objectives of any user education programme vary according to its level, and the sources and services of the library. However, broad purposes of such programmes can be stated as following:

1. To collect all the published and unpublished literature in the library so as to achieve the objects of the institute.
2. To get acquaint the available resources of the library collection, so as to make it useful.
3. To makes provision for the society and its changing need of information.

4. To create confidence and faith for motivation of the use of library amongst readers.
5. To create and generate the efficiency of the readers to select the requisite information from the sources.
6. To coordinate between the teaching and library resources.
7. To train for selection of the reading material for retrieval of the information.
8. To make arrangement of the text material so that the readers may be motivated for its use.

Levels of User Education

Depending upon the type of library, needs of the users, and philosophy of the library, the user education programmes can be divided into the following four levels :

(i) User awareness

(ii) Library orientation

(iii) Bibliographic instruction

(iv) End-user searching instruction

(i) User Awareness : User awareness of library is the first step in the process of user education which aims at increasing the users' awareness of library as a primary and dependable source of information, to which they may turn for information whenever, needed. This can most effectively be started at school level. It needs a wide publicity of library resources and services in various sections of society.

(ii) Library Orientation : Library orientation is aimed at acquainting the new user with general aspects of functioning of the library. According to Stevanson, "orientation is concerned with introducing the user to the general techniques of library usage and services available in library and in particular, to the organization, services and layout of particular library". Thus, a library orientation programme is basically intended to introduce the user with the physical layout of the library, members of the staff, different types of collection and various information services, etc.

(iii) Bibliographic Instruction : Certain category of users like students of higher degree courses, professionals, researchers, etc. need to use some specialized sources to help the users to a great extent. They improve their skills and become independent in use of such sources.

Many libraries in institutions of higher learning offer such bibliographic instructions as formal courses. According to Stevanson, bibliographic instruction is "the instruction to the user of the information resources available in particular subject disciplines and techniques of making use of those resources".

(iv) End-user Searching Instruction : Libraries being social institution are affected by changes in the society. As Information Technology (IT) is increasingly being applied in all walks of life, libraries can not remain an exception. Libraries started realizing its impact in 1970s. By 1990s, it had become an integral part of library functioning and now almost all the library house-keeping functions can be performed with the help of computers. Increasing number of information sources are being issued in CD-ROMs or are made available online, and the world's largest network Internet has thrown open an unending mine of information. In this situation, when all types of information is available in abundance, even on the computer of the user at home, there is a need to retrieve relevant, reliable and quality information with in least time. End-user searching instructions are designed to satisfy this need. These instructions are intended to enable the user to effectively conduct online searches himself. The end-user searching instructions may include, training and retraining them in the use of IT- based resources and services, such as e-mail, ftp, telnet, www, browsers, search engines, opacs, databases, system software, electronic journals, newsletters, computer conferences, scholarly discussion lists, mailing lists, use net newsgroups, web-sites, web-pages, directories, guides, CDs and DVDs.

Nature of the Programmes

User education programmes vary to a great extent. On one side, they may take the shape of an informal discussion at the reference desk, while on the other, they may be offered as formal courses, where detailed study of subject specific information sources is conducted. Generally, the formal provision of user education programmes may be like library orientation in public libraries. It may be conducted on specified days of the week or month. Teaching techniques for such programmes may include, guided tours, self guided tours using audio/video tapes, printed brochure, lecture, etc.

In academic libraries, three types of programmes generally

offered are: Course related library instruction, course integrated library instruction, and formal courses in information systems.

(i) Course Related Library Instruction: Course related library instruction focuses on particular skills and tools required for a particular assignment. Practical advice is rendered to use information sources for successful completion of assignment.

(ii) Course Integrated Library Instruction: This type of instruction is provided as part of the regular academic programme. Such courses possess library as well as subject matter objectives and are generally considered as quite effective.

(iii) Formal Courses In Information System : Some institutions of higher particularly technical education offer courses aimed at introducing the user with the information communication system in their field and skills of exploiting it for the maximum use. Such courses may be elective or compulsory, or credit or non-credit courses. They are offered by different names like-bibliographic instruction, guide to sources of information, information system (e.g. agricultural), library research methods, etc.

Methods of User Education

There are various methods of user education but no any single method can achieve its objective. On the basis of their applicability, various methods can be categorized in three broad groups: group instruction, group and individualized instruction and individualized instruction as under :

(i) *Group Instruction*

Lectures	Seminars
Demonstrations	Tutorials
Guided tours	

(ii) *Group and Individualized Instruction*

Slides	Films
Video-tapes	Audio-tapes
Transparencies	

(iii) *Individualized Instructions*

Printed guides	Packaged learning
Self-instructional material	Practical exercise
Computer-aided instruction	Individual help

The important ones are briefly discussed here as under :

1. Lecture System : To be effective use of the library, lecture system is a traditional system. It's use is through some aids like black boards, projector, slides etc. Here institutions provides a program of orientation and the students & faculty members are given library orientation 'how to use your library' like program and how to make your resources fruitful.

2. Library Tour : Under this system, a student reader or a group of students or group of institutions arrange a tour of one library or many escorting with a professionally trained person. While visiting the library the readers are given and explained the study of organization and functioning of a library and the services provided. The reader is motivated to use the library and its collection in the best way at his maximum by this system. Besides, he is acquainted with the reference books to be consulted by him to get the information.

For example: to provide and select the books needed by a reader, the related study material, clipping file for a project etc.

3. Audio-Visual Methods : Recently a trend of using audio-visual aids in the education - teaching and learning is adopted and popular, for example, video cassettes, audio tapes, C.D. etc. With the help of these devices, efforts are made to get popularity to the library. Efforts are also to made for subject information, their subjects field and its organization, use of the bibliography and how to use them.

4. Printed Books : Generally well organized and service motto libraries publish a directory like 'Handbook of University Library', 'Know your library', 'Library Guide', what others say about your library, to make user education popular. These directories provides library rules, literary collections of various departments and their coordination, various types of services provided by the library. How to use library, patent reports, bibliography and its organization this all can be explained by these directories. If the reader uses this all systems himself, naturally his confidence will develop. These publications can also be posted to the readers by post or at the time of admission to the students. These directory publications should be arranged nearby at cataloguing cabinet and department of circulations.

5. Seminar, Workshop etc. : With the help of subject experts, seminar and workshop programs are arranged from time to time to train the readers to use the library in effective way. The readers are trained to use the library catalogue, bibliography and system of using the library through these seminars.

6. Orientation Week : In the western countries and now leading academic institution of India too arrange and celebrate a week at the time of new session like freshens' initiation and gives an orientation training of the library. For seven days each day is arranged to train them for the systems of cataloguing and the rules of the library.

7. Planned Instruction : Instructional teaching and learning is a slow process by which a reader is given training in a planned way by the certain methods like book, computer, audio visual aids. Under this system the teaching can be performed in the following way:

(i) **For the point of view of use:** Instructions are given to a reader or group of reader, keeping in a view their need and demand and the material is made available to them for use.

(ii) **Personalization of instruction :** Efforts are made in this system that the readers may be capable to make the use of available reading material.

8. Computer-aided Instruction : Computer-aided instruction is very useful particularly for complex bibliographical tools. Different search statements and analysis of search results can be presented to make the user understand the implications of various techniques used in the system. It has the facility of self-pacing and return to same earlier point as and when needed in an interactive mode. However, preparation of such material costs high, and requires high level of computer expertise and time.

9. Individual Help at Reference Desk : In many cases, reference desk may be an ideal place for point-of-need type of instruction. A user can be provided instructions on use of specific sources when needed in the context of a particular assignment. This type of instruction is frequently provided in academic libraries.

All the methods discussed above have their relative utility in different situations and contexts. But no individual method can be sufficient for imparting bibliographic instructions to the users. Guided tours, video- tapes, slides, transparencies, and library guide map can be useful for understanding different sections and their location. On the other hand, demonstration, practical exercise, programmed instruction, self-instructional material, computer-assisted instruction and individual help by the reference staff can be helpful for teaching identification and effective use of bibliographical sources.

Q. : How will you plan User Education program through various methods? Discuss.

or

How will you provide introduction to the new course in University and College library?

or

Bring out the need for initiating a new reader in the usage and services of public library. How would you initiate him in such a library?

or

Discuss the need for User's Education in a special library. Give your suggestions for preparing a user's education program in such a library.

Ans. A well-planned User Education Programme or UEP plays a significant role in optimum use of library resources and services. In a different way, UEPs highlight the teaching role of library professionals, and may provide a good opportunity for improving their social image by communicating what librarians can do for them.

A successful UEP needs to be carefully planned. The planning phase requires certain decisions to be taken on all related factors from amongst various options available, while designing is concerned with implementing the relevant decisions so that the programme takes a concrete shape for use.

Planning and designing of a UEP generally needs the following steps in succession:

1 : Identifying users and their information needs

Potential users of UEP and their information needs are identified. At the same time their present level of knowledge of various information sources and library tools and techniques is also identified. This will help in deciding the contents of the programme.

2 : Identifying goals and objectives of the UEP

The goals of UEP should be in general agreement with the aims of the institution of which library is a part. Goals are the long-term targets and difficult to quantify. Objectives are much more specific and achievable targets and are derived from the goals.

The goals and objectives of a UEP should be clearly outlined because other components of the programme like course content, teaching methods and teaching aides can be determined in the light of the objectives.

3 : Identifying resources

Designing of a UEP depends on the available resources for this purpose. The resources include financial, human, informational, technological and other resources. The course content and methods of instruction can be decided only after assessing the availability of the resources.

4 : Formulating course contents

Course contents may be formulated by keeping in view the objectives of the UEP. Course contents will also depend on the prior library knowledge of the users and the nature of their information needs.

5 : Selecting methods of instruction

There are quite a number of methods available for imparting instructions. Some methods are best suited for individual instructions, others are for group, and still other set of instructions may be used for both individual and group. Some do not need any teaching aid while others can not be used without the aid of instruments. Selection of the method(s) depends on the course content, users and resources available.

6 : Implementation

The course contents formulated earlier, are implemented on the pre-identified user population by using the selected instructional method at this stage.

7 : Evaluation

Evaluation is an attempt to know the extent, the UEP has been able to achieve its objectives successfully.

Another dimension of evaluation calls for user feedback on the programme and its different facets like course contents, teaching strategies, etc. This can be helpful in making the programme more useful.

User Education Programme in Different Types of Libraries

1. User Education Program in College & University Libraries

Now a days, it has been felt to use - users orientation in the college and university libraries due to following reasons:

(a) Due to drastic change in education the students are supposed to do the reports, projects etc. at its own level. Class teaching provided only a general and introductory part of the subject. To go through for dense study, they are to depend on reference books, which can not be dealt without guidance. Therefore, it becomes essential to train the students for use of these reference books.

(b) Due to limited budget, the manpower or staff in the library always remains inadequate. This inadequacy of staff restricts readers to use library freely as they themselves are not in a position to consult library without training.

Thus, it is felt that user education orientation should be provided so that students can get books, published literature its use and information retrieval. The reader should be motivated and self prepared to use this all devices.

In the college & university libraries, the user orientation is performed by the following ways :

(i) Library tour

(ii) Lecture

(iii) Planned directions

(iv) Audio visual material

2. User Education Program in Public Libraries:

The readers in these libraries comes with varying interest, and their needs too quite different than readers of academic libraries. The format program is not suitable to these institutions. Therefore, voluntary programme are arranged so that the user can take it on need. Audio visual aids provide them very useful help. Some aids are given for their need as well as entertaining keeping in a view of use of library. The readers are inspired to use library collection and directed "How to use Encyclopedia Britannica" etc. User education in public libraries is divided into following two categories :

1. Consultation of catalogue, collection and its organizations, reference books.
2. To avail the facility of literature so as to enable them to use library introductory, organization of sources of information, knowledge of sources of information.

Thus, user education programmes are arranged in different types of libraries.